The

College

Handbook

of

Creative Writing

Fourth Edition

Robert DeMaria
Dowling College

WADSWORTH
CENGAGE Learning·

Australia • Brazil • Canada • Mexico • Singapore • United Kingdom • United States

WADSWORTH
CENGAGE Learning·

The College Handbook of
Creative Writing,
Fourth Edition
Robert DeMaria

Editor-in-Chief: Lyn Uhl

Publisher: Michael Rosenberg

Associate Development
 Editor: Daisuke Yasutake

Assistant Editor: Erin Bosco

Editorial Assistant:
 Rebecca Donahue

Media Editor: Janine Tangney

Marketing Program Manager:
 Gurpreet Saran

Manufacturing Planner: Betsy
 Donaghey

Rights Acquisitions Specialist:
 Jessica Elias

Art and Design Direction,
 Production Management,
 and Composition:
 PreMediaGlobal

For product information and
technology assistance, contact us at **Cengage Learning
Customer & Sales Support, 1-800-354-9706**

For permission to use material from this text or product,
submit all requests online at **cengage.com/permissions**
Further permissions questions can be emailed to
permissionrequest@cengage.com

Library of Congress Control Number: 2012950572

ISBN-13: 978-0-8400-3079-5

ISBN-10: 0-8400-3079-7

Wadsworth
20 Channel Center Street
Boston, MA 02210
USA

Cengage Learning is a leading provider of customized learing
solutions with office locations around the globe, including
Singapore, the United Kingdom, Australia, Mexico, Brazil and
Japan. Locate your local office at **www.cengage.com/global**

For your course and learning solutions, visit **www.cengage.com**

Purchase any of our products at your local college store or at
our preferred online store **www.cengagebrain.com**

Instructors: Please visit **login.cengage.com** and log in to
access instructor-specific resources.

Printed at CLDPC, USA, 10-21

Contents

11 | IMAGES AND SOUNDS   220

Preface

In the Beginning

Long ago, in another century, there was no such thing as a course in creative writing. By the middle of the century the colleges and universities were busy developing courses in Freshman English. The textbook publishers competed in the large market for composition handbooks. The successful ones were very much alike and concentrated on essays or "themes" as they were often called. The subjects were limited, mostly personal or editorial. "How I spent my summer vacation" or "My favorite movie." Pretty soon Freshman English became a boring subject on most college campuses.

When I was a young instructor in a large West Coast university, there was only one course called Creative Writing. I was assigned three sections of Freshman English. Our load was four sections. The chairman said, "The only course left is this Creative Writing thing. I don't suppose you want to do that. Nobody wants to teach it because there are so many stories to read and mark. There are no textbooks and no guidelines. What do you think? Have you done any writing?"

Fortunately, I had done some writing—secretly, of course, without any publications. I hastily summarized a story I was hoping to write. I was a New Yorker and dreamed of capturing the music of the city through the eyes of a young man, suspiciously like myself. The chairman was an aging Harvard man. He listened blankly for a few minutes and then took a watch out of his vest pocket. "All right," he said. "I'll put you down for English X. We don't know what to call it yet."

I was thrilled, not only because it meant I would not have to teach four courses of Freshman English, but because I would have a course of my own. I went to work immediately and created a crude outline. It was the beginning of a long and difficult effort to reduce a complex subject to a set of principles that made it teachable.

I went back East, finished my doctorate, and had a novel published by the Macmillan Company. From then on I was able to teach creative writing whenever I wanted to. I was, however, still haunted by the possibility that it was an unteachable subject. In most creative writing courses students read something aloud, something they had written. The other students were supposed to comment on what was read. All too often the students did not know how to comment, because they had not yet learned the vocabulary of criticism. Too often it was mainly the instructor who did the talking. Some instructors really believed that a person could write well only if he or she was born with that talent.

Many years passed. I became an established novelist and poet. I even had a play of mine produced off-broadway. All this time, I felt the need for a better approach to the teaching of creative writing. I approached publishers with the idea only to be laughed at. "It's not a teachable subject," they said. "It's too idiosyncratic."

They must all have been eating at the same restaurants or drinking at the same bars, I thought, because they used the same vocabulary to describe this "unteachable" subject. Their favorite word was *idiosyncratic*. I had to look it up. It meant to them that every teacher had his or her own approach to the subject. It simply did not lend itself to a "system," something that you could put in a book.

I gave up making the rounds, convinced that none of the publishers were original enough to imagine a workable approach to the problem. I decided to go it alone. I reduced the problem to logical parts and provided examples, discussions, and exercises. In short, I wrote a handbook for creative writing. Without trying it out on students or colleagues, I sent it to Harcourt Brace Jovanovich.

Almost immediately I had an answer from an editor, who said, "You may be right, but it is a very *idiosyncratic* subject." I imagined him sitting on a fence about to fall one way or the other.

"I've solved the problem," I said with enough bravado to get him to say, "Well, maybe we should take a chance. I like the way you write—so clear and simple."

It was wonderful to feel that a publisher finally agreed with my approach, and my conviction that it was possible to create a handbook for this subject called Creative Writing.

The First Edition

The structure of the book has been the same from the beginning. It was copyrighted in 1991. It was possible to use it for fiction, poetry, and drama; and it was suitable for all levels of writing from introductory to advanced. The first four chapters dealt with fundamentals: *Theme*, *Setting*, *Characters*, and *Plot*. Chapters 5 through 11 dealt with *Point of View*, *Tone*, *Description*, *Dialogue*, *Time*, *Thoughts*, and *Images*. These subjects cover just about everything that we can say about writing. To illustrate what is discussed I added examples and exercises. With these subjects we can build a course.

Additional Editions

The second edition of *The College Handbook of Creative Writing* appeared in 1993, and the third edition appeared in 1998. In each of these editions, there were improvements. One of the major additions was a chapter called *The Performance Factor*. It added a subject that many students were interested in—plays and films.

The Fourth Edition

This edition will appear in 2012, fourteen years after the third edition. Since much time has passed and there have been significant changes in subjects and styles and technology, I have added some appropriate material.

1. **The new authors** with selections in the fourth edition are:

   David Ignatow   Jay Parini
   Brigit Pegeen Kelly   Robert J. Levy
   Lydia Davis   Claire White
   John Updike   David Dabydeen
   Leonard Nathan   Joyce Carol Oates
   Lee K. Abbott   Laura Maylene Walter
   Mary Baine Campbell

2. **Increased examples.** Originally, there was a basic pattern of one short story and a single poem for each chapter. The pattern now is a story and two poems.

3. **Revised exercises.** Changes in examples in each chapter have resulted in revised exercises in both discussion and writing.

4. **Changes in chapter 14. Writing as a Career.**
   Though there is some interest in this chapter, most students are majoring in other subjects and cannot imagine themselves as professional writers at this stage of their lives. Nevertheless, I thought it would be a note worth including in this handbook. I have reduced any elaboration of the many topics that touch on a career in writing. I have, instead, just described in general what is involved for those who are interested or hopelessly inspired to chase this rainbow.

Introduction

There are several ways to approach the study of literature. Traditional *scholars* tend to emphasize the biographical and historical context of a literary work. *Critics* are interested in aesthetics and linguistic significance. *Special interest readers* who have politicized the study of literature are preoccupied with such things as race, ethnicity, and gender. *Writers* usually study the craft of writing in order to understand, pragmatically, how certain devices work. Their primary goal is to produce work that is aesthetically effective.

This handbook takes the writer's approach. It deals with the practical aspects of the craft. There are many fascinating subjects that we might explore, such as theories of reader response and the mysteries of the creative process, but such subjects could fill another whole book. However, a brief look at how writers experience the process of writing might be useful at this point. These remarks come from *Writers at Work*, collections of *The Paris Review* interviews:

> *Writers are witnesses. The reason we need writers is because we need witnesses to this terrifying century.*
>
> **E. L. Doctorow**

> *When the writing is really working, I think there is something like dreaming going on. I don't know how to draw the line between the conscious management of what you're doing and this state.*
>
> **John Hersey**

> *Poetry, after all, milks the unconscious. The unconscious is there to feed it little images, little symbols, the answers, the insights I know not of.*
>
> **Anne Sexton**

1

*Making fake biography, false history, concocting a
half-imaginary existence out of the actual drama of my
life is my life.*

Philip Roth

*I feel the story I am writing existed before I existed; I'm
just the slob who finds it, and rather clumsily tries to
do it and the character justice. . . . It is entirely ghostly
work; I'm just the medium.*

John Irving

I didn't choose poetry; poetry chose me.

Philip Larkin

*Being a writer is a condition. You're born with it and
stuck with it. You have no choice.*

Cynthia Ozick

It is obvious from the above remarks that most serious
writers attach special significance to what they are doing.
They see themselves as "witnesses." They experience the
mystery of inspiration. They feel possessed. They feel that
writing is drawn from the deep well of the unconscious
mind. In short, they attribute to writing, and perhaps to
all the arts, the highest kind of importance: the creation of
beauty and the discovery of truth.

The human need to create works of art is well established. Not only do we have the need, we have the desire
and the capacity. We have something called *imagination*. We
can make up things. We can invent. We can generalize and
abstract. Furthermore, we are capable of creating the forms
that can give expression to our dreams. When the process
is successful, we often describe the result as *beautiful*. This
value judgment may be subjective, but it is often shared by a
number of people.

Art is a more difficult word to define than *craft*. It is complex and controversial. Let's focus, therefore, on craft. That word has a nice, down-to-earth sound to it. After all, even carpenters have a craft to learn.

Carpenters learn their craft as apprentices to the master. Musicians and painters also learn this way. Their training is more obvious than the writer's training. Without the basics a musician or painter can rarely get started. Writers, too, learn their fundamentals from the masters, but it is not usually on-the-job training; it is the more private training of reading and personal consultation. It would be a mistake to assume that all writers begin their careers by reinventing the wheel. However original their ideas may be, all writers learn the essentials of their craft from what has gone before.

Our discussion of the writer's craft necessarily involves certain basic definitions and concepts. Some of them are taken up briefly in this introduction.

Creative Writing

Creative writing is a term that has taken hold in academic circles. It started to appear about 1900, and, by now, it is an established part of the jargon of education. In college catalogues you will find creative writing courses and degree programs in creative writing. The meaning of the term is very specific. It is not a value judgment. It does not mean good writing as opposed to bad writing. It means writing that involves the imagination and invention in form and content. It means *fiction*, *poetry*, and *drama*. The fiction may be long or short. The poetry may take many different forms, and the drama may be for the stage or the movies or television. All creative writing uses made-up materials of one kind or another. Its main function is not merely to convey facts or information. Its main function is to please the reader or audience aesthetically by playing with their imagination.

Some creative writing is light and superficially entertaining; some is very profound and can reveal great truths about the human condition.

Truth and Fiction

There is an old saying that "truth is stranger than fiction." It sounds good, as many epigrams do, but it is not altogether accurate. It is only a way of saying that it is sometimes hard to believe the things that really happen in this world. No one can deny that, but some of the things one finds in fiction can be equally incredible. In Kafka's *Metamorphosis*, for instance, a young man wakes up one morning and finds that he has been transformed into a "gigantic insect." The human imagination is extremely inventive.

A literary work is often a blend of fact and fiction. A literal account of someone's adventures in Vietnam is not a novel; it is a memoir or part of an autobiography. The same author might be moved by certain experiences in Vietnam to create a work of fiction. In such works the facts can be adjusted to improve the story. Anne Sexton once said: "I don't adhere to literal facts all the time; I make them up whenever needed."

It doesn't take much background reading to discover that writers draw heavily on their own experiences. Young writers are often advised to make use of the materials with which they are most familiar. That's good advice, as long as they are also prepared to violate the truth in favor of a higher truth.

Some instructors like to shock their students by saying that all writers of fiction are "liars" because they make up things, because they do not tell the truth. This is a mildly amusing remark, but it is somewhat misleading. The word *liar* has a pejorative meaning. People lie in order to conceal or deceive. Writers do not make up things in order to conceal. They invent stories in order to reveal things about human nature and experience. We do the same thing when we dream. We represent inner feelings to ourselves in symbolic form. We make up situations and characters and sometimes nightmarish happenings, but these inventions are an expression of some inner truth about ourselves. One might even argue that *fiction is truer than fact* because sometimes the real truth can only be told by indirection, by the invention of revealing situations.

In introductory workshops, students sometimes produce papers that are really essays and not short stories. They are often personal anecdotes about interesting or even horrifying events. I have read endless accounts of automobile accidents, deaths in the family, drug abuse, and various childhood traumas. Some of these personal essays are very well written. Some of them even contain good raw materials for fiction, but always I must ask: "What's the story?" A personal essay is not a short story. It is bound by the facts and does not allow for invention. What's more, its tone is often clearly autobiographical. Nevertheless, there are times when it is impossible to distinguish between fact and fiction, and it may not be all that important to do so as long as the narrative is dramatic and has form and significance.

A strong case has been made in recent years for the inclusion of "creative nonfiction" in creative writing programs. There are many brilliantly written nonfiction works. Workshops in nonfiction need no special justification, but they do need specialized textbooks.

Prose and Poetry

Prose is any kind of writing that is built essentially out of sentences and paragraphs. Fiction is prose, but so is nonfiction. Poetry, on the other hand, is built essentially with lines, and it involves the manipulation of sounds in order to create verbal music. As in the case of fact and fiction, there is a good deal of overlapping between prose and poetry. Both can have narrative elements. Both can have pleasing rhythms, characters, and conventional punctuation, but poetry relies heavily on special forms, on configurations of lines, and often on rhymes and rhythms. In effect, poetry is a hybrid art form, a cross between prose and music.

Drama and Fiction

The most obvious difference between drama and fiction is that drama is intended for performance, whether the performance is on a stage or on a screen. That difference is sufficient to establish drama and fiction as distinct literary classifications. There are, however, many similarities between these two major genres. They both involve made-up stories. They both involve characters, plot, dialogue, and description.

One might argue that a play is merely a dramatized story, but that would be an oversimplification. Performance makes an enormous difference. Every medium has its advantages and its limitations. The visual experience is not the same as the reading experience. Actually seeing a drama on stage is not the same as seeing a story in your mind. A performed drama cannot escape from its live stage or even from its electronic stage. In fiction, "all the world's a stage." The human imagination has fewer restrictions than any other medium.

Though it is possible to discuss the common denominators in these genres in pretty much the same way, it is necessary to understand the distinctive techniques employed in each genre. There are things that can be done in a play that cannot be done in fiction, and there are things that can be done in fiction that cannot be done in a play.

Variety in Theme and Form

We might ask ourselves why there is so much variety in the verbal arts. We have short stories, novellas (short novels), novels, poems, prose poems, plays, poetic plays, scripts for movies and television, docudramas, and something that Truman Capote called "the non-fiction novel" (a journalistic novel about actual events, an example of which is Capote's *In Cold Blood*). The answer is simple: we have a wide range of human experiences and a strong urge to give them some form of expression. The form we choose depends on the experience. The special thrill of a flaming sunset may not require a novel. It might be best expressed in a poem. A complicated family saga covering several generations would be difficult to squeeze into a poem, and might be expressed most effectively in a long novel or television miniseries. A brief amorous encounter might make a good short story. A highly visual adventure requiring special effects might best be treated in a filmscript. There is, of course, much overlapping. Some subjects lend themselves to several forms. For instance, there have been poems as well as short stories about brief amorous encounters, and many a novel has been made into a film. Writers should define their ideas and experiences from the beginning so that they can choose the form most appropriate for the material.

Selection

Selection is essential to all the arts. Writing can never duplicate real life in any literal sense. Real life is a lot messier than art. It is more random, less organized, full of accidents and distractions—too full, in fact, of thousands of little details. To report completely all the actions, feelings, and thoughts (conscious and unconscious) of one day in the life of one person would require an enormous volume, much larger than James Joyce's *Ulysses*, which is a seven-hundred-page novel that tries to capture a single day in the lives of some Dubliners.

Human experience is very complex. The brain operates twenty-four hours a day, every day. It is constantly receiving, interpreting, and responding to internal and external stimuli. Even an ordinary person who thinks his or her life is uneventful and boring has moment-to-moment experiences that are impossible to record completely. Think of all the microscopic details that are involved in even the simplest action. Imagine what is involved in getting up and going to work in the morning: the sound of the alarm clock, the sensation of waking into awareness, emerging from the mysterious realm of sleep with all its strange subterranean dramas, the taste in one's mouth, the feeling of warmth or cold, the texture of the bedclothes, rituals in the bathroom, the smell of soap, the sound of water, and so on. Under a microscope every moment, every sensation is expanded: dressing, eating, driving to work, reading the newspaper, meeting people, and so on.

The raw materials of life are overwhelming and without form and meaning when looked at in this way. They are given form and meaning only through a process of selection. The writer does not record experience; he or she creates a work of art from the *selected* and carefully *arranged* details of experience. The writer creates a story, poem, or play. The writer's craft makes it possible to deal with a variety of things: *theme, setting, characters, plot, point of view, tone, style, description, dialogue, thoughts, time sequences, images, patterns, and forms.* **These are the subjects covered in this handbook.**

Theme

1A **Every literary work must have a reason for having been written.**

1 | A writer can write about almost anything.

There is virtually no limit to what a writer can write about. There are *exterior* events, all those things that happen to people, and there are *interior* events, the things that happen inside a character's head. These raw materials can only be turned into fiction, poetry, and drama if they are given *form* and *significance*. A literary work can deal with complex events that take place over a long period of time or merely with an intense experience that takes place in a moment.

2 | A summary of a literary work cannot convey the full meaning of the whole work.

Nonfiction provides us with a wide range of information and ideas. Literature provides us with imagined human experience. Nonfiction *tells* us something. Literature *shows* us something. The grammar school game of "Show and Tell" is often used to clarify the distinction.

Literature is an art form made from words. It contains ideas, but goes beyond. It is as much art as music or painting, and its ultimate impact is emotional and aesthetic. No description of a literary work can take the place of the whole work, anymore than a comment on music can take the place of the music itself.

3 | We can describe what a literary work is about by examining the subject, the theme, the situation, and the plot.

Since the whole meaning of a literary work can be found only in the whole work, anything short of that is bound to be an abstraction, a classification, or a summary. Some very well-known writers have refused to discuss what their work is about. "It stands on its own," they insist. "Just read it."

It is a lot easier to describe what a piece of nonfiction is about. An essay, for instance, has a clear central idea or *theme*, which can usually be stated in a single sentence. Composition students are encouraged, even required, to use such "topic" sentences. An essay on capital punishment, for example, might take as its theme the statement that capital punishment does not deter violent criminals. This theme is developed with evidence and arguments in the full essay. It is a lot more difficult to describe what a novel such as *Crime and Punishment* by Dostoevsky is all about, or even a short story such as "The Lottery" by Shirley Jackson. When we *do* try to describe what a literary work is about, we can make use of several kinds of abstractions or summaries. We can describe the *subject*, the *theme*, the *situation*, and the *plot*.

The *subject* is the broadest classification we can use. A subject is a category, such as war, violence, revenge, compassion, kindness, honor, ambition. We can say that *Romeo and Juliet* is a play about love, for instance. How exactly it deals with that subject is revealed in the theme, situation, and plot.

The *theme* of a literary work is the author's central message or the central dramatic impact of the work. In *Romeo and Juliet* the lovers are described as "star-crossed." The theme of the play, therefore, is that some love affairs are destined to end in tragedy.

The *situation* in a literary work consists of a set of circumstances with which the work begins. For example, the situation in *Romeo and Juliet* is that the families of two young lovers are involved in a bitter feud. Everything that happens subsequently is part of the plot.

The *plot* is a summary of all the action in a literary work. A plot cannot be a list of random happenings. It must have a shape. The action must begin, rise to a crisis, and then be resolved. In other words, the plot is a summary of coherent and significant action. It is the spring that makes the clock tick.

Subject, theme, situation, and plot tell us something about the work, but the whole is greater than the sum of the parts. Therefore, describing what a literary work is about leaves us far short of experiencing it. Of "The Lottery" by Shirley Jackson (1948) we might say the following: It is a short story about tradition (subject). It is about how people blindly adhere to their traditions without knowing what these traditions are all about (theme). It is set in a typical farming community in which the residents gather for their annual lottery (situation). The events unfold in a suspenseful and significant sequence (plot). We are not told at first what the nature of the lottery is. The preparations are described in detail, as are the residents of the town. Some of the people are named and followed in greater detail. One of these is Mrs. Hutchinson, who arrives a bit late and joins her family. Another is Mr. Summers, who conducts the lottery. Still another is Old Man Warner, who defends the tradition when Mr. Adams says that "in the north village they're talking of giving up the lottery." Warner reminds them of the old saying: "Lottery in June, corn be heavy soon," and he says: "There's *always* been a lottery." There is a holiday atmosphere in the square, but also a hint of something unpleasant. We wonder, at this point, whether the person chosen will be a winner or a loser. The crowd grows tense as the time approaches for the head of each household to draw a folded piece of paper from the black box. They are called up alphabetically and told not to open their folded slips of paper until everyone has drawn. There is a breathless pause. Then the slips of paper are all opened. Mr. Hutchinson has drawn the marked slip. His wife objects, but the drawing goes on. There are five members in the Hutchinson family—husband, wife, and three children. Each must now draw from a smaller group of papers. Mrs. Hutchinson draws the slip with the black spot on it. A space is cleared around her in the crowd. The townspeople pick up stones, and, in spite of Mrs. Hutchinson's protests, they stone her to death.

This stark summary of the content and theme cannot convey fully the emotional impact and the deeper levels of meaning in this modern classic. It does, however, provide a kind of X-ray of the bones, a fleshless description of what the story is about. Much more could be said. On the other hand, one should keep in mind that, ultimately, a literary work is not merely *about* something; it *is* something.

4 | In some poems the stress is on the "statement," in others, the stress is on "language and form."

Poets who have a political or social message often use their poetry as a vehicle, which, some critics say, makes the message more important than the poem. Purists suggest that "the poem *is* the message." It is, actually, difficult to separate most poems into these two categories. Since poetry is a hybrid form that uses words and music, most poems tend to blend statement, imagery, and form. Heavy statement poems and purely technical poems have both been open to criticism. The controversy continues in many academic and artistic arenas.

1B There is enormous variety in literary themes.

1 | Some great themes have appeared frequently in our literary heritage.

The Greeks were interested in the concept of *hubris*; that is, excessive pride. Hence, the theme that mere human beings should not overreach themselves and try to be godlike.

The classical notion of tragedy is that a good person with a tragic flaw can make an error in judgment that will lead to his or her downfall.

The concept of destiny plays a role in some literary works, in which the theme, invariably, is that a person's fate is inescapable.

The struggle between good and evil is the basis of many works. Good and evil can take many forms, but these forms are usually determined by a cultural or religious context. The influence of ancient Greece and the Judeo-Christian tradition is clear in Western literature. In Shakespeare's *Othello*, Iago is pure evil. His behavior needs no other explanation. He is living evidence of the influence of Satan in the world. In *Billy Budd*, Melville describes the evil that possesses Claggart as "natural depravity." Nothing, therefore, can prevent the clash between Billy and Claggart.

Love is often dealt with as a powerful force in human experience. "Love is not love / Which alters when it alteration finds," says Shakespeare in one of his best known sonnets (116). Milton's famous remark about love makes a sexual distinction: "Love is of man's life a thing apart; 'tis woman's whole existence." In Hemingway's *A Farewell to Arms*, and in other love stories, love is described as a kind of religion. For Othello it is the very ordering force of the universe. When his love for Desdemona is threatened, he feels on the brink of chaos: "Perdition catch my soul / But I do love thee! And when I love thee not, / Chaos is come again." For some writers love may even go beyond the grave. In her often-quoted sonnet that begins "How do I love thee?" Elizabeth Barrett Browning says, "and, if God choose, / I shall but love thee better after death." Love, of course, is a subject that includes more than just the romantic attachments of men and women. It includes familial love and friendship and even, in a broader sense, such things as love of God and country.

"No man is an island," said John Donne. There are many variations on this theme. We cannot isolate ourselves completely from our fellow creatures, nor can we remove ourselves from our own humanity. Exile was a punishment worse than death in the ancient world. The wanderer, the outcast, the outsider, the exile, the stranger—all appear frequently in literature.

2 | Certain major themes have emerged in contemporary literature.

Some of the major themes in contemporary literature are focused on the *self*; others deal with a world that is full of peril, a world that breeds more anger and despair than hope.

Alienation and loneliness are common experiences in a fragmented world. The modern decline in family and community structures has elevated loneliness as a literary subject. The theme haunts the works of such modern writers as Joseph Conrad, T. S. Eliot, Albert Camus, and Gabriel García Márquez.

Coming of age in the modern world is extremely confusing. Being young has always been difficult, but in a world in which traditional modes of behavior have been challenged out of existence, the young have to create their own modes of behavior, and, in a sense, they have to create themselves. The result is considerable agony and chaos. Earlier literature rarely dealt with this subject. Today it is a major concern. This is one of the reasons why J. D. Salinger's *Catcher in the Rye* (1951) appears on so many high school reading lists.

Male-female relationships have become very complex since the so-called sexual revolution of the 1960s. Nowhere has the loss of tradition and structure in society caused more confusion than in the relationships between men and women. Romeo and Juliet may have had their problems, but they knew exactly where they stood and what was expected of them. Today's proliferation of paperback romances may be an escapist reaction to the confusion, or even a simplistic way of dealing with the new varieties of interpersonal problems. There are also, of course, many worthwhile literary works on the subject, most of them by women who have been writing with greater freedom in an atmosphere of liberation—writers such as Alice Walker and Cynthia Ozick.

There are many themes related to current issues: racial tension, drug and alcohol abuse, abortion, poverty, and the problems of the handicapped. Films made for television feast on such themes. The serious literary treatment of the experiences of minority groups has brought recognition to such minority writers as Ralph Ellison (winner of the National Book Award) and Toni Morrison (winner of the Nobel Prize for Literature).

Related to modern technology there are themes that deal with abuse of the environment and the dehumanization of society. Science fiction is full of such themes, but they also show up in other works, such as the film *Network* (1976), which was written by Paddy Chayefsky. Charlie Chaplin's *Modern Times* (1936) was an early satirical treatment of technology, which showed how the factory system turns humans into mere cogs in a wheel.

Disaster themes have become common and reflect our general anxiety. Many of these have been treated in popular movies that make use of spectacular special effects.

Philosophical confusion has followed in the wake of political and social upheaval and acceleration of scientific speculation. It is difficult to know what to think about anything. The result is often a feeling that nobody cares and that nothing matters, which may explain the blind pursuit of materialism and pleasure.

Concern about the future has lead to some dismal prophecies and fantasies, the most famous of which are Aldous Huxley's *Brave New World* and George Orwell's *1984*.

Themes dealing with crime and violence have appeared with increasing frequency, reflecting, perhaps, the frustrations of a world in confusion. Popular works of all kinds exploit these themes, which are often merely excuses for displays of bloodshed and cruelty.

1C Clarity in literature is arrived at more through descriptions of experience than through statements of ideas.

In an essay the theme is announced early on and everything that follows supports the theme. In literature the experience is uppermost, and in it the reader discovers a theme.

1 | Sometimes the theme is obvious and can be clearly stated.

Al Young's poem "New Autumn, New York" is a good example of a poem with a clear theme.

NEW AUTUMN, NEW YORK

Late in the day when light is sandwiched   1
softly between slices of daytime and night,
I stroll around Gramercy Park, locked as usual
and all keyed up again for the real autumn.

To the falling of leaves in time-lapse slow
motion, I follow my feet, each crackling step
nudging me into a vaster present than this
friendly seasonal chill can circumscribe.

There is no end to the inward adventure of
journeying October to the edge of November.   10

Source: From Al Young, The Blues Don't Change: New and Selected Poems.
Copyright 1982. Reprinted by permission of Louisiana State University Press.

2 | Sometimes the theme is difficult to express.

It is not always possible to reduce certain experiences to a
purely intellectual statement. The proportions of head and
heart in a given work will vary enormously. Symbols may be
artistically powerful but are often difficult to interpret. This
poem by William Blake (1757–1827) has been the subject
of considerable discussion and controversy:

THE SICK ROSE

O rose, thou art sick.
The invisible worm
That flies in the night
In the howling storm

Has found out thy bed
Of crimson joy,
And his dark secret love
Does thy life destroy.

What is this destructive "invisible worm"? Is it some moral failure, some corruption? Or is it more literally a disease?

1D There are many degrees and kinds of significance in literary works.

The broad literary spectrum ranges from the silliest kind of romance or comic book adventure to the works of such major literary figures as Herman Melville and Jane Austen. There is enormous variety in literature. Some critics try to draw the line and create criteria for what they call true literature, as opposed to mere entertainment or downright junk. Drawing a precise line is always a bit arbitrary, and not really necessary. What we have is a continuum from the very trivial to the very important. Since the range is very wide, some of the material between these extremes can prove quite interesting without actually being worldshaking. What good fiction, poetry, or drama does for us is to leave us with the feeling that our experience has been expanded vicariously and that perhaps we know something afterward that we did not know before. In other words, good literature has an impact that, in some way, changes the reader. Trivial literary entertainments such as thrillers and romances and television dramas, however, cannot be dismissed with contempt. They have a role to play in the lives of many people, and many of the writers involved find such work a pleasant and profitable form of employment, though significance in such works is clearly minimal. Their aim is to thrill, chill, and titillate. Frank Lloyd Wright once described television as "chewing gum for the eyes." It's an excellent description of that medium and might also apply to most of our light literature. Chewing gum gives you a lot of action but no nutrition. Great literature, on the other hand, is full of emotional, spiritual, and intellectual nourishment.

EXAMPLE 1A

THE INVISIBLE MAN
Ric Weinman

The invisible man is the main attraction. They come from all over to see him. Our small town circus has always been popular, but now they come a thousand miles and all they want to see is him.

The invisible man does only one show each night. He says the shows are very exhausting. When asked why he does the shows at all he replies that it is to make people happy.

His show is always the last show of the night. The tent in which the show is held goes quite dark, and the people in the audience, knowing what is to come next, hush their voices to a thick whisper. Suddenly, two bright spot lights are projected on the rear of the stage. In one of them is standing a short, slight, dark-skinned man with black curly hair and a very somber-looking face. In the other spot light is a piece of wooden floor. There stands the invisible man. The crowd cheers.

After a few minutes, the somber-looking man holds up his hands and the crowd falls silent. "The invisible man sends you all his greetings," the somber-looking man usually says. These words, even in his low, gravelly voice, evoke more cheering. He is the invisible man's helper. He is the only one who can hear what the invisible man says. But even he doesn't claim to be able to see the invisible man. No one can do that. He is quite entirely invisible. There is a popular rumor that under a full eclipse of the sun the invisible man will suddenly become visible, but as of yet, no full eclipse of the sun has occurred in our small town to either prove or disprove this for a fact.

The crowd squeezes together like marshmallows, trying to get as close to the stage as possible. Those who stand in the front row are pressed so hard against the chest-high stage that it is often difficult for them to breathe. They all swear it is worth it though, and quite worth the long wait they endured to reach that strategic position. Those who want to be in the front row usually get in line right after the show ends the night before.

A balding, middle-aged man in a rumpled but expensive-looking business suit standing in the front row waves his arm furiously. The somber-looking man points to him. "Do you ever think of joining the State Department?" the middle-aged man asks. There is a short pause in which the whole tent is wrapped in a dense silence. "No," the somber man says. "The invisible man says that he never feels like joining the State Department because he doesn't feel himself to be part of the state. He feels that he is his own state and that his political responsibilities lie within those boundaries." The business man, having been called upon and given an excellent answer, seems to glow with an intense joy. He looks like one who has been blessed.

More hands are in the air. A little girl, perhaps four years old, is called upon. "I'd like to know if you would give me a kiss?" She asks shyly. The crowd is suddenly very tense. The audaciousness of the little girl's request angers them. They feel she is being denigrating. They feel she has no right to make such a request that can only be refused. "The invisible man says he will kiss you," the somber man says. The crowd relaxes, both surprised and pleased. "How wonderful of him," someone says. The little girl is lifted onto the stage and sticks her head forward with her eyes closed, her lips curled up in an expectant pout. The crowd becomes very still. "The invisible man says he has kissed you," the somber man says. "He did?" she exclaims, opening her eyes. Suddenly she knows it is true. A beautiful smile lights up her face and the crowd cheers. The little girl is lifted back down.

"To what do you attribute your invisibility?" This question is from a young woman. The crowd groans. It is an often-asked question and the answer is well known to most of those present. Mainly, though, it's the waste of a precious question—the invisible man answers only four questions each night. "The invisible man says that when he was a young boy his father died and his mother became a drunkard. Since there was no one to pay him much attention, he stopped believing he existed. As many wise men know, belief creates reality. Not long afterwards he started to fade from visible existence." Hands fly in the air.

"Does the invisible man think he'll ever meet an invisible woman?" This question from a teenage boy. "Please direct your question to the invisible man, not to me," the somber man says. The boy looks confused for a moment. His mother whispers something in his ear. The boy nods his head and smiles. "Do you think you'll ever meet an invisible woman?" The crowd is excited. They like this question. They anxiously await the answer. "The invisible man says that he does in fact already know an invisible woman but that he is not yet ready to introduce her to the world." For a moment the crowd is so shocked by the answer, there is no break in the silence. Then there is an amazed whisper. And another. And another. Suddenly the whole tent is alive with whispers which flow together and rise and fall like waves of the ocean, like a great tide washing against the shores of incomprehensible time. "An invisible woman." "An invisible woman." "An invisible woman." It sounds something like a chant the old ones used to sing. The somber-looking man holds up his hands but it is some time before the crowd is again silent.

"As you know," he begins slowly, his weak, scratchy voice somehow a perfect match for the rough tent and expectant faces, "before we conclude each night's ceremony we try to see if we can't bring the invisible man into the visible world, even for just the briefest of fleeting moments. If you'll all hold hands as best you can and try to concentrate on the invisible man becoming visible, there's a slight chance that the power of your thoughts will make him solid enough to enable you to catch a quick glimpse of him." By the time he finishes speaking, everyone is already holding hands. A hush falls on the tent and the meditation begins. For five minutes the silence is so intense a man with a slight asthma in the back of the tent can be heard all the way up front by the stage. Finally there is a whisper. "I think I saw him." "I think I saw him, too." "I saw him, I know I did." "I saw him, too. He was about six feet tall and had light-brown hair." "Yes, he had light-brown hair." "Did you see his hair?" "Yes, it was light brown and he was about six feet tall." At least half the people are certain they've glimpsed him and another third thinks they did but are not absolutely sure. They all agree though: he is about six feet tall with light-brown hair. Of this there can be no doubt.

The crowd files out of the tent and disperses into the night. Some of them will dream of him tonight. In their dreams the invisible man may take many forms.

Source: "The Invisible Man," by Ric Weinman, From Intro 10. Copyright 1979. Reprinted by permission of author, Ric Weinman.

EXAMPLE 1B

WARNING: NUCLEAR WASTE DUMP
Mary Baine Campbell

This poem has to last   1
Ten thousand years
And be translated
Into every language
In the world.

Whoever conquers New Jersey
Must come equipped
With this poem, or die.

The poem must not depend
On music for its beauty   10
Since it must be equally beautiful
In every language
There will ever be.

It has to be so beautiful
That people will say it
For five hundred generations.
It must be universal
And timeless.

Millions of lives depend
On the beauty of this poem   20
But it cannot change
From ear to ear:
The critic who discovers
Its figurative sense
Must be silenced,

For the poem means
Exactly what it says.

We must find a way
To teach the birds
And the animals   **30**
To say it too,
And the trees, and water.

EXAMPLE 1C

WITNESS
David Ignatow

We can't write ourselves into eternal life   1
and that is the sorrow and waste of writing,
but those who would write in this knowledge
have found a subterfuge by which to let
themselves be prompted, in heady confidence
of meaning: the wealth of self
spread among the readers who themselves
will read for reasons of earth:
that they have been witness
to their birth, growth and death   10
and shared the earth with earth.

Source: From Poetry, Vol. CII, Nos. 1–2, 1987. Copyright © David Ignatow. Reprinted by permission of Yaedi Ignatow.

EXERCISES

Discussion

1. What is the theme of "The Invisible Man"?
2. Is the invisible man just an entertainment at a carnival? Is he supposed to be a religious figure? If so, is the author's attitude positive or negative?
3. What is the theme of "Warning: Nuclear Waste Dump"?
4. Why do you think the author used such huge exaggerations?
5. What is the theme of the poem "Witness"? Comment on the first line: "We can't write ourselves into eternal life."

Writing

1. Write a story or play in which there is an invisible character.
2. Write a poem that uses the same kind of exaggeration used by Mary Campbell.
3. Write a poem about an important event you experienced as a child.

Setting

Every literary work has to take place somewhere, even if the setting is only minimally implied, as it often is in poetry. In any story something happens (plot), and it happens to someone (characters), sometime and someplace (setting). The role that a setting plays can vary from negligible to vital. It often provides a good source for images and symbols. Think of deserts, mountains, caves, the raging sea, and steaming jungles. And think of Faulkner's South, Baldwin's Harlem, and Hemingway's Paris and Spain. But how important are the settings in Jane Austen's novels? And is there any setting at all in the poems of Emily Dickinson?

2A A literary work can be set anywhere, from the inner space of a dream to the outer space of science fiction.

1 | Some settings are merely the landscape of the author's mind.

Most poems refer to specific circumstances with an implied or an actual setting, but some poems seem to be general comments on life or outbursts of emotion. Sometimes these feelings are translated into metaphorical landscape terms. Some of these poems may be reveries, memories, or dreams that name no other setting. Some, however, hint at specific incidents, and therefore vaguely suggest a setting in the outside world. Emily Dickinson's outbursts of emotion provide good examples. In "Wild Nights" the reverie implies a love affair of some kind, and the dreamlike imagery creates a symbolic setting.

WILD NIGHTS! WILD NIGHTS!

> Wild Nights—Wild Nights!
> Were I with thee
> Wild Nights should be
> Our luxury!
>
> Futile—the Winds—
> To a Heart in port—
> Done with the Compass—
> Done with the Chart!
>
> Rowing in Eden—
> Ah, the Sea!
> Might I but moor—Tonight—
> In Thee!

In this poem we hear the longing of a lonely character, and we might imagine that these thoughts are provoked by a stormy night, and that the narrator is lying awake in bed, a solitary soul in a remote place.

2 | Some external settings are minimal and generic.

Some literary works take place in a setting that is never identified as a specific or real place. It might merely be a living room, a bar, a boat, a castle, a village, a battlefield, or, as in that famous stage direction, "another part of the forest." Fairy tales and folk tales tend to be vague about locations. They often begin: "Once upon a time in a kingdom by the sea . . ." or something to that effect.

Many plays are preoccupied with a human drama or a comic situation and merely specify a single set—a room, a pub, a railroad station. The generic setting for Luigi Pirandello's *Six Characters in Search of an Author* is simply "the stage of a theatre."

The settings in poems are often minimal and unnamed, though they may give rise to significant experiences. In the following poem by Seamus Heaney the setting is merely described as "the slopes of the cutting." No country or town is mentioned. It is, in a sense, a generic rural setting. The emphasis is on the young boys and their revelations about the world outside their little place.

THE RAILWAY CHILDREN

When we climbed the slopes of the cutting
We were eye-level with the white cups
Of the telegraph poles and the sizzling wires.

Like lovely freehand they curved for miles
East and miles west beyond us, sagging
Under their burden of swallows.

We were small and thought we knew nothing
Worth knowing. We thought words travelled
      the wires
In the shiny pouches of raindrops.

Each one seeded full with the light
Of the sky, the gleam of the lines, and ourselves
So infinitesimally scaled

We could stream through the eye of a needle.

Source: "Railway Children" from POEMS 1965–1975 by Seamus Heaney. Copyright © 1980 by Seamus Heaney. Reprinted by permission of Farrar, Straus and Giroux, LLC and Faber & Faber Ltd.

In "The Lottery," Shirley Jackson uses a generic small American town as the setting for a shocking and primitive ritual. In Hemingway's "A Clean, Well-Lighted Place" the setting is a generic Spanish café. It doesn't really matter exactly where it is. The vagueness of location in stories such as these tends to give them a universal quality.

3 | Some literary works take place entirely in dreams.

The dream setting can be effective, suggestive, and symbolic. In a dream almost anything can happen. Locations can be realistic or fantastic. The setting can shift suddenly. The subconscious mind is cavalier about such things. The result is often surrealistic.

One of the most famous dream poems is Samuel Taylor Coleridge's "Kubla Khan: or a Vision in a Dream." It was actually written immediately after the author woke up from an opium dream.

Students in writing workshops are rather fond of dream settings. Perhaps it unleashes the imagination. Unfortunately, they are equally fond of the alarm clock that wakes up the protagonist at the very peak of the suspense. The sudden discovery by the reader that the whole adventure was merely a dream can prove extremely disappointing.

4 | Some settings are pure fantasy—places in imaginary worlds.

Writers have been using imaginary journeys to imaginary places—past, present, or future—since ancient times. Plato imagines a Spartan utopia in *The Republic*. Dante descends into hell in *The Divine Comedy*. Lewis Carroll's Alice goes down a rabbit hole into a mad, fantastic world. In more recent times we have *A Modern Utopia* by H. G. Wells, Aldous Huxley's *Brave New World*, and Charlotte Haldane's

Man's World, which, like Huxley's novel, rejects a world shaped by science, technology, and materialism. The *Star Wars* and *Star Trek* series indicate the popularity of lighter science fiction, in which futuristic heroes fight it out with the forces of evil in countless galaxies and solar systems that are largely imaginary.

5 | Most literary works have realistic settings.

Since literature is essentially about human experience, readers find it easy to empathize with realistic characters in realistic settings. A great many writers, using a great variety of styles, have chosen real locations for their works. We think of James Joyce's Dublin, of Thomas Hardy's Dorset, of Tennessee Williams' New Orleans, and Woody Allen's New York. A reader does not have to be familiar with the specific setting to appreciate the work. There are common denominators in human experience that allow us to identify with characters in England or France or Russia, in rural or urban areas, in New England, in the South, or in the Midwest. That is why we can all read a novel about a dull doctor in a provincial French town who is married to a restless and romantic woman who becomes involved in a series of love affairs that lead her, eventually, to a tragic end. The novel is *Madame Bovary* by Gustave Flaubert.

6 | Some realistic settings have fictitious names.

When it comes to selecting a setting and naming it, writers have three choices. They can use:

1. A real place with a real name,
2. A real place with a fictitious name,
3. A fictitious place with a fictitious name.

Setting a story in a real place such as New York and calling it New York is no problem, since anything can happen in New York, and, in any case, nobody knows everything that goes on in such a big city. Setting a story in a very small town, however, and calling it by its real name can cause some problems. In some small towns everybody knows everything that ever happened there. It is difficult to insist that certain events took place and certain characters existed when, in reality, they did not. Some writers avoid this problem by using a fictitious name for a real town. If there is no special reason for choosing a certain location, some writers will simply make up a place, perhaps a typical American small town. It might resemble a lot of towns without actually being modeled after any particular place.

Thomas Hardy used the fictitious name Wessex for Dorset, a real county in England. William Faulkner used the name Yoknapatawpha county for a real region in his home state of Mississippi. On the other hand, Dorothy Parker, Saul Bellow, James Baldwin, and Woody Allen simply call New York by its real name.

2B The accuracy of the setting depends on its importance to the story.

In some literary works the setting is *incidental*, and the main concern is plot or character. In other works the setting plays a *major role*. In poetry the setting itself is sometimes the *central focus* of the work. William Wordsworth writes about the countryside above Tintern Abbey. Dylan Thomas describes his town in Wales in musical detail. Robert Frost contemplates the walls and woods of his New England landscape.

1 | Some settings require personal and detailed knowledge.

Many writers make use of their hometown or the various places in which they have lived. And why not? These are the places one knows best. In autobiographical works they often play a significant role. It would have been difficult for James Baldwin to write *Go Tell It on the Mountain* if he had not grown up in Harlem. There is a long list of important writers whose works depend heavily on an intimate knowledge of the settings they use. James Joyce had to have an intimate knowledge of Dublin to write *Ulysses*, and William Faulkner could not have written such works as *The Sound and the Fury* and *Absalom! Absalom!* without being a native southerner. Flannery O'Connor also drew on her southern background to write her fiction, including the brilliant novel *Wise Blood*.

2 | Some settings do not require an intimate knowledge of the place.

Many a Hollywood or television script has been set in places never even visited by the writer. Almost any well-known place in the world can be conjured up with stereotypes and stock shots. The Eiffel Tower in Paris, the White House in Washington, Big Ben in London, a crowded marketplace in Casablanca. Old Hollywood films are especially notorious for creating sets out of stereotypes—the French café, the canals of Venice, the imaginary jungles through which Tarzan swung. A high degree of accuracy was not necessary.

The central focus of these works was action, adventure, romance, intrigue. Even excellent human dramas made use of these theatrical sets. *Casablanca* did not become one of the most popular movies of all time because of the accuracy with which the place was depicted. It was important because of the love story, the conflict, the illusion of important events, and the incredible number of quotable lines.

3 | Settings in historical fiction and drama depend on careful research.

Although stereotypes are sometimes used in works set in the past, a serious attempt to deal with a historical period should involve a careful and accurate reconstruction of that period. Stock shots of Roman orgies and gladiators may do for junk films and adventures with a comic book sense of history, but a novel such as *I, Claudius* by Robert Graves requires a much more thorough background. For most historical periods there is plenty of material in libraries, including books on everyday life. Useful for the writer are books with pictures, not only of historical characters but of the artifacts, architecture, and geographical locations. For modern periods personal visits have a distinct advantage, but it is amazing what one can find in books, on video tapes, and CDs.

4 | Excessive attention to the setting can be distracting; too little attention can lead to vagueness.

The degree of accuracy and the amount of detail you use must depend on the nature of your project. If the setting is very significant, you should know it well and weave details carefully into the fabric of events. If the setting is not very significant, do not burden your reader with unnecessary details. Too much description can get in the way of the story. On the other hand, a reader always likes to know where the action is taking place. Do not be too vague. Try to be convincing without being intrusive.

2C The significance of the setting varies from work to work.

1 | In autobiographical works the setting can tell us something about the author.

A *novel of emergence* is a novel about the early years and young adulthood of a character. Since children are very sensitive to their environment, the setting of such a novel is significant. Charlotte Brontë's *Jane Eyre*, set in Yorkshire, and Charles Dickens' *David Copperfield*, set in London, are such novels. In D. H. Lawrence's *Sons and Lovers*, the dismal life of a coal mining family in Nottingham figures prominently, and in James Baldwin's *Go Tell It on the Mountain*, the background is Harlem in New York.

2 | Sometimes the setting itself is the main subject of the work.

One might argue that the main character in Faulkner's *Absalom! Absalom!* is the South itself, and that Thomas Sutpen is merely a symbolic or mythological figure.

There have been many attempts to capture the way of life in a typical small town in America. One of the best is *Our Town*, a play by Thornton Wilder, which is a portrait of a fictional place called Grover's Corners, New Hampshire.

3 | Some settings are used symbolically.

In Conrad's *Heart of Darkness* the journey up the Congo River is hardly treated as a mere travelogue. It is a journey back to the primitive state of man and to certain shadowy and violent regions of the human mind and heart. In Melville's *Moby Dick*, the sea, the whale, and the whaling ship are all treated symbolically. The novel is not just an adventure story; it is an ambitious metaphysical masterpiece. In drama we have the bleak landscape of Samuel Beckett's *Waiting for Godot* or the bare room in hell in Jean-Paul Sartre's play *No Exit*.

4 | Some settings present obstacles that influence or determine the action.

Jungles, deserts, rivers, mountains, and islands all have figured in light or serious literature. Who can forget the white-water journey in *Deliverance* or the desert across which Lawrence of Arabia led his Arab troops to attack the Turks?

Such settings are often difficult enough in themselves, but when visited by natural disasters, as they often are, they provide truly dramatic stages for suspense, heroism, and disaster. At sea there are typhoons. In the mountains there are avalanches. Islands are swept by hurricanes and tidal waves. Forests become blazing infernos.

5 | Some settings are satirical.

Some of the imaginary places in utopian and prophetic literature are designed to criticize contemporary life. Huxley's *Brave New World* is a prime example, as is Samuel Butler's *Erewhon*, in which illness is considered a crime and crime is considered an illness. In a novel called *The Fixed Period*, Anthony Trollope invented an island named Britannula, ruled by a president named Mr. Neverbend.

Satire can be very amusing and significant. In order to use it well you not only have to create a convincing imaginary setting, but you also must have a good understanding of the real place that is being satirized.

EXAMPLE 2A

BARCELONA
Alice Adams

In the darkened, uneven cobbled square, in the old quarter of Barcelona, the Barrio Gótico, the middle-aged American couple who walk by appear to be just that: American, middle-aged. The man is tall and bald; his head shines dimly as he and his wife cross the shaft of light from an open doorway. She is smaller, with pale hair; she walks fast to keep up with her husband. She is wearing gold chains, and they, too, shine in the light. She carries a small bag in which there could be—more gold? money? some interesting pills? They pass a young Spaniard lounging in a corner whose face the man for no reason takes note of.

Persis Fox, the woman, is a fairly successful illustrator, beginning to be sought after by New York publishers, but she sees herself as being in most ways a coward, a very fearful person; she is afraid of planes, of high bridges, she is overly worried by the illnesses of children—a rather boring list, as she thinks of it. Some years ago she was afraid that Thad, her husband, who teaches at Harvard, would take off with some student, some dark, sexily athletic type from Texas, possibly. More recently she has been frightened by accounts everywhere of muggings, robberies, rapes. She entirely believes in the likelihood of nuclear war. She can and does lie awake at night with such thoughts, for frozen hours.

However, walking across these darkened cobbles, in the old quarter of Barcelona, toward a restaurant that Cambridge friends have recommended, she is not afraid at all, only interested in what she is seeing: just before the square, an arched and windowed walk up above the alley, now crenellated silhouettes, everywhere blackened old stones. Also, she is hungry, looking forward to the seafood for which this restaurant is famous. And she wishes that Thad would not walk so fast; by now he is about five feet ahead of her, in an alley.

In the next instant, though, before she has seen or heard any person approaching, someone is running past her in the dark—but not past; he is beside her, a tall dark boy, grabbing at her purse, pulling its short strap. Persis' first instinct is to let him have it, not because she is afraid—she is not, still not, afraid—but from a conditioned reflex, instructing her to give people what they want: children, her husband.

In the following second a more primitive response sets in, and she cries out, "No!"—as she thinks, Kindergarten, some little boy pulling something away. And next thinks, Not kindergarten. Spain. A thief.

He is stronger, and with a sudden sharp tug he wins; he has pulled the bag from her and run off, as Persis still yells, "No!"—and as (amazingly!) she remembers the word for thief. "Ladrón!" she cries out. "*Ladrón!*"

Then suddenly Thad is back (Persis has not exactly thought of him in those seconds), and almost before she has finished saying "He took my bag!" Thad is running toward the square, where the thief went. Thad is running, running—so tall and fast, such a sprint, as though this were a marathon, or Memorial Drive, where he usually runs. He is off into the night, as Persis yells again, "*Ladrón!*" and she starts out after him.

Persis is wearing low boots (thank God), not heels, and she can hear Thad's whistle, something he does with two fingers in his mouth, intensely shrill, useful for summoning children from ski slopes or beaches as night comes on. Persis, also running, follows the sound. She comes at last to a fairly wide, dimly lit street where Thad is standing, breathing hard.

She touches his arm. "Thad—"

Still intent on the chase, he hardly looks at her. He is not doing this for her; it is something between men. He says, "I think he went that way."

"But Thad—"

The street down which he is pointing, and into which he now begins to stride, with Persis just following—this street's darkness is broken at intervals by the steamy yellow windows of shabby restaurants, the narrow open door of a bar. Here and there a few people stand in doorways, watching the progress of the Americans. Thad sticks his head into the restaurants, the bar. "I don't see him," he reports back each time.

Well, of course not. And of course each time Persis is glad—glad that the boy is hidden somewhere. Gone. Safe, as she and Thad are safe.

They reach the end of the block, when from behind them a voice calls out, in English, not loudly, "Lady, this your bag?"

Thad and Persis turn to see a dark, contemptuous young face, a tall boy standing in a doorway. Not, Thad later assures Persis, and later still their friends—not the thief, whom he saw as they first crossed the square, and would recognize. But a friend of his?

The boy kicks his foot at something on the cobbles, which Thad walks over to pick up, and which is Persis' bag.

"I can't believe it!" she cries out, aware of triteness, as Thad hands over the bag to her. But by now, now that everything is over, she is seriously frightened; inwardly she trembles.

"Well, we got it." Thad speaks calmly, but Persis can hear the pride in his voice, along with some nervousness. He is still breathing hard, but he has begun to walk with his purposeful stride again. "The restaurant must be down here," he tells her.

Astoundingly, it is; after a couple of turns they see the name on a red neon sign, the name of the place they have been told about, where they have made a reservation.

The kitchen seems to be in the front room, next to the bar: all steam and steel, noisy clanging. Smoke and people, glasses rattling, crashing. "I really need a drink," Persis tells Thad, as instead they are led back to a room full of tables, people—many Americans, tourists, all loud and chattering.

At their small table, waiting for wine, with his tight New England smile Thad asks, "Aren't you going to check it? See what's still there?"

Curiously, this has not yet occurred to Persis as something to be done; she has simply clutched the bag. Now, as she looks down at the bag on her lap, it seems shabbier, a battered survivor. Obediently she unsnaps the flap. "Oh good, my passport's here," she tells Thad.

"That's great." He is genuinely pleased with himself—and why should he not be, having behaved with such courage? Then he frowns. "He got all your money?"

"Well no, actually there wasn't any money. I keep it in my pocket. Always, when I go to New York, that's what I do."

Why does Thad look so confused just then? A confusion of emotions is spread across his fair, lined face. He is disappointed, somehow? Upset that he ran after a thief who had stolen a bag containing so little? Upset that Persis, who now goes down to New York on publishing business by herself, has tricks for self-preservation?

Sipping wine, and almost instantly dizzy, light in her head, Persis tries to explain herself. "Men are such dopes," she heedlessly starts. "They always think that women carry everything they own in their bags. Thieves think that, I mean. So I just shove money and credit cards into some pocket. There's only makeup in my bags."

"And your passport." Stern, judicious Thad.

"Oh yes, of course," Persis babbles. "That would have been terrible. We could have spent days in offices."

Gratified, sipping at his wine, Thad says, "I wonder why he didn't take it, actually."

Persis does not say, "Because it's hidden inside my address book"—although quite possibly that was the case. Instead, she says what is also surely true: "Because you scared him. The last thing he expected was someone running after him, and that *whistle*."

Thad smiles, and his face settles into a familiar expression: that of a generally secure, intelligent man, a lucky person, for whom things happen more or less as he would expect them to.

Persis is thinking, and not for the first time, how terrible it must be to be a man, how terrifying. Men are always running, chasing something. And if you are rich and successful, like Thad, you have to hunt down anyone who wants to take away your possessions. Or if you're poor, down on your luck, you might be tempted to chase after a shabby bag that holds nothing of any real value, to snatch such a bag from a foreign woman who is wearing false gold chains that shine and glimmer in the dark.

Source: "Barcelona," from Return Trips by Alice Adams. Copyright © [1984] by Alice Adams. Reprinted by permission of International Creative Management, Inc.

EXAMPLE 2B

LAND OF LITTLE STICKS, 1945

James Tate

Where the wife is scouring the frying pan
and the husband is leaning up against the barn.
Where the boychild is pumping water into a bucket
and the girl is chasing a spotted dog.

And the sky churns on the horizon.
A town by the name of Pleasantville has disappeared.
And now the horses begin to shift and whinny,
and the chickens roost, keep looking this way and that.
At this moment something is not quite right.

The boy trundles through the kitchen, spilling water.
His mother removes several pies from the oven, shouts
    at him.
The girlchild sits down by the fence to stare at the horses.
And the man is just as he was, eyes closed, forehead
against his forearm, leaning up against the barn.

Source: "Land of Little Sticks" from Constant Defender (Eccho Press, 1983).
Reprinted by permission of author.

EXAMPLE 2C

WORKING THE FACE
Jay Parini

On his belly with a coal pick   1
mining underground:
the pay was better for one man
working the face.
Only one at a time could get
so close, his nose
to the anthracite, funneling
light from a helmet, chipping,
with his eyes like points of fire.
He worked, a taproot   10
tunneling inward, layer
by layer, digging
in a world of shadows,
thick as a slug against the floor,
dark all day long.
Wherever he turned, the facets
showered a million stars.
He was prince of darkness,
stalking the village at 6 P.M.,
having been to the end of it,   20
core and pith
of the world's rock belly.

EXERCISES

Discussion

1. Is the setting significant in the story "Barcelona" by Alice Adams? Would the story have the same effect if it was set in New York or some other large city?

2. How does the author describe the main characters? Why is the husband so determined to catch the thief?

3. James Tate has written a poem that is entitled "Land of Little Sticks, 1945." What does that title mean? The name of the town is Pleasantville. Is this a satire?

4. With what do you associate the year, 1945? Is the poem possibly about the testing or the use of an atomic bomb? If so, what kind of a setting is this? Is it specific or generic?

Writing

1. Describe your hometown or any other place that is familiar to you.

2. Describe life on an imaginary planet called Cronos.

3. Write a story that is set in a typical New England or Southern town.

4. Write a short story that takes place in a foreign country that you have never been to.

5. Write a poem about a natural setting, such as a forest, river, desert, beach, or mountain.

6. Write a poem or a story that takes place in a dream.

7. Write a story set in Pleasantville, the town referred to in "Land of Little Sticks, 1945." Make up a plot and a catastrophe that is consistent with whatever is suggested by the poem.

Characters

3A Since literature is about human experience, all literary works have characters.

1 | A character is usually an imaginary person created to play a role in a literary work.

Some characters are pure creations of the writer's imagination, and some are drawn from the writer's experience. Occasionally, specific people can even be identified as the models for certain characters. And in historical fiction, of course, real people are brought to life again, with varying degrees of accuracy. Wherever the characters come from, they are, in a sense, *created* and become part of the literary work, which is an artifice or vision, an act of the imagination. When a work is devoted to presenting the life of a real person in a factual way, we have biography, not fiction.

2 | Literary characters are created for a purpose, but real-life people just are what they are.

Fictitious characters exist in the author's mind and on paper. Since they are created for a purpose, they usually have a certain coherence and definition. At simple extremes they are heroes and villains. In most realistic works they are more complex, but the bottom line is that they are "employed." Their employer is the writer, who has a job for them to do in his or her literary project. Living a real life is not the same as being specifically created to play a role in a drama or a novel. Literature is not life; it is *about* life.

3 | Nonhuman characters figure prominently in some forms of literature.

In works such as *Aesop's Fables*, in children's literature, and in animated cartoons, we find a lot of animals that can talk. We also find trees that can talk, and rocks, and other things in nature, such as the wind and thunder. Actually, all of these things, when they appear in stories, in poems, in dramas, and movies, are humanized. This convention is known as *anthropomorphism*, not strictly in the sense that a human form is given to a nonhuman thing, but in the sense that human speech and feelings are attributed to this thing. In general, animals and inanimate objects can be used in literature only if they are given some human characteristics. One can describe a duck in scientific terms or as a farmyard animal that is part of the setting, but that duck is not the same as Donald Duck, who has a human personality.

4 | How much the reader should know about a character depends on the nature of the literary work.

In a long work a character may be presented from the cradle to the grave, but often a literary work is like a view through a keyhole. We see only a portion of a character's life. The rest of the character's life is implied, and there is only the impression that the character has a real life. In order to create this illusion, the writer has to know more about the character than is revealed to the reader. Some writers prepare detailed biographical notes on their characters before beginning their play or story, and many a writer has felt that, in a sense, the characters really exist. Flaubert said: "Everything one invents is true, you can be sure of that. Beyond a doubt my poor Bovary is suffering and weeping in twenty French villages at this very moment." Woody Allen toys with this idea in "The Kugelmass Episode," a short story in which the protagonist is able to go back in time and have a love affair with Madame Bovary. Later, Emma is able to walk right out of her novel and the nineteenth century to visit her lover in modern New York.

The gimmick is amusing, and certainly there are characters who are so effectively depicted that they become real in the reader's mind, but that does not mean that either the author or the reader knows *everything* about them. In fact, it is not necessary to know everything in order to create the illusion of reality. What is necessary for that illusion is depth of understanding and skillful presentation.

5 | Characters in literature can be presented with the help of a number of literary devices.

The people in fiction are not any different from the people in poetry or drama, but there may be some differences from genre to genre in the devices used to bring them to life. On the other hand, there are certain devices that are common to all the forms of creative writing (see the chapters on *description*, *dialogue*, and *thoughts*). What we are concerned with here are the broader goals you hope to achieve when you present your characters. Those goals can be discussed in terms of the following questions:

1. What do your characters look like? (appearance)
2. What are your characters thinking? (depth)
3. Why do your characters do what they do? (motivation)
4. How believable are your characters? (plausibility)

The balance of this chapter will deal with these four points.

3B There is often some literary significance in a character's physical appearance.

1 | A character's physical appearance is sometimes influenced by literary traditions.

Some of the literary traditions about the appearances of characters seem simplistic today, and even objectionable; nevertheless, the influence of those traditions is sometimes still felt. For instance, there was a time when it was customary in literature, and especially in the theater, to assume that internal good or evil is reflected in the external qualities of a character. Heroes are attractive, villains are ugly. Richard III was portrayed as a hunchback by Shakespeare. Desdemona, who was innocent and pure, was an unblemished beauty. This tradition influenced the vintage films of the Hollywood era. To a lesser degree that influence continues in all the popular media, but there are more and more exceptions. Now there are even very handsome villains. Even serious works are occasionally touched by this tradition, though in modern times there is more subtlety and flexibility. What's more, the concept of the hero has given ground to the concept of the antihero, who is not a villain, but simply an ordinary person. Much of our good literature is no longer about a struggle between a hero and a villain; it is often about a wide variety of people and circumstances. There was a time when the common person was not considered worthy of a central role in any literary work. In modern times literature has become democratized. Central characters are drawn from every segment of society. Willy Loman, for instance, is the pathetic hero of Arthur Miller's *Death of a Salesman*. A very poor and old black woman named Phoenix Jackson is the heroine of Eudora Welty's "A Worn Path."

Though we still have stereotypes in modern writing, we also have unique individuals—a broad range of individuals. The writer has to decide what they look like. Most writers have minds like old attics, in which a lifetime of odds and ends are stored. They tend to be very inquisitive and observant. They walk down a street and notice things: a smile, a glance, a scar, a limp, the face of a young woman, the yellow skin of an old man, the eyes of a child. Writers are scavengers. They are people-watchers, photographers, psychologists, and a lot of other things. A good writer must pay attention to everything he or she encounters—everything! It is from this attic full of fragments that characters are constructed.

Some writers borrow the faces and features of people they know. Often, it's nothing personal, just the need for a model, a need to visualize a character. A *roman à clef*, however, is actually about real people who are presented as thinly disguised fictional characters. This is a special situation.

When writers choose the physical appearance of characters, they already have something deeper in mind. They already have a plot or a set of circumstances, and they already have a general feeling for the fictional persons involved. They simply have to flesh out the characters. Their choices will be influenced by the personality of the characters and by the roles they play. Even though stereotypes are not involved, the appearance of the characters must be appropriate. It is, in a way, part of their costumes.

2 | In some works the physical appearance of a character is merely implied or is left entirely up to the reader's imagination.

Hemingway made famous this kind of economy in fiction. In the opening paragraph of "A Clean, Well-Lighted Place" we are introduced to a man in a café. All we are actually told about him is that he is old and deaf, but almost instantly we can picture him. Hemingway uses tone, imagery, and dialogue to help along the reader's imagination:

> It was late and every one had left the cafe except an old man who sat in the shadow the leaves of the tree made against the electric light. In the day time the street was dusty, but at night the dew settled the dust and the old man liked to sit late because he was deaf and now at night it was quiet and he felt the difference. The two waiters inside the café knew that the old man was a little drunk, and while he was a good client they knew that if he became too drunk he would leave without paying, so they kept watch on him.

In fairy tales, fables, and folktales we often get an even sparser description of the appearance of the character. In Somerset Maugham's "Appointment in Samarra" (see Chapter 12) we have a merchant, a servant, and a woman who is the spectre of death. None of them is described. They don't even have names.

The amount of physical detail provided by the author involves questions of style and is influenced by the conventions of the genre.

3C Characters in literary works should have a certain depth of development.

1 | Characters can be classified as *flat* or *round.*

Some characters are superficial or two-dimensional; other characters are three-dimensional and more fully created. They are as complex and convincing as real people. Flat characters have very little depth and are often stereotypes— the tall, dark, handsome lover in a romance, for instance, and his beautiful, virtuous, and devoted sweetheart. Entertainment literature does not require characters with depth. It needs only stock characters to amuse us or help us wile away our leisure time. It is devoted largely to love, sex, and violence. It needs heroes and villains, and, especially, husbands and wives and lovers with all the romantic agonies humanly imaginable.

2 | The deeper qualities in round characters are those qualities that make the characters more lifelike and meaningful.

What is it that we want to know about the characters in serious literature? "It is easier to know man in general than to understand one man in particular," said La Rochefoucauld in 1665. This fascination with the complexity of the individual is age-old. Science and psychology may not have all the answers. Literature is sometimes a more effective way to explore human experience. In his Nobel Prize acceptance speech William Faulkner said that literature concerns itself with "the eternal problems of the human heart."

At the greeting-card level human experiences are described in clichés. Love is a valentine message that begins, "Roses are red, violets are blue." When serious writers such as Emily Brontë, Gustave Flaubert, or D. H. Lawrence write about love, it is a profound exploration of a complex emotion. We are still deeply moved by the story of Heathcliff and Catherine in *Wuthering Heights*, and we still talk about Emma Bovary's love affair with love, and about Lady Chatterley's passionate affair with the gamekeeper. If people weren't so complicated and fascinating, we wouldn't go on writing about them the way we do.

We want to know what they are *really* like, in what ways they inescapably participate in human nature, and in what ways they can be distinguished one from another. We want to know how they feel, what they think, and how they act in a variety of circumstances.

Even physically no two people are exactly alike. They differ in many ways: body language, posture, mannerisms, patterns of speech, attitudes, moods, overt desires and hidden desires, ordinary fears and secret fears, obsessions, neuroses, ways of seeing things and ways of seeing themselves. Discovering *everything* about a single individual, including ourselves, is like dropping a stone into a very deep lake and following its progress to the murky bottom. Sooner or later we lose sight of it because the absolute bottom is not visible.

3D   The behavior of a three-dimensional character has to be logically motivated.

In superficial adventures the good guys are simply good and the bad guys are simply bad. It is the action that counts, not the characters. In more serious literature, motivation is very important. It is often more interesting than the action itself. Understanding the motivations of literary characters helps us to understand human nature and ourselves.

When we talk about Hamlet we talk less about the action than we do about the character, his strange behavior, his indecision, his anger, his sexuality. He is, in fact, a character who suddenly finds himself incapable of action. We want to know why. What's wrong with this guy? Does he want to avenge his father's death or not? He accuses his uncle and mother of incest, but perhaps it is he himself who has incestuous longings.

Your characters need not have the classical stature of Hamlet; they can be ordinary people in the grip of some conflict or obsession. Understanding ordinary people is not much easier than understanding Hamlet, and certainly not less significant.

1 | Every human action is motivated by some internal or external factor.

In Albert Camus' *The Stranger*, motivation is at the very heart of the novel. With minimal provocation Mersault kills a stranger. It is not really self-defense, and, what's more, after shooting him once, Mersault then empties the gun into him. In court Mersault cannot explain his actions and refuses to testify in his own defense. He is called an emotional monster by the prosecutor, and he is sentenced to death. Existentialists see in the incident the philosophical significance of the gratuitous act of violence, but the novel can also be read as a psychological study in repressed violence.

Where there is an effect there is a cause. Whatever you allow your characters to do, make sure that you understand what motivates them and that you make these motives clear to the reader.

3E Proper development makes characters believable.

1 | Some characters are not plausible because they are fantasy figures and not realistic human beings.

Many implausible characters appear in science fiction and stories of the supernatural, but some, such as the monster in Mary Shelley's *Frankenstein*, appear in more serious works and have a kind of literary credibility. Conan the Barbarian belongs in a comic book along with Wonder Woman and the Incredible Hulk. A bit more might be said for King Kong, because the movie touches on the theme of beauty and the beast and perhaps the theme of nature versus civilization, but it's hardly profound. Godzilla is ridiculous, but Moby Dick has an interesting and mysterious presence and takes part in a great symbolic work of art. In mythology there are many incredible but meaningful characters, such as Prometheus and Sisyphus. Lewis Carroll's Alice and Jonathan Swift's Gulliver come closer to being believable characters, except for the fact that they experience incredible adventures. *The Strange Case of Dr. Jekyll and Mr. Hyde* by Robert Louis Stevenson is a weird tale, but it is also an interesting way of exploring the split personality and perhaps the good and evil in all of us. Flat or round, mythological or ordinary, some characters can achieve universality because they touch on ideas and feelings that can be understood by all people in all ages.

2 | Realistic characters must be believable.

In order to be effective as a writer you must persuade your readers that your fictional characters would react in real life just the way they do in fiction.

When you breathe life into your characters and set them in motion, they take over and only do the things that they are capable of doing or would naturally do when confronted with certain situations. You cannot force your characters to do things that they would not naturally do or things that they are incapable of doing. You cannot create a shy girl like Laura in *The Glass Menagerie* and then expect her to seduce a gentleman caller or to shoot someone. You cannot create a character like Ruby in "Ruby Tells All" (Example 9b) and have her sneaking off to the barn to read Marcel Proust. Some people get impatient with Hamlet. Why can't he just get it over with, they think. Why can't he just knock off his uncle and assume the throne of Denmark? The problem is that *as a character, he can do only what he can do.* This is not mere fatalism; it is a matter of psychological consistency. In good literature you have to tell the truth. And the truth is that Hamlet is in a state of high confusion, and that Persis Fox in "Barcelona" (Example 2a) thinks men are a bit ridiculous, and that the old man in "A Clean, Well-Lighted Place" is in despair, and that Ruby will never be a middle-class suburban housewife.

EXAMPLE 3A

THE ALPHA MALE
Joan Frank

Something about the way he came into Dan's apartment that night. Long, sure strides. Brisk and easy. Certain of his impact. The wind he generated blew along my cheek. I was talking to Maxine, the violinist. Sprung from a long work-week, hair still drying from the workout, my arms loose and floaty, brain pleasantly softened by endorphins and champagne on an empty stomach. Glancing up at his cocky entrance, I caught his face a moment, glanced back to my friends, resumed talking with an eye on him.

He carried himself tall, though he wasn't. Graceful in his dense frame. Bit of a Nicolas Cage lookalike—must have known it—the requisite black everything; the leather jacket, the brown curly hair in a quasi-fifties sweep. Normally I laughed at this image, but—there was something about his face. I knew him from somewhere. When he approached, I stared at him and then it flooded back. "I know you. We met at Dan's last party. You were with the computers. We talked about your moving to the country after living in the city so long. . . ." He shrugged. Maybe I'd embarrassed him. Maybe I was too ugly for him.

I was wearing a simple shirt and jeans and a down vest, my wet hair still pinned back on each side, which always made me look kind of sexless, I thought—the way women will, measuring ourselves against the acknowledged beauty model of the day and certain we fall hopelessly short of it by the end of a stupefyingly lonely night. I always think then of Laughton's Quasimodo—especially the final scene, when he murmurs to the heinous carved gargoyle beside him: "O that I were made of stone, like thee."

I did remember this one from my composer friend Dan's last party. He had been bored and restive, almost rude. All I'd sought then was polite chat. Social noise. He'd made it clear I didn't fit his agenda. Not on his dance card. *Tant pis*, little boy, I thought then, and wandered away. *Tant pis*, I thought now, and turned back to the others.

But he looked . . . different this time. I glimpsed him as he moved, so blatantly fond of himself, a touching caricature of suave control. Making just the right kinds of contact with the gathered crowd. Light on his feet, artful, shrewd, knowing just when to duck in and duck out. It was like watching ballet, or really good jump-rope. People looked into his face with frank admiration, and the women showed a bit of extra shine to their eyes.

Something in me made a tiny *click* as I watched him. I got up, went into the bedroom full of coats. Shed the down vest, removed the hairpins and brushed out my drying hair. Then I went back. A little experiment. What the hell.

Men are amazing. Soon I caught him sneaking glances at me. Each time I pulled my eyes away, and turned back to the others. But the young musicians were wearing on me. They were critical of the old ones, critical of the elders who continued to concertize even when they were old and (these young ones indicated) atrophied. They were haughty, these young ones, impatient to claim their own renown. They wanted their pathetic elders out of the way. "Why, Isaac Stern *bought* his own career," one young woman said. It made me feel rancid.

Then the Nicolas-type put on good dance music, music with a deep and sexy *thrum* that made you want to move. He moved a little to it. Across the room, I moved a little to it. Good music. I tried not to look at him moving so nice. I kept my face toward the people around me.

After a while the face began to ache from holding an interested expression toward the uncharitable noise of young musicians. I knew I had popped all the juice there was from these bright, tart berries. Another socially correct, useless evening: drag yourself to parties; follow the self-imposed mandate to Meet People; end up pondering Quasimodo. I made ready to leave and was making my way to bid my host goodbye. As I walked past him, Nicolas II said: Yo.

Yes?

Would you like to dance. He stood sort of sideways, looking sideways at me. I thought, Well. I didn't imagine it.

Yes. Sure. Wait. I ran away, brushed my hair again, heart thudding, came back, thinking: *don't think.*

Then I was moving with him in the darkened middle room, on a floor that was nice and rough-smooth like a real dance floor. We started to tell our lives. As he moved, he bragged about his career: his position, his talent, his power. Hilarious, yet his earnestness touched me. I told him the artists' colony had accepted me, but at that moment somehow it sounded obscure and puny, some bit of old lint in a camphor-soaked closet. Blinking only a moment to absorb and measure the possible import of this news, he pressed on: trips and cars and computers, foreign languages and prestige. Finally I decided to bite: Aren't you afraid of losing your soul, I asked.

Soul, no—heart, maybe, he said as we walked deep into the dark backyard, beyond the back porch, and sat down on some old lawn furniture. It was the most amazing night. The wind blew cool, but not cold, and there was a quickening in it: one felt currents moving inside and outside. Vines hung long around us, and they smelled of deep, cool summer, and the soft fragrance hung there in the damp, dark yard, old roses and jasmine, even there in the middle of the city, and we both thought suddenly of Faulkner and the South. Had I read him, he asked. Long ago, I said, when I was too young to understand. Suddenly there was a breathlessness between us; I recognized it—everything would seem fulsome and important now, as if we needed to hold up a million little mirrors to each other, and agree, and agree, and agree.

The way he sat pleased me: open-lapped, elbows on thighs, hands open, shaping the air between his knees. He yammered on and on, of trying to transcend the high-powered corporate spin he commandeered. Of therapies and counseling. Of spirit and matter, of tantric yoga and tantric sex, of a cyber-punk future. It felt sweet and bold for me to listen with dancing eyes. He stretched harder with his bragging: Joyce and Cummings and chakras, his college work: philosophy, logic, Japanese . . .

I wanted to laugh, but for some reason it all moved me. All of it. He was trying so hard. I put my chin in my hand and gazed at him in the windy, cool semi-dark and wanted him, and thought about what he'd be like. I kept pushing my hair back, letting my eyes dance but keeping the rest of my face grave and neutral, a full professor of the fragrant vines and the windy night.

Then he said something that faded my smile, something that gave back the rancid feeling. He said he believed he was an "alpha" male. A type who . . . had something extra. That he could take the lead anywhere, he said, any time he chose—if he chose—and that people would follow. I knew this was true as he said it, and loathed him for saying it. It was as if he'd told me he came from extreme royalty, but traveled incognito. Or that he had X-ray vision, or could fly or walk on water, but tried to use the gift responsibly. There I was: living evidence, a moth at the flame of his irresistible charisma, sitting rapt at his knees, having let something in me—that knew better—be eclipsed.

There is always that moment when you look at someone, and you realize how it could go either way. The vision shimmers in, and shimmers out. One moment they're a shining hothouse bloom of wit and warmth: the next they are a cold turd, an ugly absurdity. You can't decide. You want to get lost in their arms. You want to slap them away.

I felt angry, tired, and foolish. Tired of all the work of it. The chasm was too wide. I rose; snapped something like watch out for being subsumed by all those fancy toys. I wanted to fly away, to dissolve—at very least to shut up my brain's dull monologue, the old man in the bathrobe who paces under a pale bulb in some stinking room, muttering an endless rosary of bitter imprecations. My own little *noir* Jiminy Crickett.

He followed me back in. We stood a stupid moment in the room where the coats lay. I gathered my things.

Suddenly he blurted: would you like to go dancing.

What? When, I said.

Right now, he said.

I glanced at the clock; it was 1:00 A.M. Maybe another time, I said.

Then I looked at him again in the dim light, at the attentive kindness in his face. Damn. When he offered to walk me to the car, I heard myself say yes, that I would like that; it was a rough neighborhood. I knew then that we would kiss, and my heart began to pound.

As we walked, he started it all up again—the same boasting patter as in the dark yard, and again I felt weary. I tried to get back that first tender, amused feeling. How much *isn't that fascinating, aren't you just amazing* can anyone say? But as we got to the car, the wind blew hard, blew away all knowing better. It was a cold wind by then, and my heart raced with it. I leaned back against the car, searching his face, and after some more words at last he leaned toward me—just a brush of lips past lips—chaste, tentative. Stillness.

He stood back. I looked at him. We looked at each other and my eyes said, please more. And he leaned again, and more. Soft, flow and careful, feeling it out. Trying to see how we might fit. A little open, and my tongue moving to touch inside his mouth, a soft animal darting to touch a moment and be gone, and then more, and more, and we kept trying to find the ways that fit.

And then came that flooding surge of heat that makes a woman know she is meant to love men, an electrical flush from the chest to all extremities. My body seemed to be moving to its own choreography: pressing to him, breasts pushing against his chest, hands diving inside his jacket to circle his warm middle, pulling his hips to me, one hand moving up to cup the back of his neck, into his hair. It had been so long.

But there was no surge from him: instead, just a kind of steady, calm willingness. He tasted as fragrant as the summer air, as the Faulkner vines. The kisses were long, exploratory, information-gathering. I pressed into him: deep sweetness was there, but I had to work hard to get some. I was a hummingbird laboring at the nectar stem. I longed to see tenderness, to feel him surge. His gaze was steady. No surge. From time to time I put my lips to his neck, and sighed.

We looked at each other. He said, very soft, Do you want to be together tonight.

My chest tightened. Many gears whirred, and spun out a ticker-tape code. I was able at least to think this far: to read the internal telegram: *not this night*. But I wanted to kiss forever. I wanted to kiss until we floated into effortless, dreamy lovemaking on the bed of the cold night wind.

Let's wait, I said. It's more—I searched—tantric that way. Laughter.

I was sleepy and shivering. He began to rattle on some more, this time about his plans. He wanted to arrange an elite commune, to have his children by 35 . . .

Then something funny happened.

As he talked, a full-color Disney cartoon flamed up on a big screen just behind his head. I saw Sleeping Beauty there, this young man's life-mate, the brilliant goddess who would assume the throne alongside her prince one hallelujah day and bear his exquisite children. She had fairy-tale blond hair to her tiny waist, smiled beatifically, and moved among her admiring lessers like a kindly ballerina.

He was droning along: And the really neat thing about robotics is when . . .

I stood there smiling vacantly past his talking head, watching the film. I spotted myself in it, an elder hand-maiden: one in a series. Pouring sherry at the princely pit stop. My job was to grace his training table, full-breasted, well-seasoned. Refine his technique for the real challenges, the true conquests before him. He would resume his jour-ney refreshed, with clear conscience, good, noble, and true. A comic-book hero with well-muscled legs.

Alpha-Man.

I looked on.

I saw his life stretching before him as the sea does be-fore a child—gleaming, vast. All the time in the world. And I was a colorful postcard tacked to his wallboard, a bit of something shiny, pretty souvenir of his worldliness.

I thought this: Born when I was in high school. A raw, red, wet, squawling thing when I was having regular men-strual periods. I could have birthed him.

I almost gasped aloud.

He waved as I ducked into my car. Blithe, serene. Pleased with his own equanimity. Reconfiguring his plans. I knew that I would never see him again.

And the kisses?

The kisses were a gift, I think. A gift from my fortieth sum-mer, laughing as it waved goodbye in the cool night wind.

Source: "Alpha Male," by Joan Frank. From Sun Dog: The Southeast Review, Volume 11, No. 1. Reprinted by permission of the author.

EXAMPLE 3B

DADDY
Sylvia Plath

You do not do, you do not do
Any more, black shoe
In which I have lived like a foot
For thirty years, poor and white,
Barely daring to breathe or Achoo.

Daddy, I have had to kill you.
You died before I had time—
Marble-heavy, a bag full of God,
Ghastly statue with one grey toe
Big as a Frisco seal.   10

And a head in the freakish Atlantic
Where it pours bean green over blue
In the waters off beautiful Nauset.
I used to pray to recover you.
Ach, du   15

In the German tongue, in the Polish town
Scraped flat by the roller
Of wars, wars, wars.
But the name of the town is common.
My Polack friend.   20

Says there are a dozen or two.
So I never could tell where you
Put your foot, your root,
I never could talk to you.
The tongue stuck in my jaw.   25

It stuck in a barb wire snare.
Ich, ich, ich, ich,
I could hardly speak.
I thought every German was you.
And the language obscene   30

An engine, an engine
Chuffing me off like a Jew.
A Jew to Dachau, Auschwitz, Belsen.
I began to talk like a Jew.
I think I may well be a Jew.   35

The snows of the Tyrol, the clear beer
    of Vienna
Are not very pure or true.
With my gypsy ancestress and my weird luck
And my Taroc pack and my Taroc pack
I may be a bit of a Jew.   40

I have always been scared of *you*,
With your Luftwaffe, your gobbledygoo.
And your neat moustache
And your Aryan eye, bright blue.
Panzer-man, panzer-man, O You—   45

Not God but a swastika
So black no sky could squeak through.
Every woman adores a Fascist,
The boot in the face, the brute
Brute heart of a brute like you.   50

You stand at the blackboard, daddy,
In the picture I have of you,
A cleft in your chin instead of your foot

But no less a devil for that, no not
Any less the black man who   **55**

Bit my pretty red heart in two.
I was ten when they buried you.
At twenty I tried to die
And get back, back, back to you.
I thought even the bones would do   **60**

But they pulled me out of the sack,
And they stuck me together with glue.
And then I knew what to do.
I made a model of you,
A man in black with a Meinkampf look   **65**

And a love of the rack and the screw.
And I said I do, I do.
So daddy, I'm finally through.
The black telephone's off at the root,
The voices just can't worm through.   **70**

If I've killed one man, I've killed two—
The vampire who said he was you
And drank my blood for a year,
Seven years, if you want to know.
Daddy, you can lie back now.   **75**

There's a stake in your fat black heart
And the villagers never liked you.
They are dancing and stamping on you.
They always *knew* it was you.
Daddy, daddy, you bastard, I'm through.   **80**

EXAMPLE 3C

SEXUAL TERRORIST
Mary Baine Campbell

1   I want to be in a rock and roll band so bad.
     I want to make my sins public
     In a special little dress made of gold or fur
     With one of those nuclear violins
     Strapped on around my neck
     And a couple thousand watts for a halo.
     I want to make so much noise
     That even God can't interrupt
     And the 24-hour business of heaven
10   Just grinds to a halt, and the angels
     Dangle in the sky like secretaries
     In an air raid.
     I want to make those tight wires
     Scream under my hands like bombs
     Dropping for miles over miles
     Of empty Arizona sand, and whimper
     Like animals when the sky goes black
     And the scales stampede
     And there's no cover to run for
20   Cause the cover's on fire and the earth is so hot
     The lizards have to dance to stay alive.
     And when I stop I'm gonna go backstage
     Where it's real, real dark and take prisoners
     All night. It could be you
     Or anyone. Get ready.
     If the ransom's rich enough I'll sing
     That long, low note that makes the sun come up.

Source: From Mary Baine Campbell, The World, the Flesh, and the Angels.
Copyright 1989 by Beacon Press. Reprinted by permission of the author.

EXERCISES

Discussion

1. What is revealed about the narrator of "The Alpha Male" in the very first paragraph? Can you form a first impression of her at that point?

2. After you have read the whole story, describe the narrator's physical appearance and personality.

3. What is meant by an "alpha male"? What is the narrator's attitude toward the concept and the man she is with?

4. Explain the last paragraph of the story: "The kisses were a gift, I think . . ." Who gives the gift and who receives it?

5. Is "Daddy" a character study of the father or of the daughter?

6. What do we learn about the narrator and her father?

7. Do you think the narrator is mentally unbalanced? Is she ranting, or is this good poetry? Can both be true?

8. What does the title of Mary Campbell's poem mean?

9. Compare the style of "Sexual Terrorist" with an earlier poem by Mary Campbell (Example 1b).

10. Both poems by Campbell are highly emotional. Compare these poems with "Daddy" by Sylvia Plath. What is revealed by the authors of these poems? Which poet do you prefer and why?

Writing

1. Describe a stereotypical (*flat*) character, such as a lawyer, business person, professor, criminal, private detective, waiter or waitress, librarian, entertainer, or athlete.

2. Write a short story in which there is an incredible character, suitable for science fiction, fantasy, or the supernatural.

3. Write a story or play in which a character with some *depth* confesses to a very close friend that he or she once did something terrible that has, until now, remained a haunting secret. Make the situation *plausible* and try to convey the *motives* of the character.

4. Write a poem about an interesting stranger that you noticed on the street or on a bus or in the park. Concentrate on *appearance* and what it reveals.

5. Write a scene (fiction or drama) in which a man and a woman meet for the first time at a party.

6. Describe yourself in the third person as though you were talking about a character in a story.

7. Write a poem or story about someone (real or imaginary) whom you hate.

Plot

4A The term *plot* is often used too vaguely.

To avoid vagueness, you should understand the meanings of *story*, *action*, and *plot*, and how these three things are related.

1 | Story usually refers to the whole work.

A *story* is a work of fiction that includes a *setting* in which *characters* who *talk and think* become involved in *significant action*. It is the whole work, including its special *tone and style* and *point of view*.

In a broader sense, the word *story* can be applied to any narrative, whether it is fiction, nonfiction, drama, or poetry, as long as significant action is involved. We use "story" in such expressions as: The Watergate story, the story of Adam and Eve, the story of Romeo and Juliet.

2 | Action refers to all the things that happen in a story, especially those things that involve the characters.

Action is anything that happens, anything from the incidental to the epic. Since the term is very broad, the following useful distinctions should be made:

Internal and external action

Internal action happens inside a character's mind, consciously or unconsciously. *External action* refers to things that happen outside of the character's mind, things done *by* the character or *to* the character. A dream is an internal event. A hurricane is an external event.

Real-life action

In real life there are all kinds of actions, from the trivial to the catastrophic. A lot of real-life action is *random*. Some things just happen. A dog barks, the weather turns bad, someone gets sick. Some happenings are more *significant*. There is a major decision to be made, there is a premeditated act of violence, an extremist group plans a military coup.

In real life a lot of things can happen simultaneously. In writing it is difficult to record simultaneous action because writing itself is sequential—one sentence follows another. A writer can only suggest that several things are happening at the same time. On stage or screen this is an easier task.

Fictional action

In literary works all action is *significant*, not random. Every action is carefully selected. In written fiction all action is presented *sequentially*. A writer cannot present two things at exactly the same moment. However, as noted earlier, simultaneous events can be presented in a performed drama.

There are two kinds of action in fiction: *habitual action* and *unique action*. The routine things that a character does, such as going to work or eating lunch, are habitual. The unusual things that occur, such as falling in love or getting lost in a jungle, are unique. Fairy tales usually make this distinction clear at the very beginning: "Once upon a time in the land of Anglia there was a miserly king who was in the *habit* of counting his money every day. *One day* he was interrupted by an evil dwarf."

3 | Plot refers to the meaningful arrangement of the significant action in a story.

The plot of a literary work is a summary of the unique and significant action in that work. It is an artistically arranged sequence of events that serves as the skeleton for the whole story, which has to be completed or fleshed out by setting, characterization, description, dialogue, style, and tone. A good plot usually has the following elements: *conflict, suspense, development, resolution.*

4B Conflict refers to whatever causes the central dramatic tension in a story.

In literature the term *conflict* has a very broad meaning. In its most obvious sense it suggests a clashing of forces, as in good versus evil, but it also means any problem, external or internal, that a human being experiences and longs to resolve.

Since conflict is an aspect of plot, it is most often discussed in relation to fiction and drama, but it can frequently be applied to poetry as well, even though many poems do not have much of a plot. The following anonymous poem, for instance, written more than five hundred years ago, clearly has a conflict but only hints at a plot:

WESTERN WIND

> Western wind, when wilt thou blow,
> The small rain down can rain?
> Christ, if my love were in my arms
> And I in my bed again!

The author seems to be far from home, perhaps at sea or on some marauding or military adventure. Apparently the coming of the west wind will mean a gentle rain and a homeward journey.

Why does conflict give rise to literature? There is an old saying that it is the sick oyster that produces the pearl, meaning that a grain of sand sets up an irritation, which the oyster tries to deal with by developing a pearl around it. The saying suggests that all artists are driven by some disturbance or problem and that their art is an attempt to relieve the disturbance or resolve the problem. It seems to be the unpleasant destiny of human beings to be plagued by problems and, therefore, to be fascinated by problem solving. In literature one can find the drama of conflict and resolution rehearsed over and over again.

Since there are many different kinds of conflict, they are sometimes conveniently classified as follows: *people versus people, people versus society, people versus nature,* and *people versus themselves.*

1 | People versus people.

War is the most obvious and massive indication that all too often people cannot live together in peace. It is a fundamental flaw in human nature. Wars have affected so many people in so many horrible ways that it is no wonder so much literature, great and trivial, has dealt with the subject. Homer's *Iliad*, written almost three thousand years ago, deals with the Trojan War. Conflict in war stories is not only physical conflict; it often involves questions of honor, glory, betrayal, and guilt. In Hemingway's *A Farewell to Arms*, for instance, the hero falls in love and deserts the army to flee to Switzerland with his beloved.

Crimes clearly involve people versus people, though sometimes an author concentrates on the sociological implications or on the internal, psychological drama, as in the case of Dostoevsky's *Crime and Punishment* or Stendhal's *The Red and the Black*.

Conflicts between individuals are too numerous to list or classify. People can disagree about almost anything—property, politics, principles, family affairs, and love. In "The Ballad of Reading Gaol," Oscar Wilde says:

> Yet each man kills the thing he loves,
> By each let this be heard,
> Some do it with a bitter look,
> Some with a flattering word,
> The coward does it with a kiss,
> The brave man with a sword!

Oscar Wilde's approach to love may have been rather eccentric, to say the least, but there is no doubt about the frequency with which love conflicts appear in literature, and love tragedies may be more popular than happy tales of love. Romeo and Juliet die. Desdemona is strangled. Madame Bovary and Anna Karenina commit suicide. Heathcliff hears the ghost of his beloved call his name. Two men kill each other over a woman in Lorca's *Blood Wedding*. And Rhett Butler leaves Scarlett O'Hara with the famous line: "Frankly, my dear, I don't give a damn."

Though love conflicts abound in literature, other conflicts between people appear with considerable frequency. King Lear is betrayed by his two evil daughters. In Conrad's *Victory* a man and a woman living on a remote island are terrorized by three evil men. In the movie *Chinatown* a domineering father seduces his own daughter, who bears his child. In *Citizen Kane* the central figure is in love with money and power, and lets no one stand in his way.

2 | People versus society.

Any individual who resists the rules and values of his or her society runs the risk of criticism or even punishment. Benign eccentrics, including artists, are sometimes exceptions. If the rebellion against society is extreme, the individual can expect a very hard time, indeed, whether the rebellion is a question of conscience or a violent crime. A lot of people were arrested in the 1960s because they took part in civil rights or antiwar demonstrations. In literary works rebels are often portrayed as heroes. Ordinary criminals are usually portrayed as villains. A fairly recently coined expression for a chronic offender is *sociopath*, someone who simply can't get along with society.

Technology and the problems of big cities and sprawling suburbs have created many conflicts between the individual and society. Governments have grown larger. Ordinary people feel helpless against their remote governments. Farmers find it difficult to survive. The family has eroded. There is loneliness in the cities and suburbs. There is racial and ethnic tension. There is polarization between rich and poor. Violence and drug use continue to increase. These subjects appear in serious literature as well as on television and in mass-market paperbacks.

An early modern example of a literary work about the conflict between the individual and society is Ibsen's *An Enemy of the People*, a play first performed in 1882. The hero is a doctor who discovers that the water in a resort town is polluted. The town's economy depends heavily on its health-giving baths. The mayor and businessmen want to cover up the medical report. The doctor finds himself standing virtually alone against the conventional majority.

The most famous counterculture poem produced by a member of the Beat Generation is Allen Ginsberg's long poem "Howl" (1955), the angry tone of which is apparent from its opening lines. Richard Wright's brilliant novel *Native Son* (1940) is about a black man victimized by a white society. In more recent years this conflict has been the basis of many works, from Ralph Ellison's *The Invisible Man* (1952) to Alice Walker's *The Color Purple* (1982).

3 | People versus nature.

By *nature* we usually mean the tangible world around us that is shaped by natural forces, not by humans. We mean the sea, the wilderness, the animal kingdom, and the vastness of outer space. Some people would include the concept of God and destiny, depending on their philosophical persuasions. In literature we find people in conflict with nature in both simplistic and profound works. Disaster and survival stories have exploited all the ancient elements—air, earth, fire, and water. There have been stories of hurricanes, avalanches, towering infernos, and tidal waves. There have been stories of killer ants, killer bees, killer tarantulas, and even killer tomatoes. Beyond such low-level entertainments we find some more interesting efforts, such as *The Rains Came* and *The African Queen*. Even a classic as great as *Moby Dick* might be considered a novel about the conflict between man and nature, and it may have inspired the popular novel *Jaws* by Peter Benchley.

4 | People versus themselves.

Sometimes a story focuses on a character's internal conflict. This conflict can be triggered by circumstances, or it can be the result of some psychological disorder. Hamlet has a terrible internal conflict. He feels he must avenge his father's death, but he is filled with doubts and other confusing feelings. Lady Macbeth's ambition and sense of guilt drive her mad. In more modern works we find characters struggling with alcoholism (*Under the Volcano*) and drug addiction (*Naked Lunch*). Sheer madness figures in many horror stories and films, of which one of the most famous is Hitchcock's *Psycho*. The most dramatic treatment of the divided self is *The Strange Case of Dr. Jekyll and Mr. Hyde* by Robert Louis Stevenson.

4C Suspense is a condition created by uncertainty.

Suspense is a state of curiosity, uncertainty, or anxiety about a conflict or problem, the outcome of which cannot as yet be determined. It is a natural human response to certain situations, whether the situations are real or fictitious. In real situations the anxiety is direct. In fiction, it depends on *empathy*, our ability to identify with the feelings of others, including made-up characters. Once the story or drama is over, our curiosity disappears, along with our uncertainty and anxiety, whether the ending is tragic or happy. In good literature there is also a residue of wisdom or aesthetic exhilaration. In lighter entertainments there is only a satisfied curiosity. People who gobble up romances and murder mysteries or routine television dramas readily admit that they forget about them almost instantly, as soon as they find out "whodunit" or whether or not a pair of lovers will work out their problems and live happily ever after.

In any literary work that has a plot, suspense begins as soon as the conflict or problem is introduced, which is usually at the very beginning. A ship is wrecked on the shores of a deserted island and only a man and a woman survive. What will happen to them? Three prospectors set out to search for gold in the dangerous Sierra Madre area of Mexico; a mercenary is hired to assassinate a rebel leader in Central America; and so on.

In stories of pure adventure, suspense is all-important. Suspense follows a formula and can be diagrammed. First there is the *problem*, then there are *complications* that heighten the sense of danger or mystery, sometimes to the point at which our hero is hanging (literally or figuratively) from the edge of a cliff (hence the term *cliffhanger*), and then there is a *resolution*, a happy or unhappy ending.

Suspense is an intolerable state that demands a resolution, even an unpleasant one.

In more complex literary works it may not be as easy to find the basic diagram of suspense. There may be ideas or characterizations that rival the suspense in importance, but very often even works of great literary merit are full of suspense. Certainly, we want to know what happens to Ahab and his mad pursuit of the white whale, and, certainly, we want to know what happens to Emma in *Madame Bovary* and what becomes of Willy Loman in *Death of a Salesman*.

4D *Development* refers to the events that grow out of a conflict before it is resolved.

1 | Every narrative needs movement.

Creating a conflict is only a starting point in literature. In nature nothing stands still. A wound will either heal or fester. A person on the ledge of a tall building has to jump or fall, or somehow get back inside. However, you can't simply present your problem and then immediately resolve it. You can't say that a person crawled out onto a ledge and then jumped to his or her death. You can't leap from conflict to resolution. That would not only kill your character but all the suspense, and you wouldn't have much of a story. You need *development*. You have to hold the interest of your readers. You have to involve them by exploring the situation and the character more deeply, not merely through exposition but through *action*.

Development often makes up most of the plot. A conflict can be stated in a sentence or a paragraph, and some resolutions are swift and sudden, but what you must do in between is to heighten the reader's curiosity by devising a series of events that reveals the true nature of the situation and leads to a conclusion that, afterward, seems inevitable to the reader.

If there is a "man on the ledge" in your story, the reader wants to know why he is out there. Does he really want to commit suicide, or does he just want attention? Perhaps he is a rejected lover who is trying to punish the woman who rejected him. If he is psychologically disturbed, what exactly is his psychological problem? Has he just had a fight with his domineering mother? Is he a paranoid character who feels that everyone is plotting against him? There has to be some sort of *motivation* for his behavior. Furthermore, something has to happen before the resolution. Perhaps the police send for a priest who knows the man. Perhaps they get in touch with his psychiatrist or the woman who rejected him or his mother. Someone tries to talk him down. The police spread a net. A friend crawls out onto the ledge to calm him down. Perhaps the friend slips and almost falls, but is saved by the man who thought he wanted to commit suicide. Saving another person's life may make him realize suddenly that he is needed and that his life has some value and meaning after all.

2 | The sequence of events must develop logically.

When you create a sequence of events in your development, you have to be sure that every event has some significance and that these events build toward a climax. One of the most serious mistakes made by amateur writers is to try to reveal everything all at once. Development needs pace. A story or drama is most effective when it is a gradual and ascending revelation. Details of character and setting can be revealed as you go. It is not important to tell us everything about everybody in the first paragraph. It is much more important to indicate the nature of the problem and to set things in motion. Many opening sentences or paragraphs contain a hook to capture the reader's attention. "The invisible man is the main attraction," is the opening sentence of "The Invisible Man" (Example 1a). If you spend too much time on your setting and cast of characters at the beginning, especially in a short story, you might confuse or bore your reader.

If your sequence of events is going to build toward a climax, the situation has to grow more intense before it is resolved.

In "Barcelona" (Example 2a), we begin with a middle-aged American couple in the darkened streets of a seedy neighborhood in a foreign city. The sense of danger is heightened. Suddenly, a thief snatches the woman's purse. The man chases the thief. He searches restaurants and bars, but to no avail. He is about to give up when a stranger who is not the thief points to the abandoned purse in the street and says, "Lady, this your bag?" In the final scene we explore the reactions of the couple as they recover in a restaurant. The real meaning may be in these reactions, but there would not have been a story without a significant sequence of events.

4E Every conflict must have a resolution.

1 | The resolution must fit the plot.

You can't drop a completely random ending on your reader, like a concrete block that accidentally falls from a high building. An ending is absurd if it is not a plausible conclusion to a certain sequence of events. You can't select a conflict and create characters and develop a dramatic and cohesive series of events without ending the whole process with a meaningful and believable *resolution*.

The word *resolution* may be misleading to some people. It sounds as though the problem you began with must be solved. That's not the case at all. You are a writer solving an artistic problem. You are not a therapist solving human problems. If all conflicts and problems were solved in that way in literature, every story would end happily. As we know, many do not. The unhappy or tragic ending can often be a more logical resolution artistically than the happy ending.

2 | Some resolutions are clear and simple; others are more complex and subtle.

In light entertainments, in which there are conflicts between good guys and bad guys, or problems between lovers, the usual resolution is that good prevails over evil or, in the case of romance, that love conquers all. In more serious literature a resolution may involve a dramatic change in the main character, a spiritual revelation, a significant decision, an act of violence or of self-destruction.

Though some of the old dramas seem to end with a bang, and some of the more contemporary works seem to end with a whimper, the good ones all have significance. Oedipus blinds himself and Othello strangles Desdemona, but all that happens in "The Invisible Man" (Example 1a) is that the circus performance ends with the audience imagining that they actually saw an invisible man; all that happens at the end of "Barcelona" (Example 2a) is that Persis Fox has a few thoughts about how difficult it must be to be a man, and about how men don't quite understand women. Modern literature does not require a stage littered with corpses anymore than it requires characters larger than life. Subtle endings involving ordinary people can be just as moving and just as meaningful as the louder events of antiquity. In all cases, however, a resolution is a *literary conclusion*, not a real-life conclusion.

EXAMPLE 4A

THE HANDSOMEST DROWNED MAN IN THE WORLD
A Tale for Children
Gabriel García Márquez[1]

The first children who saw the dark and slinky bulge approaching through the sea let themselves think it was an enemy ship. Then they saw it had no flags or masts and they thought it was a whale. But when it washed up on the beach, they removed the clumps of seaweed, the jellyfish tentacles, and the remains of fish and flotsam, and only then did they see that it was a drowned man.

They had been playing with him all afternoon, burying him in the sand and digging him up again, when someone chanced to see them and spread the alarm in the village. The men who carried him to the nearest house noticed that he weighed more than any dead man they had ever known, almost as much as a horse, and they said to each other that maybe he'd been floating too long and the water had got into his bones. When they laid him on the floor they said he'd been taller than all other men because there was barely enough room for him in the house, but they thought that maybe the ability to keep on growing after death was part of the nature of certain drowned men. He had the smell of the sea about him and only his shape gave one to suppose that it was the corpse of a human being, because the skin was covered with a crust of mud and scales.

They did not even have to clean off his face to know that the dead man was a stranger. The village was made up of only twenty-odd wooden houses that had stone courtyards

---

[1] Translated by Gregory Rabassa.

with no flowers and which were spread about on the end of a desertlike cape. There was so little land that mothers always went about with the fear that the wind would carry off their children and the few dead that the years had caused among them had to be thrown off the cliffs. But the sea was calm and bountiful and all the men fit into seven boats. So when they found the drowned man they simply had to look at one another to see that they were all there. That night they did not go out to work at sea. While the men went to find out if anyone was missing in neighboring villages, the women stayed behind to care for the drowned man. They took the mud off with grass swabs, they removed the underwater stones entangled in his hair, and they scraped the crust off with tools used for scaling fish. As they were doing that they noticed that the vegetation on him came from faraway oceans and deep water and that his clothes were in tatters, as if he had sailed through labyrinths of coral. They noticed too that he bore his death with pride, for he did not have the lonely look of other drowned men who came out of the sea or that haggard, needy look of men who drowned in rivers. But only when they finished cleaning him off did they become aware of the kind of man he was and it left them breathless. Not only was he the tallest, strongest, most virile, and best built man they had ever seen, but even though they were looking at him there was no room for him in their imagination.

They could not find a bed in the village large enough to lay him on nor was there a table solid enough to use for his wake. The tallest men's holiday pants would not fit him, nor the fattest ones' Sunday shirts, nor the shoes of the one with the biggest feet. Fascinated by his huge size and his beauty, the women then decided to make him some pants from a large piece of sail and a shirt from some bridal brabant linen so that he could continue through his death with dignity. As they sewed, sitting in a circle and gazing at the corpse between stitches, it seemed to them that the wind had never been so steady nor the sea so restless as on that night and they supposed that the change had something to do with the dead man. They thought that if that magnificent man had lived in the village, his house would have had the widest doors, the highest ceiling, and the strongest floor, his bedstead would have been made from a midship frame held together by iron bolts, and his wife would have been the happiest woman. They thought that he would have had so much authority that he could have drawn fish out of the sea simply by calling their names and that he would have put so much work into his land that springs would have burst forth from among the rocks so that he would have been able to plant flowers on the cliffs. They secretly compared him to their own men, thinking that for all their lives theirs were incapable of doing what he could do in one night, and they ended up dismissing them deep in their hearts as the weakest, meanest, and most useless creatures on earth. They were wandering through that maze of fantasy when the oldest woman, who as the oldest had looked upon the drowned man with more compassion than passion, sighed:

"He has the face of someone called Esteban."

It was true. Most of them had only to take another look at him to see that he could not have any other name. The more stubborn among them, who were the youngest, still lived for a few hours with the illusion that when they put his clothes on and he lay among the flowers in patent leather shoes his name might be Lautaro. But it was a vain illusion. There had not been enough canvas, the poorly cut and worse sewn pants were too tight, and the hidden strength of his heart popped the buttons on his shirt. After midnight the whistling of the wind died down and the sea fell into its Wednesday drowsiness. The silence put an end to any last doubts: he was Esteban. The women who had dressed him, who had combed his hair, had cut his nails and shaved him were unable to hold back a shudder of pity when they had to resign themselves to his being dragged along the ground. It was then that they understood how unhappy he must have been with that huge body since it bothered him even after death. They could see him in life, condemned to going through doors sideways, cracking his head on crossbeams, remaining on his feet during visits, not knowing what to do with his soft, pink, sea lion hands while the lady of the house looked for her most resistant chair and begged him, frightened to death, sit here, Esteban, please, and he, leaning against the wall, smiling, don't bother, ma'am, I'm fine where I am, his heels raw and his back roasted from having done the same thing so many times whenever he paid a visit, don't bother, ma'am, I'm fine where I am, just to avoid the embarrassment of breaking up the chair, and never knowing perhaps that the ones who said don't go, Esteban, at least wait till the coffee's ready, were the ones who later on would whisper the big boob finally left, how nice, the handsome fool has gone. That was what the women were thinking beside the body a little before dawn. Later, when they covered his face with a handkerchief so that the light would not bother him, he looked so forever dead, so defenseless, so much like their men that the first furrows of tears opened in their hearts. It was one of the younger ones who began the weeping. The others, coming to, went from sighs to wails, and the more they sobbed the more they felt like weeping, because the drowned man was becoming all the more Esteban for them, and so they wept so much, for he was the most destitute, most peaceful, and most obliging man on earth, poor Esteban. So when the men returned with the news that the drowned man was not from the neighboring villages either, the women felt an opening of jubilation in the midst of their tears.

"Praise the Lord," they sighed, "he's ours!"

The men thought the fuss was only womanish frivolity. Fatigued because of the difficult nighttime inquiries, all they wanted was to get rid of the bother of the newcomer once and for all before the sun grew strong on that arid, windless day. They improvised a litter with the remains of foremasts and gaffs, tying it together with rigging so that it would bear the weight of the body until they reached the cliffs. They wanted to tie the anchor from a cargo ship to him so that he would sink easily into the deepest waves, where fish are blind and divers die of nostalgia, and bad currents would not bring him back to shore, as had happened with other bodies. But the more they hurried, the more the women thought of ways to waste time. They walked about like startled hens, pecking with the sea charms on their breasts, some interfering on one side to put a scapular of the good wind on the drowned man, some on the other side to put a wrist compass on him, and after a great deal of *get away from there, woman, stay out of the way, look, you almost made me fall on top of the dead man*, the men began to feel mistrust in their livers and started grumbling about why so many main-altar decorations for a stranger, because no matter how many nails and holy-water jars he had on him, the sharks would chew him all the same, but the women kept piling on their junk relics, running back and forth, stumbling, while they released in sighs what they did not in tears, so that the men finally exploded with *since when has there ever been such a fuss over a drifting corpse, a drowned nobody, a piece of cold Wednesday meat*. One of the women, mortified by so much lack of care, then removed the handkerchief from the dead man's face and the men were left breathless too.

He was Esteban. It was not necessary to repeat it for them to recognize him. If they had been told Sir Walter Raleigh, even they might have been impressed with his gringo accent, the macaw on his shoulder, his cannibal-killing blunderbuss, but there could be only one Esteban in the world and there he was, stretched out like a sperm whale, shoeless, wearing the pants of an undersized child, and with those stony nails that had to be cut with a knife. They only had to take the handkerchief off his face to see that he was ashamed, that it was not his fault that he was so big or so heavy or so handsome, and if he had known that this was going to happen, he would have looked for a more discreet place to drown in, seriously, I even would have tied the anchor off a galleon around my neck and staggered off a cliff like someone who doesn't like things in order not to be upsetting people now with this Wednesday dead body, as you people say, in order not to be bothering anyone with this filthy piece of cold meat that doesn't have anything to do with me. There was so much truth in his manner that even the most mistrustful men, the ones who felt the bitterness of endless nights at sea fearing that their women would tire of dreaming about them and begin to dream of drowned men, even they and others who were harder still shuddered in the marrow of their bones at Esteban's sincerity.

That was how they came to hold the most splendid funeral they could conceive of for an abandoned drowned man. Some women who had gone to get flowers in the neighboring villages returned with other women who could not believe what they had been told, and those women went back for more flowers when they saw the dead man, and they brought more and more until there were so many flowers and so many people that it was hard to walk about. At the final moment it pained them to return him to the waters as an orphan and they chose a father and mother from among the best people, and aunts and uncles and cousins, so that through him all the inhabitants of the village became kinsmen. Some sailors who heard the weeping from a distance went off course and people heard of one who had himself tied to the mainmast, remembering ancient fables about sirens. While they fought for the privilege of carrying him on their shoulders along the steep escarpment by the cliffs, men and women became aware for the first time of the desolation of their streets, the dryness of their courtyards, the narrowness of their dreams as they faced the splendor and beauty of their drowned man. They let him go without an anchor so that he could come back if he wished and whenever he wished, and they all held their breath for the fraction of centuries the body took to fall into the abyss. They did not need to look at one another to realize that they were no longer all present, that they would never be. But they also knew that everything would be different from then on, that their houses would have wider doors, higher ceilings, and stronger floors so that Esteban's memory could go everywhere without bumping into beams and so that no one in the future would dare whisper the big boob finally died, too bad, the handsome fool has finally died, because they were going to paint their house fronts gay colors to make Esteban's memory eternal and they were going to break their backs digging for springs among the stones and planting flowers on the cliffs so that in future years at dawn the passengers on great liners would awaken, suffocated by the smell of gardens on the high seas, and the captain would have to come down from the bridge in his dress uniform, with his astrolabe, his pole star, and his row of war medals and, pointing to the promontory of roses on the horizon, he would say in fourteen languages, look there, where the wind is so peaceful now that it's gone to sleep beneath the beds, over there, where the sun's so bright that the sunflowers don't know which way to turn, yes, over there, that's Esteban's village.

Source: "Handsomest Drowned Man in the World," from *Leaf Storm and Other Stories* by Gabriel Garcia Marquez. Copyright © 1971 by Gabriel Garcia Marquez. Reprinted by permission of HarperCollins Publishers.

EXAMPLE 4B

YOUNG WIFE'S LAMENT
Brigit Pegeen Kelly

1   The mule that lived on the road
where I was married
would bray to wake the morning,
but could not wake me.
How many summers I slept
lost in my hair. How many
mules on how many hills singing.
Back of a deep ravine
he lived, above a small river
10   on a beaten patch of land.
I walked up in the day and walked down,
having been given nothing
else to do. The road grew no longer,
I grew no wiser, my husband
was away selling things to people who buy.
He went up the road, too, but
the road was full of doors for him,
the road was his belt and,
one notch at a time, he loosened it
20   on his way. I would sit
on the hill of stones and look down
on the trees, on the lake
far away with its boats and those
who ride in boats
and I could not pray. Some of us
have mule minds,
are foolish as sails whipping

in the wind, senseless
as sheets rolling through the fields,
30   some of us are not given
even a wheel of the tinker's cart
upon which to pray.
When I came back I pumped water
in the yard under the trees
by the fence where the cows came up,
but water is not wisdom
and change is not made by wishes.
Else I would have ridden something,
even a mule, over
40   those hills and away.

Source: From To the Place of Trumpets, 1988. Reprinted with the permission of Yale University Press.

EXAMPLE 4C

PARADISE FISH
Robert J. Levy

1   Purchased on a whim, plunged recklessly
     into my cramped aquarium,
     she was the perfect girlfish, a pink chiffon
     of fins adrift in artificial light.
     Black mollies blanched and neon tetras
     dimmed perceptibly as she trailed
     her silent taffeta past rigid swordtails,
     pudgy cichlids, lowly snails. Endless nights
     watching her hover midway between

10   gravel and glass sky—a living jewel
     nestled in black velvet—I would marvel
     at loveliness so unearthly, and think:
     How amazing she was *all mine*. Restive,
     listless and plagued by less effulgent fish,
     she spent her days avoiding tankmates
     who found her plumage something good to eat.
     Unable to seize the tubifex worms
     and daphnia I offered her for fear

     of being ripped to shreds, she languished
20   among leaves—hollow-bellied, starved.
     One time I pinched some dried food between
     my fingertips and held it out to her.
     With soft fins, she brushed my hand—a briny
     butterfly kiss—then nibbled daintily,
     and soon, accustomed to this finger-food,

she pressed against my wrist. Cupping her
in my hand, I raised her from the tank:

In the safe haven of my palm-sized pool,
I stroked the length of her body
30   with one finger. She lay completely still.
When I released her, she swam off
without the slightest urgency,
done with her flirtation in parched heaven.
Once returned, her torments only worsened:
Guppies slashed her fins to tattered flags
of finery while stray catfish

hounded her in corners. And then,
one day at feeding time, I found her
beached on the floor in front of the fishtank,
40   gone mad from too much personhood too soon.
The thin, pink crepe of her body crackled
like a dried leaf when I lifted her.
All mine, I thought, as I sent her off,
far from any human aquarium,
back to the ocean of her origin.

Source: Originally printed in Southwest Review, Spring 1991. Reprinted by
permission of the author.

EXERCISES

Discussion

1. What are some of the things that give García Márquez's story a folktale quality? What are the main characteristics of a folktale?

2. Analyze the suspense in this story. Where does it begin? How is it sustained?

3. Compare the attitudes of the men and the women of the village toward Esteban, the drowned man.

4. Is there any significance to the drowned man's immense size and the elaborate funeral given to him?

5. After Esteban is buried in the sea, everything changes for this village. What does it all mean?

6. In the poem "Young Wife's Lament" what does the title mean?

7. What do the references to mules mean in this poem?

8. Explain the title "Paradise Fish."

9. Try to translate this poem into a brief prose statement.

Writing

1. Write a short story or play involving one of the basic conflicts: *people versus people, people versus society, people versus nature, people versus themselves.*

2. Write a story that has the conventional characteristics of a folktale.

3. Write a story with an ironic ending.

4. Write a one-act play called *Woman on the Ledge* or *Man on the Ledge.* Use a room with a window as the set. Try the same subject as a short story.

5. Make use of the following situation: Two men who are in love with the same woman go on a hunting trip. One of the men imagines that the other man is trying to kill him.
6. Write a haunted-house story in which you emphasize suspense.
7. Write a poem that tells a story.

Point of View

We are all *voyeurs*. The movie or television screen is like a window, as is the stage. The usual point of view in a performed drama is defined by the simple relationship between audience and play. Something happens and the audience watches. Complexities of point of view can also be used within the play, as in the case of the soliloquy, which may allow us to share the private thoughts of one character but not another.

In poetry and fiction we view things through the mind's eye. There is a good deal of variety in that vision, and the writer is allowed considerable flexibility.

There are certain conventional categories for the various possible points of view: the *first person*, *second person*, *third person limited*, and *third person omniscient*. There is also the *persona* to consider, the voice that speaks the poem or story.

5A Persona refers to an invented narrator, often no more than a voice that tells the story.

1 | The voice that presents the story or poem is not necessarily the voice of the author.

In Latin, *persona* means "mask," suggesting an assumed personality, as in a play. For every literary work, even if it is autobiographical or confessional, the author as artist must choose a voice with which to present the material. Some authors have worn many masks in their work and spoken with many different voices. Choosing a persona is part of choosing the right style and tone for a particular story or poem. Writing is a performance, not a real-life conversation. It is an artifice, a manipulation of language and form. In a self-portrait the author (or painter) is not only the *subject* but the *creator* of the work of art. In works that are not auto-biographical it is easier to see that the voice that speaks the story or poem is not the author's personal voice. It is often the voice of a nameless tale-teller, a disembodied voice, the voice of a noncharacter, uninvolved in the action, detached and objective. On the other hand, the persona is sometimes an invented narrator who does have some degree of involve-ment in the action, possibly even a central role.

5B   In first-person narrative the speaker is a character in the story.

When a narrative is told in the first person (*I*, *we*), the speaker becomes a character. We hear his or her voice. The voice may belong to a well defined character or one who reveals little about himself or herself. The narrator may have an important role in the story, or no role at all. These are the major possibilities:

- a narrator who seems to be the author,
- a narrator who is an invented character (major or minor),
- a narrator who heard the story from another person, or
- several narrators, each of whom tells part of the story or his or her own version of the whole story.

1 | A first-person narrator can seem to be the author.

There are several advantages to using a narrator who seems to be the author. First of all, the reader knows immediately who is talking. Second, the story or poem is very convincing, since the author seems to be talking about something he or she knows firsthand. It has some of the effect of non-fiction, even though it may be entirely a fabrication. This point of view is used frequently in personal poetry. In such poetry we can't deny that the authors themselves are speaking to us, but we must keep in mind that they are speaking to us through an art form and that they may be taking a few poetic liberties with the truth in order to give wider significance to their experiences.

2 | A first-person narrator can be an invented character (major or minor).

When an invented character is used, we know that we are not listening to the author's voice but to the voice of someone the author has created. Nevertheless, hearing the narrative from someone who participated in the action, even if it is fictional action, gives the work an air of authenticity. If it is the central character who speaks, we feel that we are in direct touch with the character. Hearing the voice of the narrator helps us to know the person, even to visualize him or her (see "Ruby Tells All," Example 9b). The character comes to life instantly. When a minor character is used as narrator, the character's role is usually to tell us about the central figures. Their comments as outsiders can often be objective and valuable. *Moby Dick* begins "Call me Ishmael." He's the narrator, but the novel is rarely about *him*.

The main limitation of this use of the first person is that narrators can only tell us what they know and what they think. Some events may be unknown to them or passed on to us secondhand as hearsay. There is also some risk of being bored by hearing only one voice, especially in longer works. This can be avoided by having the narrator report a fair amount of dialogue instead of just summing up what happens.

3 | A first-person narrator may have heard the story from another person.

This device gives the impression that what was told to the narrator was a true story. Similar to this approach is the author (persona) who tells us that he or she has found an old manuscript or other documents in which there is an interesting story. The materials may be diaries or letters or newspaper clippings, or anything of that sort that will help in the suspension of disbelief. A good example is Hawthorne's *The Scarlet Letter* (1850).

4 | Several first-person narrators can be used, each of whom tells part of the story or a version of the whole story.

This approach is commonly used in courtroom dramas or criminal investigations in which direct testimonies are given in the first person. The reader often has to decide who's lying and who's telling the truth. Sometimes no one is really lying. Certain apparent contradictions may be merely a matter of perception or point of view, as in the movie *Rashomon*, by Akira Kurosawa.

This technique is also used in complex works such as Faulkner's *Absalom! Absalom!* The multiple point of view allows us to see the central figure, Thomas Sutpen, through the eyes of several characters, and it allows us to understand these participating characters better. In *The Collector* by John Fowles, the story of a kidnapping is told first by the young man who did the deed and then by the young woman he kidnapped.

5C   The second-person point of view invites the reader to identify with one of the characters.

The second person (*you*) was popular for a while some years ago in detective stories and in satires of the genre. For example,

> You are a private eye. You're sitting in your office in San Francisco when the phone rings. It is a woman with a voice that can melt ice-cubes long-distance. You pour yourself another drink and listen more to her voice than to her problem. . . .

The second person sometimes has the same effect as the first person. What the narrator is really saying is, "Pretend that you are me." The narrator could have said as easily, "*I* am a private eye. . . ." The second person used with the present tense moves toward the immediacy of a film-script and has occasionally been used successfully in recent fiction, such as *Bright Lights, Big City* (1984). Since the second person has many limitations, it is not widely used.

5D   The third-person narrative employs an "invisible narrator."

The first-person point of view may have the edge in poetry, but in fiction it is the third person that has traditionally been more common (*he, she, they*). In recent fiction, however, the first person has gained ground. *The Norton Anthology of Contemporary Fiction* contains stories that are about equally divided between the two points of view.

The third-person approach has many variations. There is usually no identifiable narrator, as in the first person, but the persona as invisible narrator can tell the story or poem in a variety of voices and tones, with degrees of objectivity, and with limited or unlimited knowledge. The four conventional subdivisions of the third-person point of view are: (1) complete objectivity (2) limited objectivity (3) limited omniscience (4) complete omniscience.

1 | Complete objectivity refers to the point of view in stories that are written as though seen on a stage or screen.

The completely objective point of view is like the view from a seat in the theater. The author describes only what might be seen and heard from a certain distance. In such an approach there can be no commentary or intrusive analysis. The thoughts of characters cannot be presented directly. We cannot be told anything about the past or circumstances beyond those immediately before us. Everything must be revealed through description, dialogue, action, and occasionally voice-over thoughts, monologues, or soliloquies. Fortunately, we can learn a good deal this way, as we know from stage and screen productions. In fiction, examples of pure objectivity are rare. More often we will find substantial objectivity with occasional comments or added information from the narrator. Since the advantage of third-person narration is that it allows the *persona* to comment, pure objectivity seems, at times, unnecessarily limited. One might as well write a play or film-script.

2 | Limited objectivity refers to the point of view in stories presented through the eyes of one of the characters.

Although objectivity can be limited in a variety of ways, the most common way is to tell the story in the third person, from the point of view of one of the characters. This means seeing things through the eyes of either the central character or one of the less important characters. The narrator who uses this approach knows only what goes on in the mind of one character. He or she knows how that character thinks and feels, and uses the character to give us impressions of other people in the story. The narrator knows the background of the character, birthplace, childhood, and so on, often commenting on the character and revealing secret fears and desires. These are all limitations on pure objectivity and move toward limited omniscience.

This technique is used in "Barcelona" (Example 2a). The narrator comments extensively on Persis Fox, the woman whose purse is stolen. When the incident takes place, we see it entirely from her point of view:

> In the next instant, though, before she has seen or heard any person approaching, someone is running past her in the dark—but not past; he is beside her, a tall dark boy, grabbing at her purse, pulling its short strap. Persis' first instinct is to let him have it, not because she is afraid—she is not, still not, afraid—but from a conditioned reflex, instructing her to give people what they want: children, her husband.

The narrator never gets directly into the mind of any of the other characters, including the woman's husband. The narrator's actions and reactions all reach us through Persis Fox.

3 | Limited omniscience refers to the point of view in stories told by a narrator who has some knowledge but not total knowledge of what is happening.

The knowledge of the narrator can be limited even if everything is not seen through the eyes of one of the characters. We may be told what several of the characters feel and think without having the impression that the narrator is omniscient. Furthermore, the narrator must reveal whatever he or she knows gradually in order to create suspense. This gives us the feeling that limited discoveries are being made all along. In a mystery story we must not be told whodunit at the very beginning. We must not even feel that the persona knows. This is the feeling we have in Shirley Jackson's "The Lottery." The story is told in an aloof voice. The narrator is anonymous and unobtrusive, aware more than we are, but not necessarily all-knowing. This is clearly established in the opening paragraph:

> The morning of June 27th was clear and sunny, with the fresh warmth of a full-summer day; the flowers were blossoming profusely and the grass was richly green. The people of the village began to gather in the square, between the post office and the bank, around ten o'clock; in some towns there were so many people that the lottery took two days and had to be started on June 26th, but in this village, where there were only about three hundred people, the whole lottery took less than two hours, so it could begin at ten o'clock in the morning and still be through in time to allow the villagers to get home for noon dinner.

4 | Complete omniscience refers to the point of view in a story told by a narrator who knows everything that is going on in the story.

The narrator who knows everything seems to be godlike. Such a narrator can never be a character, because all characters have a limited point of view. Such a persona is only a voice, a convention in fiction or poetry. The reader, who has suspended disbelief, doesn't even wonder who the narrator is, though he or she may give credit to the author for skillful writing. The omniscient narrator is the author's designated tale-teller and can tell us anything the author decides is worth telling. It is only in this sense that the narrator is godlike and omniscient (of course, nobody really is). Such narrators seem to know everything about the characters, including what they are thinking and anything they've ever done. The narrators can comment and analyze. They know everything about history and geography, all the names of all the people in the character's hometown, and so on. Naturally, they don't tell us all these things. They have to be selective because their goal is to tell us a good story, not to write an encyclopedia. Some writers who use this point of view try to jam too much information into their work and wind up boring the reader with irrelevancies. It is important to remember that only *significant* details count. Guy de Maupassant was a master at using the omniscient point of view. Here is the opening paragraph of "The Necklace":

> She was one of those pretty and charming girls who are sometimes, as if by a mistake of destiny, born in a family of clerks. She had no dowry, no expectations, no means of being known, understood, loved, wedded by any rich and distinguished man; and she let herself be married to a little clerk at the Ministry of Public Instruction.

5E Unity and consistency in point of view can be achieved by avoiding accidental shifts.

One of the fundamental responsibilities of the writer is to establish a clear vantage point for the reader. That vantage point has to be established at the very beginning. It can be any of the points of view just described, and once it is established the writer should stick with it. Accidental shifts in point of view can be disturbing and disruptive. They may even be distracting enough to shatter the reader's *suspension of disbelief* (a term that describes the reader's willingness to accept fiction as truth). This does not mean that you can't consciously use multiple points of view if the material lends itself to such an approach. They are sometimes used even in short stories, but they are much more common in novels. The reader can accept any approach that is artistically viable. If, however, you start out writing a story that is *completely objective*, as though seen on a screen or stage, and then start to make elaborate editorial comments, you may confuse the reader. If you start out in the third person, you shouldn't shift accidentally into the first person. If you want your reader to hear directly the voice of one of your characters, you can use the first person or you can make use of dialogue, internal monologue, and such things as letters and diaries, all of which can be contained within a basically third-person point of view. Whatever you do, make sure that the point of view from which your story is told is absolutely clear.

EXAMPLE 5A

THE FOX
Paul Ruffin

From where she was sitting at the kitchen table, her hands deep in the ball of dough in a green bowl, she could see him cross the creek beyond the lower pasture and angle up toward the house. He stopped to lean on the fence that bordered the remains of the summer garden, where the bean poles still stood at odd angles beside the all-but-leafless okra stalks. Drought had brought the garden to an early end as it almost always did.

She was dumping the dough out onto the counter when his shadow mounted the steps and filled the doorway. The screen door squawked open, then slammed to behind him. She did not look around at him.

"There was a fox," he said, sliding a chair back from the table and sitting down, "a red one, in the back field. Near the low-water crossing." He leaned and lifted the coffee pot from the counter and filled the cup that he had already emptied twice that morning before leaving the house. The sun, still morning low, slanted into the small kitchen, brightening what inexpensive things she had scattered across it on table and counter and walls over the thirteen years that they had lived there. Dust specks spun in the rays.

"He had one leg hanging silly to the side and dragging and leaving blood." He looked to see whether she had heard. She kept shaping the ball of dough. "He was so close I could see his eyes. I swear they looked like, like he was blaming me for what trouble he'd been in." He reached over and slid open the box of matches by the stove, one-handedly, lifted one out and struck it across the table top and lit a cigarette. Blue smoke curled up and ribboned in the sun.

She dusted her hands with flour and flattened out the dough, rolled it, and lifted the sheet over a pie plate and dropped it into place. With a paring knife she sliced off the excess, leaving a neat edge around the rim of the plate.

"What you making?" he asked.

"Pie."

"What kind? Something special?"

"No. Just a blueberry pie, from them berries I picked back earlier and froze." She stirred the berries again for good measure and lifted them from the burner.

"His eyes. I can't get over his eyes. They looked like cracked marbles, only black and cold. I was almost afraid he was going to come after me, he looked so mad at the world."

She poured the berries into the dough-lined plate and patted them level with her hand with short little strokes to avoid burning herself, then dropped another sheet of dough over the top. Her hands were stained a deep purple. Using the tines of a fork, she crimped the top shell onto the bottom and ran the knife around the rim again, leaving the pie picture-perfect and ready for baking. She struck three vent slits in the top and slid it into the oven.

"One of them old coon traps likely." He looked at her. "I guess that's what he got into. Hell, I ain't checked them things in years. I left maybe four, five right near where he was."

She dried her berry-stained hands on her apron front, walked to the back door, and looked off toward the smoky morning woods. Crows were zipping in and out of a tree by the creek, cawing, diving in, wheeling up and out, cawing and diving in again. "Owl," she said quietly, "they must be after an owl or something."

"What?" He turned toward her.

"Nothing. I was just talking out loud to myself." She returned to the table and sat down across from him, not because she wanted particularly to be there but because there was no place she could get off to in such a small house where his voice would not find her, rising in insistence until she came. She was not certain that he even cared whether she listened or not. She was just another living thing his voice could drive into or bounce off of—she was something to keep him from talking to himself, which even he must have known was proof positive that he had crossed over into craziness.

"He must have got into one last night, broke his foot or leg, might even have gnawed it off to get out, though I couldn't see the tip of it to be sure." He squinted as smoke coiled about this face. "He crawled under the fence and got off into Mason's corn, what there is of it, not much more than enough to hide a fox, I'd say. Could have been the one that killed them chickens last month, same size, same color. Not likely to get at 'm again."

Their relationship, from her intense hatred of him when they were in grade school together through an infatuation in high school that was consummated in her father's hayloft one Sunday afternoon, had come finally full circle, back to something that she thought at times was hate, at other times mere indifference. If she wished him harm, as she found herself doing some days when he was off in the fields and she was alone in the little house or out in the garden, she was almost happy to see, once he appeared at the door, that none had come to him. Those times the hate swung much too quickly to something like love.

It was the indifference that she nurtured, the cold distance that she put between herself and him even when he was close enough that she could see the hardness of his eyes. It was the calm deadness of indifference that allowed her to continue, day after day, to endure the hill and house and his voice and, each night that he rose to it, to accept his heavy roughness as he drove into her until he shuddered and rolled off onto his side of the bed.

"You shoulda seen them eyes. Like he was blaming me."

She stared past him, past the dust specks in the beam of sun that crossed his face, past the dreamlike haziness of the screen, to the wall of woods where the crows were still zipping in and out of the tree where she was sure some owl crouched, or hawk, something wiser or nobler than crows.

"May die from it, may not. Lucky he didn't die in the trap. He's got something to be glad of there."

And there were the times she was sure that she wished him dead, gone, so that she could try to find some value again in her life, some meaning, before she was stooped and gray and broken like her mother before a merciful onslaught of pneumonia took her out of it, leaving her father so alone that even he, in all his hardness, lasted only another year. She was not so old now—though you could not tell it looking at her hands and face, where the wind and sun and contact with all the things that sting and slash and burn on a farm had done their damage—that she could not smooth over and grow graceful, as her mother had wanted, had taught her to be. She did not even have a child to pass her dreams on to, no matter what their possibilities or impossibilities. She was not even certain that his savage seed, which burned in her like a burst of flame, could beget anything softer than a boy, who would be a copy of him.

"I guess I ought to get the shotgun and go finish him off. If he ain't got too far by now." He flicked his cigarette toward the ashtray and dropped the butt into the last of his coffee. It extinguished with a short hiss.

She walked over to the oven, swung the door down, and checked on the pie. The smell billowed up and out and filled the kitchen.

He slid his chair back and walked into their bedroom, where she heard him fumbling in the closet, getting his gun and shells. He emerged, broke the shotgun open, slipped in two red shells, and stood there watching her bent over the pie. "I don't know how long I'll be gone."

She straightened. The sun had crept along the floor now until the corridor of light from the door was only half as long as it had been. Its reflection off the linoleum gave his face an almost blessed look, like that of the saints in pictures she had seen, but his eyes were still dark and merciless, and the hard lines in his face stood out. He smiled and reached to touch her hand where it lay on the counter. She pulled it away.

"You . . .," he began, then turned to the door to go.

Watching out of the corner of her eye as his shadow darkened the doorway, paused, and disappeared, she took the pie out of the oven and set it onto a back burner to cool. The house quieted then, dropped so far into silence that she could hear nothing but the wind stirring the okra stalks and the distant chatter of crows. She walked to the screen and saw him blend into the woods. A fierce smile on her face, she looked once around the little kitchen and walked over to the stove, where she poised her hand at the edge of the pie and then plunged it into the hot, dark center, where it stayed until the burning stopped and there was no feeling left at all.

Source: "The Fox," originally published in Ploughshares, included in The Man Who Would Be God, by Paul Ruffin. Copyright © 1988 by Paul Ruffin. Reprinted by permission of the author.

EXAMPLE 5B

THOSE WINTER SUNDAYS
Robert Hayden

Sundays too my father got up early
and put his clothes on in the blueblack cold,
then with cracked hands that ached
from labor in the weekday weather made
banked fires blaze. No one ever thanked him.

I'd wake and hear the cold splintering, breaking.
When the rooms were warm, he'd call,
and slowly I would rise and dress,
fearing the chronic angers of that house,

Speaking indifferently to him,
who had driven out the cold
and polished my good shoes as well.
What did I know, what did I know
of love's austere and lonely offices?

EXAMPLE 5C

HELLO BONES
Robert DeMaria

Hello bones!
I hear you rattling down there
Inside my fat flesh.
Just do your job and shut up.
I don't have to be constantly reminded
That you support me,
That your joints ache,
That your marrow is overworked.
Don't talk to me about early retirement.
What the hell do you think I am, anyhow,
A federal penitentiary?
I'm only human. I need you.
Where would I be without you?
I'd fall apart.
I'd collapse like an empty coat
Dropped in a heap on the floor.
And then what?
Then what?

Source: Reprinted by permission of the author.

EXERCISES

Discussion

1. Analyze the point of view from which "The Fox" (Example 5a) is told. Is it *objective*? Is it *omniscient*? Is it something in between? Which character do we learn more about? How is this accomplished? Does the persona make comments that do not come from either character's point of view?

2. Are there any shifts of point of view in this story? Is there a clear and unified vantage point?

3. Would the story be more successful if it were told by the woman in the first person?

4. Analyze the point of view in "Those Winter Sundays" (Example 5b).

5. Who is the speaker in "Hello Bones"? Is this poem a fantasy? How can anyone speak to his or her bones? Is this point of view effective?

Writing

1. Using the *first-person* point of view, write a poem or story about a childhood experience.

2. Write a story or poem from a *completely objective* point of view, without the benefit of any commentaries or explanations.

3. Write a story or poem about two former lovers who have not seen each other for several years. Use a *multiple* point of view, telling the story first through the man's eyes, then through the woman's eyes.

4. Write a story from the *third-person omniscient* point of view. Perhaps your main character has witnessed a crime and is reluctant to tell the police because the person who committed the crime is a close friend or relative.

5. Write a story or poem in which the writer speaks to something inanimate, such as a computer, a car, a river, or tree.

Tone and Style

6A It is important to understand the terminology usually used in discussions of tone and style.

1 | Tone refers to the feelings, moods, and attitudes that are reflected in the way a work is written.

Although it is difficult to separate tone from style, we usually think of *tone* as reflecting the feelings and attitudes of the writer. Tone is not content; it is the particular way in which the content is expressed. The tone of a light literary work might be described, for instance, as flamboyant, farcical, or whimsical. The tone of a more serious work might be elegiac, heavy, or mournful. The tone of a particular work is achieved through certain stylistic devices.

2 | Style refers to writing techniques.

A writer's *style* can be described in terms of such things as vocabulary, syntax, imagery, figurative language, the handling of dialogue and point of view, and other technical peculiarities.

6B There is a wealth of variety in the terminology used to discuss tone and style.

Since many students are not accustomed to discussions of tone and style, they do not know what words are available to them. Here are some words on which you can draw when you talk about tone and style:

abstract Theoretic, without reference to specifics.

ambiguous Having two or more possible meanings.

analytical Inclined to examine things by studying their contents or parts.

anecdotal Involving short narratives of interesting events.

angry Resentful, enraged.

austere Stern, strict, frugal, unornamented.

bland Undisturbing, unemotional, and uninteresting.

boring Dull, tedious, and tiresome.

cinematic Having the qualities of a motion picture.

classical Formal, enduring, and standard, adhering to certain traditional methods.

colloquial Characteristic of ordinary and informal conversation.

concise Using very few words to express a great deal.

confessional Characterized by personal admissions of faults. Used more recently to describe very personal, autobiographical writing.

contemptuous Expressing contempt or disdain (as opposed to *contemptible*, which means deserving of contempt).

conventional Ordinary, usual, conforming to established standards (can be applied to language as well as to manners or values).

cool Unaffected by emotions, especially anger or fear. In modern slang there are many shades of meaning: great, really fine, calm, composed.

cynical A tendency to believe that all human behavior is selfish and opportunistic. (Iago in *Othello* is a cynical character. Some writers are cynical.)

decadent Marked by a decay in morals, values, and artistic standards. Deplored by some writers, applauded by others.

derivative Coming from something or someone else. (When a writer's style is derivative, it seems to stem from the style of an earlier writer or group of writers.)

dreamlike Having the characteristics of a dream. (In literature events are sometimes portrayed as though they are happening in dreams, which often contain symbols and distortions of reality.)

dreary Depressing, dismal, boring.

earthy Realistic, rustic, course, unrefined, instinctive, animal-like (sometimes applied to the language of characters who live close to the earth or soil).

elegiac Expressing sorrow or lamentation. (An elegy is a mournful poem, often a lament for the dead.)

emphatic Using emphasis or boldness in speech, writing, or action.

epigrammatical A tendency to make use of epigrams, which are terse, witty, or pointed sayings ("Any time that is not spent on love is wasted," said Tasso).

evocative Having the ability to call forth memories or other responses. (Imagery in literature tends to be evocative.)

experimental Inclined to try out new techniques or ideas (used of writers who break new ground, such as James Joyce).

fashionable Conforming to whatever the current fashion is in dress, manners, language, or any field of endeavor, including literature.

farcical Humorous in a light way, as in a farce, a play in which the comedy depends a good deal on the situation, often a ridiculous situation.

fatalistic Believing that everything that happens is destined, and therefore, out of the hands of the individual. (See "Appointment in Samarra" in Chapter 12.)

flamboyant Conspicuously bold or colorful.

gimmicky Tricky, sometimes excessively, as in contrived endings.

heavy Profound or serious. (There are various informal modern meanings: *excellent, difficult, tragic*.)

heroic Bold, altruistic, like a hero. (*Heroics* refers to extravagant language, especially that written during the Restoration.)

hysterical Uncontrollably or violently emotional. (It is possible to be hysterical with laughter as well as with fear or rage.)

incoherent Without logical connections, as in speech or writing that cannot be understood.

ironic Characterized by an unexpected turn of events, often the opposite of what was intended. (It was *ironic* that when Oedipus searched for the mysterious cause of the plague, he discovered that he himself was the cause.)

irreverent Showing disrespect for things that are usually respected or revered.

journalistic Characterized by the kind of language usually used in journalism, sometimes pejoratively called *journalese*.

juvenile Immature or childish (a fault in adults, but a standard category in publishing—that is, literature intended for children).

lyrical Intense, spontaneous, musical.

melodramatic Having the characteristics of melodrama, in which emotions and plot are exaggerated and characterization is shallow.

metaphorical Making use of metaphors, which are figures of speech, nonliteral comparisons ("We recognize that flattery is poison, but its perfume intoxicates us."— Marquis de La Grange).

metaphysical Preoccupied with abstract things, especially the ultimate nature of existence and reality.

minimalist Inclined to use as few words and details as possible (a fairly new word used to describe a current trend in literature).

monotonous Tiresome or dull because of lack of variety.

mournful Feeling or expressing grief. (Certain literary forms are devoted to the expression of grief, such as elegies and eulogies.)

mystical Having spiritual or occult qualities or believing in such things. (Some writing is supposed to be divinely or mysteriously inspired, and the writer is supposed to be merely a medium used by a higher power.)

nostalgic Inclined to long for or dwell on things of the past (suggests a certain sentimentality).

objective Uninfluenced by personal feelings. Seeing things from the outside, not subjectively.

obscure Unclear, indistinct, hard to understand (compare *obscurantism*, which is the deliberate use of obscurity and evasion of clarity).

ominous Indicating or threatening evil or danger, as dark clouds indicate that a storm is coming. (*Foreshadowing* is a device in writing that provides hints to the reader that something, usually bad, is going to happen.)

parody A satirical imitation of something serious, such as the endless comic takeoffs on *Romeo and Juliet.*

philosophical Interested in the study of the basic truths of existence and reality. Also, inclined to have a calm and accepting attitude toward the realities of life.

poetical Having the qualities of poetry, such as pleasing rhythms or images. (The prose of some fiction writers, such as Virginia Woolf, has been described as poetical.)

polemical Involving a controversial argument or disputation.

political Involved in politics. Sometimes political literature tends to be polemical, intellectual, or satirical. It can also fall to the level of propaganda.

pompous Displaying one's importance in an exaggerated way. Sometimes a quality in comic characters.

pragmatic Preferring practical action and consequences to theory and abstractions.

precious Being affected in matters of refinement and manners, sometimes ridiculously so. (Some language can be described as *precious*.)

pretentious Having and displaying an exaggerated view of one's own importance.

profound Having penetrating insight, deep.

psychological Having to do with the human mind and human behavior. (The development of modern psychology influenced literature and produced the so-called psychological novel and a kind of clinical approach to characters.)

puritanical Strict or severe in matters of morality (as were the English Puritans of the sixteenth and seventeenth centuries).

realistic Inclined to represent things as they really are (not necessarily as they appear to be).

repetitious Tediously repeating the same thing (such as words or ideas).

rhythmic Characterized by certain patterns, beats, or accents (as in dancing, music, poetry).

romantic Having feelings or thoughts of love, but when associated with nineteenth-century literature or any such literature it suggests a style that emphasizes freedom of form, imagination, and emotion.

sarcastic Inclined to use nasty or cutting remarks that can hurt people's feelings.

sardonic Mocking, taunting, bitter, scornful, sarcastic.

satirical Using sarcasm and irony, often humorously, to expose human folly. (Satire is a commonly used device in literature that is politically or socially critical.)

sensuous Taking pleasure in things that appeal to the senses. (*Sensual* suggests a strong preoccupation with such things, especially sexual pleasures.)

sentimental Expressing tender feelings, sometimes excessively, hence the phrase "sloppy sentimentality."

sharp Precise, biting, or harsh (as applied to words). One can be said to have a sharp tongue, meaning that he or she says harsh or nasty things.

stilted Very formal, sometimes excessively, as in *stilted* prose.

sophisticated Worldly and experienced when applied to people, intricate or complex when applied to things. In writing, a sophisticated style may suggest complexity or considerable experience in the craft.

stark Plain, harsh, completely (as in "stark raving mad"). Simple or bare, when applied to style; sometimes even bleak or grim.

subjective Relying on one's own inner impressions, as opposed to being objective. (Literature that is presented mainly through the thoughts and feelings of characters is often described as subjective.)

subtle Delicate in meaning, sometimes elusively so.

superficial Shallow, trivial, dealing only with the surface of things.

surrealistic Stressing imagery and the subconscious and sometimes distorting ordinary ideas in order to arrive at artistic truths (a modern movement in art and literature).

symbolic Using material objects to represent abstract or complex ideas or feelings. (Moby Dick is obviously symbolic.)

trite Stale, worn out, as in trite expressions.

urbane Sophisticated, socially polished.

vague Unclear, indefinite, imprecise, ambiguous.

venomous Poisonous, malicious.

whimsical Inclined to be playful, humorous, or fanciful.

witty Being able to perceive and express ideas and situations in a clever and amusing way.

wordy Using more words than necessary to say what you have to say.

6C The writer can use various literary devices to establish the right tone.

To achieve the desired tone a writer can use many devices from manipulation of word choice and syntax to imagery, irony, and satire.

To demonstrate varieties of tone and style, let us examine three passages on exactly the same subject and situation, each with a distinct tone and style.

1 | A witty, sardonic tone can be established stylistically by irony, satire, and wordplay.

If the city were merely a jungle, we'd all be a lot safer. What goes on in the jungle is a natural process of growth and decay. There is that nasty old food chain, of course. I mean, some lovely little creatures get eaten up. They, in turn, find something even smaller to eat. Nobody seems to mind, at least not in the way that we do. There is no memory, no guilt, no conscious anxiety—only *flick!* The long tongue of a giant frog hauling in an insect. Then crunch, crunch, wriggle, wriggle, and it's all over. You don't have to make up resumés and look for another job because you have become obsolete or redundant, not to mention fat and bald and mystified by the world of computers. Insects are always employed until the big bullfrog gets them. Instinct tells them what to do. I sometimes wish the city *were* a jungle, instead of what it really is—an obscene marketplace. I'd rather be a frog croaking love songs in a swamp than a terminated advertising executive croaking of anonymity in a three-room apartment cluttered with the cosmetic debris of some stranger who calls herself my wife. So, here I am with my severance check in my pocket. Perhaps I should use it to sever myself from all this nonsense and buy myself a one-way ticket to Tahiti. Gauguin did it. Why can't I?

The *tone* of this passage is lively, witty, satirical, sardonic, sophisticated, and urbane. The narrator may be unhappy with his situation, but he makes his point with humor, even if it is bitter humor. This is achieved by using *stylistic devices* such as:

(a) *Irony*: In the opening sentence, for example, he says, ironically, that the jungle is safer than the city.

(b) *Word choice*: Witty and informal, as in "nasty old food chain"; onomatopoetical, as in *flick, crunch,* and *wriggle*; sharp and critical, as in *terminated, anonymity,* and *cosmetic debris.*

(c) *Word play*: For example, in the two meanings of *croak* and the play on *severance.*

(d) *Satire*: In his amusing and biting references to the "obscene marketplace," for example, and the business world, and the prejudice against older employees; and his reference to marriage in the sardonic expression, "some stranger who calls herself my wife."

2 | A dreary tone can be established stylistically by imagery, a pattern of word choice, and repetition.

There was a dead rat on the sidewalk when he came out of the bolted vault of his apartment house on the West Side. He looked furtively at the hunched group of winos outside the burnt and boarded *bodega*. In the dull light and sticky summer air they looked like a group of ragged apes, and the city itself seemed like a kind of jungle that required special instincts for survival. Fear was his constant companion—fear of attack, fear of losing his job, fear of displeasing his wife, fear of being laughed at because he was fat and bald, and even the minor terror of stepping in dog dung and having to carry the smell of it with him into the transient grave of the subway, and the more permanent grave of his dreary office on Madison Avenue.

The tone of this passage is serious, dreary, and emotional. The dominant feelings are fear and disgust. The atmosphere is gloomy and dangerous. This is achieved by using literary devices such as:

(a) *Imagery, metaphors*, and *similes*: His opening reference to a dead rat sets the tone. The winos are like ragged apes. The city is like a jungle. The subway is a transient grave, and his office is a permanent grave.

(b) *Word choice: furtively, hunched, burnt, boarded, dull, sticky, ragged, survival, dog dung, grave.*

(c) *Repetition*: He repeats the word *fear* five times, and he repeats *grave* in an effective comparison.

3 | An objective, serious tone can be established stylistically by an analytical approach.

He thought of New York as a city that had failed, and he knew that it was just a matter of time before he would have to leave. The rents were too high. The traffic was unbearable. The air was foul. Two thousand people a year were murdered in the city. Over two hundred thousand were hooked on heroin, and over thirty-five thousand were homeless. New York was not a jungle; it was a sociological disaster that offended his sense of order and justice. He hated the polarization of rich and poor. The glass and aluminum functionalism of the towering buildings was as unattractive in its own way as the desolation of the South Bronx.

Though it is still full of negative feelings, the tone of this passage is more objective and impersonal than the tone of either the first or second passage. Stylistically, this is achieved by an analytical and factual approach.

Analysis: The opening sentence contains the broad statement that New York is a city that has failed. It is followed by a series of statements, each of which describes a specific way in which the city has failed—high rents, unbearable traffic, foul air, high crime rate, many drug addicts, many homeless people, polarization of rich and poor, ugly architecture.

6D There are as many varieties of tone and style as there are writers.

The three passages analyzed earlier are contrived illustrations. Let us now consider a few actual works, some of which are included in this book and some of which are so widely known that they can be considered without being included.

"Barcelona," by Alice Adams (Example 2a)

Tone: ominous, psychological, sensitive, and subtle (a familiar modern sound).
Style: cinematic and visual, but also subjective because of the strongly focused point of view. The language level is very contemporary, as is the use of the present tense, which has recently become quite fashionable.

"The Railway Children," by Seamus Heaney (see page 29)

Tone: nostalgic, wistful, with a childish innocence and a sense of awe and adventure.

Style: lyrical with a narrative element. Selective, sharp, descriptive details, and strong, suggestive word choice, as in "sizzling wires," the "burden of swallows," and the raindrops "seeded full with the light."

"Ruby Tells All," by Miller Williams (Example 9b)

Tone: earthy, colloquial, wistful, philosophical (as an attitude of acceptance of life).

Style: Though Ruby speaks in a confessional and autobiographical way, the poem cannot be called "confessional" in the same sense as can Sylvia Plath's or Anne Sexton's poetry. There is no end-line pattern, but the lines are measured (blank verse). It is very narrative, almost like prose, except for the line structure and distillation of events into poetic phrases, often enhanced by the earthy language (a style not uncommon in southern writers).

"Do Not Go Gentle into That Good Night" by Dylan Thomas (see page 262)

Tone: sad and affectionate, a powerful, plaintive exhortation.

Style: a villanelle, which is highly rhymed, using only two rhyming sounds throughout its nineteen lines. A traditional form, but used here with powerful and sometimes unusual phrasing, and with frequent alliteration, which adds up to a poem that is very musical and reflects the ethnic background of the author (the Welsh are famous for their love of music and the lilt in their language).

"Daddy" by Sylvia Plath (Example 3b)

Tone: confessional, angry, hostile, violent, desperate, and a little hysterical and paranoid.

Style: melodic, partly because of the skillful use of repetition. Magnificent and sometimes shocking imagery and word choice. (*Confessional* is a term that is sometimes used to describe style as well as tone.)

This analytical approach to tone and style is designed to give you some insight into an aspect of writing that is all too often treated with a good deal of vagueness. In actual practice a writer is not likely to be this analytical or self-conscious. Most writers automatically integrate content, tone, and style. They have an instinct for selecting the appropriate voice, language, attitude, and literary devices. In the act of creation a writer is often like an athlete who unconsciously performs with spectacular grace. After the fact, neither the writer nor the athlete can explain exactly what happened.

EXAMPLE 6A

THE LAST MOON
Andre Dubus

The murder began someplace in her heart, a place she had never been: it was like a shadowed mountain pass, then a brilliant plain. The plain drew her. She stepped into it one night in bed with the sixteen-year-old boy. They lay naked in the dark room; it was late winter and cold still, and the light of streetlamps came through the windows. The boy held her; his breath was slowing now, and he pushed his hair away from his left eye. Soon he would be ready again. She was twenty-five; she was a guidance counselor at the only high school in town; her husband coached three sports. Now it was basketball, and he was thirty miles away, at a game.

She was on the bed she had chosen with her husband nineteen months ago, when they bought the house and began to buy things to put in it. They were engaged then, and they married a month later. Now she did not feel the bed holding her, or the room, the dead witness of its walls; she felt only her body, as when running early in the morning in this New England town where trees shaded lawns and the park and her office at school, she felt only her blood and muscles and breath, and not the earth her feet struck; as on the high diving board she felt only her gathered flesh, and not the board that held her above air and water. She said: "We could kill him."

Her voice, her words, seemed to stay in the air above their faces, as though, looking at the boy's eyes, she could reach up and with a finger touch each word. She could look at them; she could listen to her voice: it was low and strong, and slightly buoyant, enough so she could brush away the words, scatter them in the dark air, say she did not truly intend them; and in her tone was muted anticipation of the boy saying yes, and so taking the words from the air, making them part of his body, and of hers. The boy said: "Why?"

"I'd have the house. There's insurance on the mortgage. And another policy for two hundred thousand. We could do anything."

He believed her, and he would tell the detectives this, when they broke him; and he would say it on the witness stand, crying, looking again and again at his mother and father. He would tell it first on a warm spring afternoon to a boy who had been his friend since they were six; the boy would be horrified and, after days of pain, would tell his older brother, then his parents.

She was not lying about the house and the money, but they were not the truth. The truth was in this place where she breathed and her heart beat as she lay in the boy's arms. She felt the boy's breath on her cheek, felt her own going out of her parted lips, and she could see how to do it. She could see him doing it, and she could see herself at that moment sitting in the café, drinking tea. She knew now that he would say yes. He had said "Why?" and he would say *How?* and then he would say yes, not with that word alone, but with many words. She would use many words, too; that is how they would plan it. She would talk about the house and the money, and where they could go with the money, when he was older, when he did not live at home; she would say: "We can make love in Spain." But she would never tell him where they were truly going. She would plead not guilty, and people would hear and read what the boy said about the house and the money. In prison she would tell the truth only to her pale and thin girlfriend, weeping as she told it, because she was young and smart, strong and pretty, and she was in prison forever.

In bed the boy stared; they had been lying in the dark long enough for her to see the light in his eyes. No naked girl had kindled this boy until she did. In her office, before she invited him to her house, his eyes were bright, as they were now: he sat in the chair in front of her desk and he could not look away from her; he looked at her hands on her desk, her shoulders beneath pale blue cotton, her blond hair, her mouth; he could not look at her eyes. This was in autumn, and she wanted his frenzy inside her. In bed that night in late winter, the skin of her face felt his eyes, as if their focused light were a point of warmth. He said: "He's really big."

"You could use a gun."

"I've never shot one."

"You'll be close. Can you get a gun?"

"My brother-in-law has some."

"You could take one. Then put it back."

"Where would he be?"

"In his car. You'll wait in the backseat. At night while they're playing a game on the road."

"What if guys are in the parking lot?"

"He does things in his office. He always goes home last. I'll give you a key. You'll take his money and his watch, and throw the watch in the river."

"Do you hate him?"

"He's just ordinary. I can do better."

The boy thought better meant him; she saw this in his eyes.

On the winter night of the murder, she sat in the café, at a table covered with a white cloth, and drank tea with a slice of lemon. She wore a brown sweater and jeans and hiking boots; her leather purse was on the table, and her dark blue parka hung on the back of the chair. She lifted the cup with her thumb and forefinger, felt the solid curve of its handle, the heat of tea in her mouth and throat. She glanced at her watch, knowing the time before she saw the gold hands. She felt each second in her chest and stomach, faster than her breath, slower than her heart. She watched a graying man and woman wearing sweaters and eating cake at a table; they put forks of cake in their mouths, looking at each other, as if they were speaking, or smiling. She watched the large and pleasant woman in a loose green blouse, sitting behind the counter and looking out the window, where people from the movie theater were on the sidewalk.

It would be soon now, the boys leaving the locker room, her husband in his blue suit and white shirt unbuttoned at the collar, the knot of his maroon tie pulled down from his throat, standing in the doorway of his office, talking to the boys as they left. In the car the boy lay waiting, the revolver warm in his hands, the boy afraid of failing and afraid of not failing, afraid of his parents and police and prison; but he was ablaze; he would do it. She watched two teenaged girls drinking Cokes at the counter, and saw the boy on the floor of the car and her husband at his desk in his office; they were inside her, in that place where she lived now.

This place would not have come to her if she had not taken the boy. Before she took him, she knew: even as she waited for him at her house on the first night, she knew that he was not what she wanted, that the boy and her desire were the form of something else she moved closer to when he rang the bell and she opened the door, and pulled him inside and closed the door, and locked it. People she knew, people she had always known, would call it passion, or happiness. They did not know. They were someplace behind her—they always were—and people like them came into the café now, moviegoers sitting at the counter and tables. She watched them. She had watched her husband, these days of snowfall and sunlight, these nights since the one when she said: "We could kill him," and in her heart then he was dead and she was in motion; and for the next eleven days and twelve nights she heard and saw him from that distance, and she made love with him because it was dazzling. The boy was behind her, too; she believed she would keep him for a while, and someday spit him out of her, return him to the place she watched herself watching now: people eating cake and sipping tea.

While beneath her fast heart, her husband left his office and the gymnasium, his gray overcoat unbuttoned, his head bare as he walked into the parking lot under his last moon. The boy lay in the dark and her husband opened the door, and dim light was in the car, and he got inside and closed the door, and it was dark again. The boy rose, and her husband's head and the revolver and the bullet and the boy were poised. In her body she saw the flash, heard the explosion of powder, saw the sudden hole and the spray of blood, her husband's dead eyes and falling face. Her hands rested on the table. It could be in this second; or the next; or the one a minute ago. Her right hand moved toward the cup, and she felt that her arm could reach through the night sky, her thumb and forefinger open to hold the moon.

EXAMPLE 6B

TRIANGLE OF LIGHT
Pamela Harrison

Perhaps it was nothing so much
as the tone of my mother's voice
that stopped me dead in the hall
as she talked softly to my brother,
5   in the kitchen, unaware—a tone
golden as the light that slants
beneath the trees late in August,
warming the gate, the path,
the gently sloping, green and gold field.

10   Even now, I see the shape of that long hall,
in whose deep recesses every possibility
waited to be realized, and the light
spilling in a triangle from the kitchen—

You must imagine the flooding gold
15   of that triangle of light, how it slid
across the threshold, heavy with its own
fullness, tilting like a wave cresting
to break into the shadows of the hall
where I was stranded, listening,
20   gulping knowledge like a burning cup.
Then imagine what
the Siamese twin must feel, the searing
fire along his breastbone where the knife
severs him from half he ever was or knew,
25   cleaving a wholeness he would spend his life
searching to complete.

Had you rounded the corner behind me then,
like a driver coming to rest behind a car
in whose rear window a plastic doll nods,
30   agreeing to everything, you might have sensed
my complicity, as something in me acceded—
no, affirmed the fitness of her choice: for *yes*,
I loved him, too, naturally, loved him
first and best, so that the moment passed,
35   breaking away. . . .

Sometimes it happens crossing a snowy yard
over whose smooth, chill expanses the evening
shadows lean, deeply blue, or, stepping
from some dim interior into the jarring
40   refractions of sunlight striking crisscross
off traffic: a moment you pause to remember
something, telling yourself you must remember
what was suddenly so present and so clear—

though, now, all you can recall
45   is the pressure of its importance, tangled
in the light, in the color, blue or gold.

Source: "Triangle of Light," by Pamela Harrison. Originally published in The Green Mountains Review. Reprinted with the permission of the author.

EXAMPLE 6C

MONEY
Mary Baine Campbell

1   We need more money.
    There isn't enough, and life
    Is too short to waste
    On being poor.

    Money in all its beautiful forms:
    The pale wampum, the bright doubloon
    Cowries blinking on the dawn shore
    The tawny oxen, the rupee
    With its ten colors.

10   We need to give each other money
    Till we are rich beyond our wildest dreams
    Until the banks of the world can't hold it
    Until we have to melt it down into spoons.

    There should be money on every tree
    Nestled in the buds for safe keeping
    Or in summer hanging heavy from the branches.
    The leaves should clink as they fall
    And the squirrels hoard nuggets of gold.

    We could buy everything
20   If we had the money:
    We could buy each other's freedom.
    It would mean the end of rock and roll.

    It would give us time to walk hand in hand
    Through the forest with our lovers,
    Like rich people do in a time of peace,
    Naming the animals.

Source: From Mary Baine Campbell, The World, the Flesh, and the Angels. Copyright 1989 by Beacon Press. Reprinted by permission of the author.

EXERCISES

Discussion

1. Describe the tone and style of "The Last Moon" by Andre Dubus.
2. If the style seems unconventional, can you explain why?
3. Is the handling of the dialogue in this story consistent with the overall style and tone?
4. Does the narrator have any special attitude toward the story? How is that attitude revealed?
5. How is the character of the teacher established? Explain the opening sentence.
6. Do we learn anything about the boy or the husband?
7. Comment on the tone and style of "Triangle of Light" by Pamela Harrison (Example 6b).
8. What pictures appear in your mind as you read this poem?
9. What is the actual event or experience described in this poem?
10. Discuss the tone and style of the following poem:

THE MAN IN THE MERCEDES
Judith Kroll

The killer will be driving a Mercedes.
Watch for a foreign-looking man,
swarthy and short.

We see him from the back of his head:

a fat neck; disappearing hair;
definitely middle-aged (a career agent)

The man in the Mercedes appears
in the supermarket. He has come
to do a demonstration
of something that changes hope
into pretzels.

Source: "The Man in the Mercedes," by Judith Kroll. From The Mediterranean Review, Volume 2, No.1, Fall 1971. Reprinted by permission of the author.

11 | Here are the opening passages of two short stories.

Discuss the tone and style of each passage. Is there anything in the writing to indicate that the story by Lawrence was written more than fifty years earlier than the story by Oates?

From "The Man Who Loved Islands" by
D. H. Lawrence:

There was a man who loved islands. He was born on one, but it didn't suit him, as there were too many other people on it, besides himself. He wanted an island all of his own; not necessarily to be alone on it, but to make it a world of his own.

An island, if it is big enough, is no better than a continent. It has to be really quite small, before it *feels like* an island; and this story will show how tiny it has to be, before you can presume to fill it with your own personality.

Now circumstances so worked out, that this lover of islands, by the time he was thirty-five actually acquired an island of his own. He didn't own it as freehold property, but he had a ninety-nine years' lease of it, which, as far as a man and an island are concerned, is as good as everlasting. Since, if you are like Abraham, and want your offspring to be numberless as the sands of the sea-shore, you don't choose an island to start breeding on. Too soon there would be overpopulation, overcrowding, and slum conditions.

Which is a horrid thought, for one who loves an island for its insulation. No, an island is a nest which holds one egg, and only one. This egg is the islander himself.

From "By the River" by
Joyce Carol Oates:

Helen thought: "Am I in love again, some new kind of love? Is that why I'm here?" She was sitting in the waiting room of the Yellow Bus Lines station; she knew the big old room with its dirty tile floor and its solitary telephone booth in the corner and its candy machine and cigarette machine and popcorn machine by heart. Everything was familiar, though she had been gone for five months, even the old woman with the dyed red hair who sold tickets and had been selling them there, behind that counter, for as long as Helen could remember. Years ago, before Helen's marriage, she and her girl friends would be driven into town by someone's father and after they tired of walking around town they would stroll over to the bus station to watch the buses unload. They were anxious to see who was getting off, but few of the passengers who got off stayed in Oriskany—they were just passing through, stopping for a rest and a drink, and their faces seemed to say that they didn't think much of the town. Nor did they seem to think much of the girls from the country who stood around in their colorful dresses and smiled shyly at strangers, not knowing any better: they were taught to be kind to people, to smile first, you never knew who it might be. So now Helen was back in Oriskany, but this time she had come in on a bus herself. Had ridden alone, all the way from the city of Derby, all alone, and was waiting for her father to pick her up so she could go back to her old life without any more fuss.

Writing

1. Write a story about an act of violence in a small town or rural setting. Establish an appropriate tone.

2. Write a story or play about a high school or college reunion. Focus on a small group of people who were once close friends.

3. Write a story or play, serious or comic, about a couple who are engaged and promise to confess to each other, before the wedding, the worst thing they ever did.

4. Write a poem or story, the tone of which can be described with one of the following sets of terms:
   a. satirical, sardonic, ironic
   b. elegiac, dreary, metaphysical
   c. metaphorical, symbolic, surrealistic
   d. psychological, ominous, fatalistic

5. Write a description of a place that you don't like. Make your negative tone clear in your writing as well as your content.

6. Write a satirical poem, story, or play in which the target of your satire is some aspect of education, politics, or television.

Description

Description should be *selective* and *significant*. It should also appeal to the five senses: seeing, hearing, smelling, tasting, and touching. It is the writer's job to create a kind of fictional reality, to make things seem real. The scientist describes the physical world with cold objectivity. The writer describes the world with physical details to create a work of art. This can best be accomplished by careful observation and skillful abstraction.

7A Abstractions as well as specific details play a part in literary descriptions.

To *abstract* means to remove. When you write an abstract (summary) of a report, you single out only the most important points. In abstract art only certain significant forms and colors are used. It is nonrepresentational. In writing, words that are abstract refer to some general quality or condition, not to a specific object. *Beauty*, for instance, is an abstract word. So is *truth*. When John Keats says "beauty is truth," he is making an abstract statement, but when Byron says the following he has someone specific in mind:

> She walks in beauty, like the night
> Of cloudless climes and starry skies . . .

An abstract statement is a generalization that is arrived at by observing many specific cases. Thus, when you say "There is a charming innocence in children," you are making a general observation about children and not a comment about a specific child. Aphorisms and proverbs are generalizations. For example, "As we grow older we grow both more foolish and wiser at the same time" (La Rochefoucauld).

So much of human thought and expression involves the use of abstractions that we can't just toss them aside when we write fiction, poetry, and drama. In many workshops, student writers are advised to avoid abstractions. This advice is a bit simplistic. What a writer has to learn to do is to use abstract language when it is appropriate and specific language when it is more effective. Most descriptive passages benefit enormously from the use of specific details that appeal to the senses.

7B Physical details are an essential part of any description.

The use of physical details allows the reader to experience what is going on in the literary work. Good writers are especially perceptive and sensitive when it comes to such details. Such writers share their observations and their sensitivity with their readers, and, thereby, provide them with vicarious experiences and insights that otherwise they might not have. That is why great writers are not considered mere entertainers. The contributions they make to their culture are important.

1 | It is important for writers to develop the habit of perception.

Some writers are born with the gift of observation; some have to learn how to look at things. It is possible for a young writer to cultivate the habit of perception. One workshop exercise involves the systematic observation of people from head to toe, and the listing of descriptive details and what they reveal about a person. One example should suffice.

What about a character's hair? What can it reveal? Hair doesn't just have a color; it has a texture, and it is done in a certain style. It also moves as the body moves or as the wind moves through it. Hair is a kind of language. How you wear it is a message to the world, sometimes a sexual message, sometimes even a political message. In the 1960s it was very political. Long hair became a sign of protest and the back-to-nature look. More recently, punk hairdos have announced rebellion. The idea is to be outrageous, even offensive. Such youthful rebellions are almost always against the stodginess and conservatism of the older generation and the establishment. Conscious and constant practice in the observation of details such as these can improve a writer's ability to describe things.

A writer's observations can be subtle or superficial. Good writers tend to have greater depth and originality. Commercial writers tend to rely heavily on stereotypes and clichés.

2 | Seeing

A writer must learn to make use of all the five senses when writing descriptions. The highest of these senses, according to Aristotle, is sight. The popularity of television may be modern evidence of how right he was. In performed dramas, of course, sight is essential, but even in poetry and fiction the visual appeal is often dominant. Notice the number of vivid details in this paragraph from "A Worn Path" by Eudora Welty:

> She wore a dark striped dress reaching down to her shoe tops, and an equally long apron of bleached sugar sacks, with a full pocket: all neat and tidy, but every time she took a step she might have fallen over her shoelaces, which dragged from her unlaced shoes. She looked straight ahead. Her eyes were blue with age. Her skin had a pattern all its own of numberless branching wrinkles and as though a whole little tree stood in

the middle of her forehead, but a golden color ran underneath, and the two knobs of her cheeks were illuminated by a yellow burning under the dark. Under the red rag her hair came down on her neck in the frailest of ringlets, still black, and with an odor like copper.

3 | Hearing

The following poem by Wallace Stevens is visually striking, but the strongest sensation is *sound*—the cry of the peacocks:

DOMINATION OF BLACK

At night, by the fire,
The colors of the bushes
And of the fallen leaves,
Repeating themselves,
Turned in the room,
Like the leaves themselves
Turning in the wind.
Yes: but the color of the heavy hemlocks
Came striding.
10   And I remembered the cry of the peacocks.
The colors of their tails
Were like the leaves themselves
Turning in the wind,
In the twilight wind.
They swept over the room,
Just as they flew from the boughs of the hemlocks
Down to the ground.
I heard them cry—the peacocks.
Was it a cry against the twilight
20   Or against the leaves themselves
Turning in the wind,
Turning as the flames

Turned in the fire,
Turning as the tails of the peacocks
Turned in the loud fire,
Loud as the hemlocks
Full of the cry of the peacocks?
Or was it a cry against the hemlocks?
Out of the window,
I saw how the planets gathered
30   Like the leaves themselves
Turning in the wind.
I saw how the night came,
Came striding like the color of the heavy hemlocks.
I felt afraid.
And I remembered the cry of the peacocks.

The mating call of the peacock is a harsh, haunting, unearthly cry. Wallace Stevens tries to describe poetically his reactions to that sound. It is not an easy task. Sounds may be more difficult to describe than sights. Consider, for instance, how difficult it is to describe music. Since the world is full of sounds, writers must learn to include them in the fabric of their work. Who can forget that terrifying line by Emily Dickinson: "I heard a fly buzz—when I died—"? And no one has captured the sound of the sea on a calm night better than Matthew Arnold in this excerpt from "Dover Beach":

The sea is calm tonight.
The tide is full, the moon lies fair
Upon the straits;—on the French coast the light
Gleams and is gone; the cliffs of England stand,

Glimmering and vast, out in the tranquil bay.
Come to the window, sweet is the night-air!
Only, from the long line of spray
Where the sea meets the moon-blanched land,
Listen! you hear the grating roar
Of pebbles which the waves draw back, and fling,
At their return, up the high strand,
Begin, and cease, and then again begin,
With tremulous cadence slow, and bring
The eternal note of sadness in.

4 | Smelling

A novel by Tom Robbins called *Jitterbug Perfume* is pre-occupied with the sense of smell, as its title might indicate. In the following scene the ultimate fragrance actually causes a riot:

> Somebody had supplied beer, cases of it, and many in the crowd had lost their reason in it. About seven o'clock, as much of Seattle was finishing its dinner, a dense, hot, rustic odor swept through the street, and as if it had one mind, one nose, the crowd spontaneously panicked. Something snapped in it, and it rushed the gate, tearing it from its hinges and throwing the guards aside.
>
> Disturbed and anxious, pursued by the smell, the people ripped loose the fairy door knocker and streamed into the mansion, where they raced from room to room, looking for the divine magic that had been denied them. And when they found nothing—no gurgling test tubes or sparking coils, no vials of purple elixirs or leatherbound books bursting with esoteric information, no files, even, that they might plunder; when they found merely a posh modern residence lacking so much as a hint of scientific activity and occupied only by a red-faced man who'd been skipping and leaping about in a

bizarre dance, and a young girl playing with potted plants, then they truly panicked.

In an earlier scene one of the characters discusses the importance of fragrance in the human experience:

Bunny: "Scent is the last sense to leave a dying person. After sight, hearing, and even touch are gone, the dying hold on to their sense of smell. Does that sharpen your appreciation of the arena in which we perfumers perform?

"Fragrance is a conduit for our earliest memories, on the one hand; on the other, it may accompany us as we enter the next life. In between, it creates mood, stimulates fantasy, shapes thought, and modifies behavior. It is our strongest link to the past, our closest fellow traveler to the future. Prehistory, history, and the afterworld, all are its domain. Fragrance may well be the signature of eternity."

There are times in *Jitterbug Perfume* when Tom Robbins gets carried away, but there is no doubt that the sense of smell is extremely important. We all know how effectively a hunting dog can follow a scent, but we are less aware of many of the subtle effects that fragrances and odors have on people. Experiments have shown that newborn babies can pick out their own mothers from a group through their sense of smell. One theory about sexual attraction claims that what is called "chemistry" between people is largely determined by smell. The popularity of perfume is further evidence that we may not be as far removed from other animals as we think. A good writer can make good use of the sense of smell in the descriptions that bring human experience to life. One of Shakespeare's most powerful lines can be found in the final couplet of Sonnet 94:

> For sweetest things turn sourest by their deeds;
> Lilies that fester smell far worse than weeds.

5 | Tasting

In this well-known poem by Delmore Schwartz the sense of taste is very effectively used:

THE HEAVY BEAR WHO GOES WITH ME
"The withness of the body" –Whitehead

The heavy bear who goes with me,
A manifold honey to smear his face,
Clumsy and lumbering here and there,
The central ton of every place,
The hungry beating brutish one
In love with candy, anger, and sleep,
Crazy factotum, dishevelling all,
Climbs the building, kicks the football,
Boxes his brother in the hate-ridden city.

10   Breathing at my side, that heavy animal,
That heavy bear who sleeps with me,
Howls in his sleep for a world of sugar,
A sweetness intimate as the water's clasp,
Howls in his sleep because the tight-rope
Trembles and shows the darkness beneath.
—The strutting show-off is terrified,
Dressed in his dress-suit, bulging his pants,
Trembles to think that his quivering meat
Must finally wince to nothing at all.

20   That inescapable animal walks with me,
Has followed me since the black womb held,
Moves where I move, distorting my gesture,
A caricature, a swollen shadow,
A stupid clown of the spirit's motive,
Perplexes and affronts with his own darkness,
The secret life of belly and bone,
Opaque, too near, my private, yet unknown,

Stretches to embrace the very dear
With whom I would walk without him near,
30   Touches her grossly, although a word
Would bare my heart and make me clear,
Stumbles, flounders, and strives to be fed
Dragging me with him in his mouthing care,
Amid the hundred million of his kind,
The scrimmage of appetite everywhere.

Source: By Delmore Schwartz, from SELECTED POEMS, copyright ©1959 by Delmore Schwartz. Reprinted by permission of New Directions Publishing Corp.

This poem is as much about appetite and taste as *Jitterbug Perfume* is about the sense of smell. It ends with "The scrimmage of appetite everywhere." The bear with which the author identifies has a passion for honey, is "in love with candy," "howls in his sleep for a world of sugar," "strives to be fed." The bear is the clumsy beast inside the poet, his double, his other self, perhaps the animal part of all of us. The bear is always there, all appetite and desire. The poet cannot even free himself from the creature to talk in a civilized way to the one he loves.

The sense of taste is closely related to the sense of smell, not only in our physiology, but in our literature. Descriptions of food require both. In some works such descriptions are convincing enough to make the reader's mouth water. There is no more famous celebration of wine and the pleasures of life than Edward FitzGerald's translation of "The Rubáiyát of Omar Khayyám," in which we find this well-known stanza.

A Book of Verses underneath the Bough,
A Jug of Wine, a Loaf of Bread—and Thou
Beside me singing in the Wilderness—
Oh, Wilderness were Paradise enow!

6 | Touching

There are obviously some things that we cannot fully understand without touching them. Just as the understanding of color requires the ability to see, the understanding of such things as heat and cold, and of physical contacts such as sex, requires the ability to feel. So important is the sense of touch to an infant that without it normal development is not possible. A famous experiment involving rhesus monkeys has proven this. Removed from physical contact with their mothers or some substitute they grow up to be incurably neurotic.

One of the sensations that writers have often tried to describe is the kiss. There are many famous passages that deal with this act, but perhaps none is more famous than the following passage from Christopher Marlowe's *Doctor Faustus*:

> Was this the face that launched a thousand ships,
> And burnt the topless towers of Ilium?
> Sweet Helen, make me immortal with a kiss.
> Her lips suck forth my soul: see where it flies.
> Come, Helen, come, give me my soul again.
> Here will I dwell, for heaven is in those lips,
> And all is dross that is not Helena.

While Tom Robbins argued that the sense of smell was the most fundamental of the human senses, August Coppola made a strong case for the sense of touch, a field in which he did a great deal of research. His interest is clearly reflected in his novel *The Intimacy* (Grove Press, 1978).

He went to the faculty lounge to rest. Then took lunch in the commons. He didn't know what had happened. It was like amnesia; he remembered nothing of those few seconds, only his hand after. He reached out at the table, not looking, and took hold of a soup spoon by his plate. His thumb fit into the depression of the backside at the top of the handle, his fingers playing lightly over the molded pattern. The curves, the cut lines, the bevels. It was an eerie sensation. Somehow the shape seemed to be teasing him, as if alive, beckoning him to touch one part, then another, always shifting elusively beneath his fingertips, cool, smooth, rounded, like the chalk. There was an excitement, something unspoken, a kind of mute urgency. He looked down at the spoon, turning it over: the pattern was an ugly little cherub face with swollen cheeks and sunken eyes, more like some primitive deity. He closed his eyes, turning the spoon over again, letting his fingers move along the underside. The sensation was suddenly frozen; he could distinguish the cheeks, the hollows for eyes, the beveled mouth—the "face"— just as he had seen it. But the other feeling that had called out to him was gone, as though two separate worlds existed, one of sight, the other of touch.

He bit his lip. It was still terrifying, that blackout, like something unknown there, waiting. And then perhaps—his mind began functioning—it was the birth of some new idea that had come so quickly it had left him mentally breathless before he could capture it. He held the spoon tight in his hand, then let it bang against the plate. The thought struck him: the ultimate reality was still touch, solidity, something to grasp hold of, yet everything in our lives seemed to be based on sight, the things we believe about ourselves, or try to appear as, our language, racial prejudice, class distinction, law and order.

He picked up the spoon, turning it over in his hand. He wondered what life would be like if known only through touch, what it would reveal, what kinds of thoughts and feelings it would give rise to. It was so simple. He couldn't imagine our existence without touch, and yet so little was known about it. He remembered the works he had read of Helen Keller. All that was talked about was the attempt to be sighted, how to turn the handicap into a compensation for the normal world, fitting back in. Never the mysteries of that dark existence she had felt—on its own terms—the things for which there were no names, no words.

The idea intrigued him, helping him to relax, to ease the pain of those few moments. He wondered if there could be a beauty there, if such a primordial beauty did exist, one that might evaporate if brought to light, or seem ugly, as did the little face on the spoon. As a new art form perhaps. Combining sensations of touch to create a new dimension of life, or a new sense of reality, or beauty that might well transport or change or re-shape or release one from all the ugliness one already felt to be real. Just as music could blend sounds to move people, and painting or film change how we see the world. It suddenly seemed to mean a lot to him. It seemed so obvious now. The oldest of all man's senses, and yet never used like that before. Why? What was really there?

Source: Excerpt from The Intimacy by August Coppola. copyright © 1978 by August Coppola. Reprinted by permission of The Estate of August Coppola.

7 | Using all five senses can produce a powerful effect.

"Digging" by Seamus Heaney is such an earthy poem that we can find in it every one of the five senses, beginning with the feeling of the pen in the author's hand moving to the "clean rasping sound" of the spade, to the sight of his father digging in the potato fields, to the taste of the milk and "the cold smell of potato mould." This appeal to the senses draws us into the experience. It is, understandably, one of Seamus Heaney's best known poems.

DIGGING

Between my finger and my thumb
The squat pen rests; snug as a gun.
Under my window, a clean rasping sound
When the spade sinks into gravelly ground:
My father, digging. I look down

Till his straining rump among the flowerbeds
Bends low, comes up twenty years away

Stooping in rhythm through potato drills
Where he was digging.

The coarse boot nestled on the lug, the shaft
Against the inside knee was levered firmly.
He rooted out tall tops, buried the bright edge deep
To scatter new potatoes that we picked
Loving their cool hardness in our hands.

By God, the old man could handle a spade.
Just like his old man.
My grandfather cut more turf in a day
Than any other man on Toner's bog.
Once I carried him milk in a bottle
Corked sloppily with paper. He straightened up
To drink it, then fell to right away

Nicking and slicing neatly, heaving sods
Over his shoulder, going down and down
For the good turf. Digging.

The cold smell of potato mould, the squelch and slap
Of soggy peat, the curt cuts of an edge
Through living roots awaken in my head.
But I've no spade to follow men like them.

Between my finger and my thumb
The squat pen rests.
I'll dig with it.

Source: "Digging" from POEMS 1965–1975 by Seamus Heaney. Copyright ©
1980 by Seamus Heaney. Reprinted by permission of Farrar, Straus and Giroux,
LLC and Faber & Faber Ltd.

7C   Selectivity is necessary in description.

A description that is literally complete is an impossibility.
Even if it were possible it would not be desirable. We don't

have to know everything about a character who appears in a literary work, and we don't have to know everything about the setting. Any attempt to be all-inclusive is bound to result in nothing but clutter and confusion.

1 | The details that are selected should be significant.

Not all descriptive details are of equal value. We must select those things that have some meaning within the context of the work. When we introduce a character, for instance, it may or may not matter how tall he or she is. If it doesn't matter, what's the point of mentioning it? Of course, if height has some bearing on the situation, then it *is* significant. The same is true of other details, such as age, weight, eye color, hair, general appearance, and ethnic background.

All too often a student writer will introduce a character as though the details were taken from his driver's license: "John Sherman was twenty-two years old, five feet eight, and had blue eyes and blond hair." This is certainly information, but it may not be significant information. What the reader wants to know is something about his defining qualities, something that brings him to life as an individual, not as a list of statistics.

In the opening paragraph of "Barcelona" (Example 2a) we are introduced to Thad and Persis Fox. The first thing we are told is that they are a "middle-aged American couple." The details that follow are carefully selected to reveal something significant about the characters and the situation in which they find themselves. "The man is tall and bald; his head shines dimly as he and his wife cross the shaft of light from an open doorway. She is smaller, with pale hair; she walks fast to keep up with her husband. She is wearing gold chains, and they, too, shine in the light. She carries a small bag in which there could be—more gold? money? some interesting pills?"

The characters here are not described in isolation; they are described in a setting, "the old quarter of Barcelona." The details of that setting are also carefully selected. There is a great deal more that we could be told about both the couple and the Barrio Gotico of Barcelona, but nothing is included that does not contribute to the story. The gold chains that Persis wears are important because in such a neighborhood she might attract thieves, and the bag she carries is important because it is about to be stolen.

In the second paragraph we are given a thumbnail sketch of Persis, with the emphasis on her somewhat neurotic nature. This is important, because the main focus of the story will be her reaction to the incident. In the next paragraph we are given some more details about the dark, cobbled streets of the old quarter. These details are significant because they create a sense of danger.

2 | Some writers are more selective than others.

As in the visual arts, the degree of selectivity is partly a matter of style. Some fiction writers are almost as selective as poets, who tend to distill their descriptions into significant and evocative images. Other writers use techniques that require more details and tend to be more analytical than poetic. Conciseness in itself is not necessarily a virtue. It can even be carried too far or become an affectation. Minimalism doesn't always work, and selectivity must not be confused with mere brevity or sparseness. Stylistically, writers like Hemingway and Faulkner are worlds apart. Hemingway is well known for his descriptive economy, and Faulkner is famous for his verbal profusion, but neither of them won the Nobel Prize for wasting words.

7D Language choice is as important as choosing the correct details.

Good description involves not only selecting the right details, but using the right words. Some writers and critics have even gone so far as to insist that finding the precise word is what good writing is all about. This notion is associated especially with Flaubert, for whom writing was sometimes an agonizingly slow process, because he was such a perfectionist. There may be more to great writing than effective word choice, but it is certainly one of the essentials, especially when it comes to description.

1 | Many factors are involved in effective language.

Choosing the right words depends on such things as the sound of the words, the shades of meaning, and the images the words evoke (see Chapter 11). The use of figures of speech can also add to descriptive effectiveness. As an example, we can use the opening paragraphs of William Faulkner's short story, "A Rose for Emily."

> When Miss Emily Grierson died, our whole town went to her funeral: the men through a sort of respectful affection for a fallen monument, the women mostly out of curiosity to see the inside of her house, which no one save an old manservant—a combined gardener and cook—had seen in at least ten years.
>
> It was a big squarish frame house that had once been white, decorated with cupolas and spires and scrolled balconies in the heavily lightsome style of the seventies, set on what had once been our most select street. But garages and cotton gins had encroached and obliterated even the august names of that neighborhood; only Miss Emily's house was left, lifting its stubborn and coquettish decay above the cotton wagons and

the gasoline pumps—an eyesore among eyesores. And now Miss Emily had gone to join the representatives of those august names where they lay in the cedar-bemused cemetery among the ranked and anonymous graves of Union and Confederate soldiers who fell at the battle of Jefferson.

The men in the town thought of Emily as "a fallen monument." This expression conjures up a number of images. She represents the Old South, but perhaps has some of the coldness or deadness of a monument. Decay and nostalgia are both suggested here. Her house is built in "the heavily lightsome style of the seventies." *Lightsome* is a literary word that means *lighthearted*. The house was, therefore, heavily decorated, but expressed the lighthearted spirit of the times. Miss Emily's house was the last one left on the street from the grand old days. It is described as "lifting its stubborn and coquettish decay above the cotton wagons and the gasoline pumps." *Stubborn* and *coquettish* suggest a Southern belle, a vivid piece of personification. The cemetery where she lies is described as "cedar-bemused," which may sound odd but somehow feels appropriate. Certainly, "ranked and anonymous graves" is a very effective way to describe the burial place of soldiers, in this case, soldiers who fell in the Civil War. There is a kind of cumulative consistency of word choice in this passage that is linked with the theme of the decay of the Old South and the ugliness that replaced it.

EXAMPLE 7A

THE HOUSE BEHIND
Lydia Davis

We live in the house behind and can't see the street; our front windows look across the courtyard into the kitchens and bathrooms of the front house, and our back windows are close up against a gray wall, the inner wall of the city. The apartments inside the front house are lofty and comfortable, while ours are cramped and graceless. In the front house, maids live in the neat little rooms on the top floor and look out upon the spires of St. Etienne, but under the eaves of our house, tiny cubicles open in darkness onto a dusty corridor and the students and poor bachelors who sleep in them must share one toilet by the back stairwell. Many tenants in the front house are high civil servants, while the house behind is filled with shopkeepers, salesmen, retired post office employees, and unmarried schoolteachers. Naturally, we can't really blame the people in the front house for their wealth, but we are oppressed by it: We feel the difference. Yet this is not enough to explain the ill will that has always existed between the two houses.

I often sit by my front window at dusk, staring up at the sky and listening to the sounds of the people across the way. As the hours pass, the pigeons settle over the dormers, the traffic choking the narrow street beyond thins out, and the televisions in various apartments fill the air with voices and the sounds of violence. Now and again, I hear the lid of a metal trash can clang below me in the courtyard, and I see a shadowy figure carry away an empty plastic pail into one of the houses.

The trash cans were always a source of embarrassment, but now the atmosphere has sharpened: The tenants from the house in front are afraid to empty their trash. They will not enter the courtyard if another tenant is already there. I see them silhouetted in the doorway of the front hall as they wait. When there is no one in the courtyard, they empty their pails and walk quickly back across the cobblestones, anxious not to be caught there alone. Some of the old women from the house in front go down together, in pairs.

The murder took place nearly a year ago. It was curiously gratuitous. The murderer was a respected man from our building, and the murdered woman was one of the only kind people in the front house; in fact, one of the few who would associate with the people of the house behind. M. Martin had no real reason to kill her. I can only think that he was maddened by frustration: For years he had wanted to live in the house in front, and it was becoming clear to him that he never would.

The murder took place one evening at twilight. I was sitting by the window. I saw the two of them meet in the courtyard by the trash cans. It was probably something she said to him, something that was perfectly innocent and friendly, yet which made him realize once again just how different he was from her and from everyone else in the front house. She never should have spoken to him—most of them don't speak to us.

He had just emptied his pail when she came out. There was something so graceful about her that although she was carrying a garbage pail, she looked and moved with a regal air. I suppose he noticed how even her pail—of the same ordinary yellow plastic as his—was brighter, and how the garbage inside was more vivid than his. He must have noticed, too, how fresh and clean her dress was, how it wafted gently around her strong and healthy legs, how sweet the smell was that rose from it, and how luminous her skin was in the fading daylight, how her eyes glimmered with the constant slightly frenetic look of happiness that she always wore, and how her light hair glinted with silver and swelled under its pins. He had stooped over his pail and was scraping the inside of it with a blunt hunting knife—for he was meticulously clean—when she came out, gliding over the cobblestones toward him.

It was so dark by then that only the whiteness of her dress would have been clearly visible to him at first. He remained silent—for he was scrupulously polite, and was never the first to speak to a person from the front house—and quickly turned his eyes away from her. But not quickly enough, for she answered his look and spoke.

She probably said something casual about how soft the evening was. If she hadn't spoken, his fury might not have been unleashed by the gentle sound of her voice. But in that instant he must have realized that for him the evening could never be as soft as it was for her. Or else something in her tone—something too kind, something just condescending enough to make him see that he was doomed to remain where he was—pushed him out of control. He straightened like a shot, as though something in him had snapped, and in one motion drove his knife into her throat.

I saw it all from above. It happened very quickly and quietly. I did not do anything. For a while I did not even realize what I had seen: Life is so uneventful back here that I have almost lost the ability to react. But there was also something arresting in the sight of it: He was a strong and well-made man, an experienced hunter, and she was as slight and graceful as a doe. His gesture was a classically beautiful one; and she slumped down onto the cobblestones as quietly as a mist melting away from the surface of a pond. Even when I was able to think, I did not do anything.

As I watched, several people came to the back door of the house in front and the front door of our own house and stopped short with their garbage pails when they saw her lying there and him standing motionless above her. His pail stood empty at his feet, scraped clean, the handle of her pail was still clenched in her hand, and her garbage had spilled over the stones beside her, which was almost as shocking to us all, in some strange sense, as the murder itself. More and more tenants gathered and watched from the doorways. Their lips were moving, but I could not hear them over the noise of the televisions on all sides of me.

I think the reason no one did anything right away was that the murder had taken place in a sort of no-man's-land. If it had happened in our house or in theirs, things would have been different: Action would have been taken—slowly in our house, briskly in theirs. But as it was, people were in doubt: Those from the house in front hesitated to lower themselves so far as to get involved in this, and those from our house hesitated to presume so far. In the end it was the concierge who dealt with it. The body was removed by the coroner and M. Martin left with the police. After the crowd had dispersed, the concierge picked up M. Martin's pail and silently returned it to his wife.

For a day or two, the people of both houses were visibly shaken. Talk was heard in the halls: In our house, voices rose like wind in the trees before a storm; in theirs, rich confident syllables rapped out like machine-gun fire. Encounters between the tenants of the two houses were more violent; people from our house jerked away from the others, if we met them in the street, and something in our faces cut short their conversations when we came within earshot.

But then the halls grew quiet again, and for a while it seemed as though little had changed. Perhaps this incident had been so far beyond our understanding that it could not affect us, I thought. The only difference seemed to be a certain blank look on the faces of the people in my building, as though they had gone into shock. But gradually I began to realize that the incident had left a deeper impression. Mistrust filled the air, and uneasiness. The people of the house in front were afraid of us here behind, now, and there was no communication between us at all. By killing the woman from the house in front, M. Martin had killed something more: We lost the last traces of our self-respect before the people from the house in front, because we all assumed responsibility for the crime. Now there was no point in pretending any longer. Some, it is true, were unaffected and continued to wear the rags of their dignity proudly. But most of the people in the house behind changed.

A night nurse lived across the landing from me. Every morning when she came home from work, I would wake to hear her heavy iron key ring clatter against the wooden door of her apartment, her keys rattle in the keyholes. Late in the afternoon she would come out again and shuffle around the landing on little cloth pads, dusting the banisters. Now she sat behind her door listening to the radio and coughing gently. The older Lamartine sister, who in the old days would keep her door open a crack and listen to conversations going on in the hallway—occasionally becoming so excited that she stuck her sharp nose in the crack and threw out a comment or two—was now no longer seen at all except on Sundays, when she went out to early morning mass with a blue veil thrown over her head. My neighbor on the second floor, Mme. Bac, left her laundry out for days, in all weathers, until the sour smell of it rose to me where I sat. Many tenants no longer cleaned their doormats. People were ashamed of their clothes, and wore raincoats when they went out. A musty odor filled the hallways: Delivery boys and insurance salesmen groped their way up and down the stairs looking uncomfortable. Worst of all, everyone became surly and mean: We stopped speaking to one another, told tales to outsiders, and left mud on one another's landings.

Curiously enough, many pairs of houses in the city suffer from bad relations like ours: There is usually an uneasy truce between the two houses until some incident explodes the situation and it begins deteriorating. The people in the front houses become locked in their cold dignity, and the people in the back houses lose confidence, their faces gray with shame. The sort of democracy the town planner might have had in mind cannot work, because people do not know how to live with others so unlike themselves.

Recently I caught myself on the point of throwing an apple core down into the courtyard, and I realized how much I had already fallen under the influence of the house behind. My windowpanes are dim and fine curlicues of dust line the edges of the floorboards. If I don't leave now, I will soon be incapable of making the effort. I must lease an apartment in another section of the city and pack up my things.

I know that when I go to say good-bye to my neighbors, with whom I once got along quite well, some will not open their doors and others will look at me as though they do not know me. But there will be a few who manage to summon up enough of their old spirit of defiance and aggressive pride to shake my hand and wish me luck.

The hopeless look in their eyes will make me feel ashamed of leaving. But there is no way I can help them. In any case, I suspect that after some months things will return to normal. Habit will cause the people here behind to resume their shabby tidiness, their caustic morning gossip against the people from the house in front, their thrift in small purchases, their decency where no risk is involved—and as the people in both houses move away and are replaced by strangers, the whole affair will slowly be absorbed and forgotten. The only victims, in the end, will be M. Martin's wife, M. Martin himself, and the gentle woman M. Martin killed.

Source: "The House Behind" from THE COLLECTED STORIES OF LYDIA DAVIS by Lydia Davis. Copyright © 2009 by Lydia Davis. Reprinted by permission of Farrar, Straus and Giroux, LLC.

EXAMPLE 7B

YOUNG MAN RUNNING
Robert DeMaria

When he was out of sight he broke into a run—
Down the dirt road,
Out of the wooded hills,
Through harvest-ready fields,
Past tractors and barns, across the two-lane road
That dead-ended at the ferry,
And then over the flat sea-level reed-land
On a path of pounded oyster shells,
All the way to the run-down potato docks,
No longer used for shipping out the crops.
He was wind.
He was pure flight.
Osprey and falcon
Moved by palpable invisibility
Into the visible whiteblue curving world of
     land and sea.

Source: Reprinted by permission of the author.

EXAMPLE 7C

HOME-COMING
Claire White

After falling asleep   1
in ten different rooms
in mountains, in plains,
facing East, facing West,

I wake in the dark
and grope for a light.
I stumble and fall
in the most foreign place

of all. Where is this
tall room of serene   10
whiteness, these floors
painted red, this smell
of clean sheets and wood-smoke?

Beyond, in a hall
with mysterious closed doors
and burnished oak chests
stairs descend to a house

filled with objects that creak
and glow in the dark.
This must be the ultimate   20
inn, where I landed

my mission fulfilled,
where the perfect decor
awaits me, reinventing
the life I inhabited all along.

Source: Reprinted by permission of the author.

EXERCISES

Discussion

1. In "The House Behind" the neighborhood described is never named. Is it a real place or a symbolic place? How are the people described? Why is there a murder? How does this event change the neighborhood?
2. Comment on the following sentence: "Naturally, we can't really blame the people in the front house for their wealth, but we are oppressed by it. We feel the difference."
3. How does the description in "Young Man Running" make everything come alive? What are some of the key words?
4. What is the poem called "Home-Coming" all about? Is it a dream? Is the description effective?

Writing

1. Describe a dream using dreamy language. Describe a violent happening using violent words.
2. Describe the faces of three different characters.
3. Write a story in which the setting is described in detail.

Dialogue

What characters say to each other can reveal an enormous amount of information. *Dialogue* can tell us what characters are like, what they think, and what others think of them. It can reveal current action, as well as action that has taken place in the past or might take place in the future. It can also tell us about things that are going on offstage.

Dialogue is clearly the main ingredient in traditional stage plays. Almost all the information we get comes through dialogue. In film and television dramas dialogue is also very important, but technology has expanded the visual dimension. More action is possible, and location changes can be instantaneous.

Dialogue gives fiction the same kind of immediacy characters might have on a stage or screen. In poetry, dialogue is used less frequently, possibly because most poems are brief and are told to us as though the poet is the speaker (*persona*), and also because poetry tends to be less narrative than fiction.

Like description, dialogue must be *selective*, *significant*, and involve careful *word choice*. Conversations should not be mere recordings of real-life exchanges, because they would be much too long and include too many irrelevancies. Only the most significant things uttered by the characters should be included, and the phrasing should be worked out carefully.

To some extent, the amount and kind of dialogue depend on the author's style. Some writers lean heavily on direct dialogue; others prefer indirect dialogue and elaborate commentaries. Subjective writers depend more on the thoughts and feelings of their characters. Objective writers are more inclined to depend on what the characters actually say.

8A There is a standard form in which dialogue is written.

1 | All spoken material is placed between quotation marks.

> "Will you marry me?" said Donna, who was pacing angrily across the floor of the penthouse living room.
> "You know how I feel about marriage," Mark said.

2 | Each time the speaker changes, a new paragraph is required.

> "Aren't you interested in how I feel?" said Donna.
> "Of course, I am," said Mark.

3 | The first word inside the quotation marks begins with a capital letter.

If the statement is interrupted by a tag that identifies the speaker and then is continued as part of a sentence that was started before the tag, then no capital is used in the continuation:

> "I come from a very conventional family," she said. "They happen to believe in marriage."
> "When we first met," he said, "you told me you didn't get along with your family."

4 | A colon should be used before a piece of dialogue, but many writers settle for a comma.

> She stopped pacing and looked at him with narrowed eyes. Finally, she said: "Do you know what I think? I think you're too self-centered to get married?"

5 | At the end of a quoted piece of dialogue various punctuation marks can be used.

A comma is most common and is used whether the dialogue is part of a sentence that will be continued or is a whole sentence followed by a tag. A period is not used at the end of a quotation if a tag follows, but is used if there is no tag. Question marks and exclamation points are used when appropriate, but the tag that follows does not begin with a capital.

> "Good grief!" he said. "Look who's talking about self-centeredness. What do you think marriage is all about?"
> "What do *you* think it's all about?"
> "Possessiveness!" he said with a cruel smile. "When women get married, it's not an act of generosity on their part, believe me."

6 | If there is descriptive material that attends the dialogue, either before or after what is spoken, it appears in the same paragraph.

She backed away from him as though he were a dangerous stranger. "You know," she said, "in time I could learn to despise you." She picked up her coat and scarf, as though she were preparing to leave.

He made no effort to stop her. "The trouble with you," he said, "is that you want all the advantages of a modern relationship and all the security of an old-fashioned marriage." He went to the door and held it open for her. "You can't have it both ways. The choice is yours."

8B Tags tell the reader who is speaking.

Sometimes tags are included; sometimes they are omitted, as long as we already know who the speaker is.

1 | Tags can be very simple.

The simplest tags are *I said, he said, she said*. Some modern writers rarely use anything else and try to use as few tags as possible. The effect of this practice is to reduce these tags almost to the level of mere punctuation, so that the reader can focus completely on what the characters are saying. Hemingway was one of the earliest, and perhaps the best, of the writers who used this technique. Here is a sample from *A Farewell to Arms*. The characters are Catherine Barkley, an English nurse, and Lieutenant Frederick Henry, an American volunteer in the Italian army in World War I. They are in a hotel room in Milan:

> "It's a fine room," Catherine said. "It's a lovely room. We should have stayed here all the time we've been in Milan."
>
> "It's a funny room. But it's nice."
>
> "Vice is a wonderful thing," Catherine said. "The people who go in for it seem to have good taste about it. The red plush is really fine. It's just the thing. And the mirrors are very attractive."
>
> "You're a lovely girl."
>
> "I don't know how a room like this would be for waking up in the morning. But it's really a splendid room." I poured another glass of St. Estephe.
>
> "I wish we could do something really sinful," Catherine said. "Everything we do seems so innocent and simple. I can't believe we do anything wrong."
>
> "You're a grand girl."
>
> "I only feel hungry. I get terribly hungry."
>
> "You're a fine simple girl," I said.
>
> "I am a simple girl. No one ever understood it except you."

2 | Tags can be varied and elaborate.

Earlier literature was more formal, and dialogue tags tended to be more complicated. In some modern writers they still are more complicated than *he said/she said*. These writers tend to vary the verb, as in *he shouted, she whispered, he whined, she cried*. Such variety is more a matter of style than necessity. One should not use old-fashioned expressions, clichés, or clumsy tags just for the sake of variety. A simple tag is better than *he expostulated* or *she blurted out*. A question in dialogue can be followed by *he said*, though often *he asked* is used.

Tags can be elaborated by adding adverbs to them, so that the way the words are spoken is described, as in: "I love you," *he said passionately*. You have to be very careful when you do this, since such elaborations can often sound ridiculous:

> "Don't touch me," she blurted out uncontrollably.
> "I need you," he growled savagely.

The best policy is to allow the dialogue to speak for itself and to avoid attracting too much attention to the tags.

8C Indirect dialogue is a description or summary of what was said.

Sometimes we learn what a character says indirectly, without the benefit of direct quotations. The narrator can describe or summarize what a character said. No quotation marks are used for indirect discourse, since the exact wording of the character's remarks is not used:

Indirect: John told Mary that he was going to Europe.
Direct: "I am going to Europe," John said to Mary.

A summarized conversation can give the reader a concise, general idea of what the characters have talked about. The whole conversation might not be worth recording word for word, especially if it is long and without enormous significance:

> *Indirect*: John and Mary spent the whole afternoon talking about the museums and art galleries they had visited in Europe.

Be careful to avoid shifts from indirect to direct discourse:

> *Shift*: What Mary wanted to know from John was "When are you going to Europe?"
> *Use*: What Mary wanted to know from John was when he was going to Europe. (indirect)
> *Or*: "When are you going to Europe?" Mary asked John. (direct)

8D   **Direct dialogue requires the use of quotation marks.**

When we use the word *dialogue*, we usually mean direct discourse, which has to be in quotation marks and tagged according to the conventions described in 8a and 8b.

1 | Some writers depend heavily on dialogue.

Writers who use a cinematic approach to fiction tend to reduce the action to stage directions and to let the characters speak for themselves. The approach is objective. There is little editorializing and little attempt to get directly into the minds of the characters. What you see (and hear) is what you get.

2 | Dialogue is usually blended with action, commentary, and indirect discourse.

Most writers do not limit themselves to just one device. Their main objective is to re-create experience in whatever way they can. Fiction limited to dialogue and stage directions is sometimes a genuine experiment in pure objectivity, but it can also be just an exercise or even an affectation, perhaps inspired by a current fad.

There is enormous variety in fiction. Some approaches use no dialogue at all, some are pure stream of consciousness, some are all commentary and analysis, but most are a blend of some sort, which does not mean that they are without consistency or distinctiveness of style.

3 | Dialogue can be used in poetry.

Since poetry can have a narrative element, it can use the usual techniques of narration, including dialogue. However, since the work is basically cast in the form of a poem, the narration is contained within that form. This means that it has certain limitations placed on it. If the narration breaks out of the poetic structure, it is liable to become a short story or simply to confuse the basic artistic concept. On the other hand, fragments of narration can be contained within a poetic whole and in themselves need not be completed in the usual way that stories are. Here is a poem by Stephen Crane that contains dialogue:

IN A LONELY PLACE

In a lonely place,
I encountered a sage
Who sat, all still,
Regarding a newspaper.

He accosted me:
"Sir, what is this?"
Then I saw that I was greater,
Aye, greater than this sage.
I answered him at once:
"Old, old man, it is the wisdom of the age."
The sage looked upon me with admiration.

8E Accents involve distinctive modes of pronunciation.

Language is in a constant state of evolution. Regional conditions, such as isolation or the influx of immigrants, can give rise to differences in pronunciation and to some strictly regional vocabulary. These differences produce an *accent*. There are many such accents in American English, among them the New York accent, the Southern and Western accents, and a variety of foreign accents.

When a variation of a language undergoes more extensive changes in its grammar as well as in its vocabulary, we have what is known as a *dialect*. Many European countries, such as Italy, Great Britain, and Spain, have distinct dialects. In less industrialized parts of the world there are enormous numbers of dialects because conditions in these places have not been conducive to standardizing the language.

When a dialect becomes truly distinct from its mother language or blends with other languages to form a mode of speech that outsiders do not understand, we have a whole new language, such as Gullah in the Carolinas or Creole in Haiti.

In the United States we have few genuine dialects. We are usually confronted, as writers, with a variety of regional or foreign accents. If we are to make our dialogue realistic, we have to learn how to capture these peculiarities of speech.

We also have to learn how to present foreign characters who are, supposedly, speaking their own language.

1 | A character can seem to be speaking a foreign language even though the story is written in English.

When characters who speak a foreign language appear in a story written in English, their dialogue can be written in their own language (with or without a translation) or in correct English, but with occasional hints of foreign syntax or idioms or even an occasional foreign word. Hemingway does this extremely well. In *A Farewell to Arms*, this is how Lieutenant Henry's Italian friend speaks:

> "One of those shot by the carabinieri is from my town," Passini said. "He was a big smart tall boy to be in the granatieri. Always in Rome. Always with the girls. Always with the carabinieri." He laughed. "Now they have a guard outside his house with a bayonet and nobody can come to see his mother and father and sisters and his father loses his civil rights and cannot even vote. They are all without law to protect them. Anybody can take their property."

In the movies it used to be a Hollywood convention to present foreign characters who are speaking their own language as characters speaking English with a foreign accent. This sometimes ludicrous device is not recommended for fiction or poetry, and is not used much anymore even in movies or television.

2 | A foreign character or a regional character often speaks English with an accent.

An author can try to capture an accent phonetically by trying to write it down exactly as the character pronounces it.

Mark Twain does this extensively, especially in *Huckleberry Finn*. In the following passage, Jim is telling Huck's fortune:

> Yo' ole father doan' know yit what he's a-gwyne to do. Sometimes he spec he'll go 'way, en den ag'in he spec he'll stay. De bes' way is to res' easy en let de ole man take his own way. Dey's two angels hoverin' roun' 'bout him. One uv 'em is white en shiny, en t'other one is black. De white one gits him to go right a little while, den de black one sails in en bust it all up. A body can't tell yit which one gwyne to fetch him at de las'. But you is all right. You gwyne to have considable trouble in yo' life, en considable joy. Sometimes you gwyne to git hurt, en sometimes you gwyne to git sick; but every time you's gwyne to git well ag'in. Dey's two gals flyin' 'bout you in yo' life. One uv 'em's light en t'other one is dark. One is rich en t'other is po'. You gwyne to marry de po' one fust en de rich one by en by. You wants to keep 'way fum de water as much as you kin, en don't run no resk, 'kase it's down in de bills dat you's gwyne to git hung.

It is also possible to capture an accent without altering the spelling but merely by providing token hints through intonation or vocabulary. Saul Bellow and Woody Allen manage this very well when their characters have a New York accent. A striking contrast to the way Mark Twain handles Jim's dialogue can be found in the way Alice Walker handles the speech of her African-American characters, who are, of course, more modern. Also, Mark Twain was using some stereotypes and comic exaggeration.

EXAMPLE 8A

SHOULD WIZARD HIT MOMMY?
John Updike

In the evenings and for Saturday naps like today's, Jack told   **1**
his daughter Jo a story out of his head. This custom, begun
when she was two, was itself now nearly two years old, and
his head felt empty. Each new story was a slight variation of
a basic tale: a small creature, usually named Roger (Roger
Fish, Roger Squirrel, Roger Chipmunk), had some problem
and went with it to the wise old owl. The owl told him to
go to the wizard, and the wizard performed a magic spell
that solved the problem, demanding in payment a number
of pennies greater than the number Roger Creature had but   **10**
in the same breath directing the animal to a place where the
extra pennies could be found. Then Roger was so happy he
played many games with other creatures, and went home
to his mother just in time to hear the train whistle that
brought his daddy home from Boston. Jack described their
supper, and the story was over. Working his way through
this scheme was especially fatiguing on Saturday, because Jo
never fell asleep in naps any more, and knowing this made
the rite seem futile.

The little girl (not so little any more; the bumps her feet   **20**
made under the covers were halfway down the bed, their big
double bed that they let her be in for naps and when she was
sick) had at last arranged herself, and from the way her fat
face deep in the pillow shone in the sunlight sifting through
the drawn shades, it did not seem fantastic that something
magic would occur, and she would take her nap like an
infant of two. Her brother, Bobby, was two, and already
asleep with his bottle. Jack asked, "Who shall the story be
about today?"

"Roger . . ." Jo squeezed her eyes shut and smiled to be   30
thinking she was thinking. Her eyes opened, her mother's
blue. "Skunk," she said firmly.

A new animal; they must talk about skunks at nursery
school. Having a fresh hero momentarily stirred Jack to creative enthusiasm. "All right," he said. "Once upon a time, in
the deep dark woods, there was a tiny little creature name of
Roger Skunk. And he smelled very bad———"

"Yes," Jo said.

"He smelled so bad none of the other little woodland
creatures would play with him." Jo looked at him solemnly;   40
she hadn't foreseen this. "Whenever he would go out to
play," Jack continued with zest, remembering certain hu-
miliations of his own childhood, "all of the other tiny animals would cry, 'Uh-oh, here comes Roger Stinky Skunk,'
and they would run away, and Roger Skunk would stand
there all alone, and two little round tears would fall from
his eyes." The corners of Jo's mouth drooped down and her
lower lip bent forward as he traced with a forefinger along
the side of her nose the course of one of Roger Skunk's tears.

"Won't he see the owl?" she asked in a high and faintly   50
roughened voice.

Sitting on the bed beside her, Jack felt the covers tug
as her legs switched tensely. He was pleased with this moment—he was telling her something true, something she
must know—and had no wish to hurry on. But downstairs
a chair scraped, and he realized he must get down to help
Clare paint the living-room woodwork.

"Well, he walked along very sadly and came to a very
big tree, and in the tiptop of the tree was an enormous
wise old owl."

"Good."   60

" 'Mr. Owl,' Roger Skunk said, 'all the other little animals run away from me because I smell so bad.' 'So you do,'

the owl said. 'Very, very bad.' 'What can I do?' Roger Skunk said, and he cried very hard."

"The wizard, the wizard," Jo shouted, and sat right up, and a Little Golden Book spilled from the bed.

"Now, Jo. Daddy's telling the story. Do you want to tell Daddy the story?"

"No. You me."   70

"Then lie down and be sleepy."

Her head relapsed onto the pillow and she said, "Out of your head."

"Well. The owl thought and thought. At last he said, 'Why don't you go see the wizard?' "

"Daddy?"

"What?"

"Are magic spells *real*?" This was a new phase, just this last month, a reality phase. When he told her spiders eat bugs, she turned to her mother and asked, "Do they *really*?"   80 and when Clare told her God was in the sky and all around them, she turned to her father and insisted, with a sly yet eager smile, "Is He *really*?"

"They're real in stories," Jack answered curtly. She had made him miss a beat in the narrative. "The owl said, 'Go through the dark woods, under the apple trees, into the swamp, over the crick——' "

"What's a crick?"

"A little river. 'Over the crick, and there will be the wizard's house.' And that's the way Roger Skunk went, and   90 pretty soon he came to a little white house, and he rapped on the door." Jack rapped on the window sill, and under the covers Jo's tall figure clenched in an infantile thrill. "And then a tiny little old man came out, with a long white beard and a pointed blue hat, and said, 'Eh? Whatzis? Whatcher want? You smell awful.' " The wizard's voice was one of Jack's own favorite effects; he did it by scrunching up his face and somehow whining through his eyes, which felt for the interval rheumy. He felt being an old man suited him.

" 'I know it,' Roger Skunk said, 'and all the little animals 100 run away from me. The enormous wise owl said you could help me.' "

" 'Eh? Well, maybe. Come on in. Don't git too close.' Now inside, Jo, there were all these magic things, all jumbled together in a big dusty heap, because the wizard did not have any cleaning lady.' "

"Why?"

"Why? Because he was a wizard, and a very old man."

"Will he die?"

"No. Wizards don't die. Well, he rummaged around and 110 found an old stick called a magic wand and asked Roger Skunk what he wanted to smell like. Roger thought and thought and said, 'Roses.' "

"Yes. Good," Jo said smugly.

Jack fixed her with a trancelike gaze and chanted in the wizard's elderly irritable voice:

" 'Abracadabry, hocus-poo,
Roger Skunk, how do you do,
Roses, boses, pull an ear,
Roger Skunk, you never fear: 120
Bingo! ' "

He paused as a rapt expression widened out from his daughter's nostrils, forcing her eyebrows up and her lower lip down in a wide noiseless grin, an expression in which Jack was startled to recognize his wife feigning pleasure at cocktail parties. "And all of a sudden," he whispered, "the whole inside of the wizard's house was full of the smell of— *roses*! 'Roses!' Roger Fish cried. And the wizard said, very cranky, 'That'll be seven pennies.' "

"Daddy."

"What?"   130

"Roger *Skunk*. You said Roger Fish."

"Yes. Skunk."

"You said Roger *Fish*. Wasn't that silly?"

"Very silly of your stupid old daddy. Where was I? Well, you know about the pennies."

"Say it."

"O.K. Roger Skunk said, 'But all I have is four pennies,' and he began to cry." Jo made the crying face again, but this time without a trace of sincerity. This annoyed Jack. Downstairs some more furniture rumbled. Clare shouldn't move heavy things; she was six months pregnant. It would be their third.

"So the wizard said, 'Oh, very well. Go to the end of the lane and turn around three times and look down the magic well and there you will find three pennies. Hurry up.' So Roger Skunk went to the end of the lane and turned around three times and there in the magic well were *three pennies*! So he took them back to the wizard and was very happy and ran out into the woods and all the other little animals gathered around him because he smelled so good. And they played tag, baseball, football, basketball, lacrosse, hockey, soccer, and pick-up-sticks."

"What's pick-up-sticks?"

"It's a game you play with sticks."

"Like the wizard's magic wand?"

"Kind of. And they played games and laughed all afternoon and then it began to get dark and they all ran home to their mommies."

Jo was starting to fuss with her hands and look out of the window, at the crack of day that showed under the shade. She thought the story was all over. Jack didn't like women when they took anything for granted; he liked them apprehensive, hanging on his words. "Now, Jo, are you listening?"

"Yes."

"Because this is very interesting. Roger Skunk's mommy said, 'What's that awful smell?' "

"Wha-at?"

"And Roger Skunk said, 'It's me, Mommy. I smell like roses.' And she said, 'Who made you smell like that?' And he said, 'The wizard,' and she said, 'Well, of all the nerve. You come with me and we're going right back to that very awful wizard.' "   **170**

Jo sat up, her hands dabbling in the air with genuine fright. "But Daddy, then he said about the other little aminals run *away*!" Her hands skittered off, into the underbrush.

"All right. He said, 'But Mommy, all the other little animals run away,' and she said, 'I don't care. You smelled the way a little skunk should have and I'm going to take you right back to that wizard,' and she took an umbrella and   **180**
went back with Roger Skunk and hit that wizard right over the head."

"No," Jo said, and put her hand out to touch his lips, yet even in her agitation did not quite dare to stop the source of truth. Inspiration came to her. "Then the wizard hit *her* on the head and did not change that little skunk back."

"No," he said. "The wizard said 'O.K.' and Roger Skunk did not smell of roses any more. He smelled very bad again."

"But the other little amum—*oh*!—amum——"

"Joanne. It's Daddy's story. Shall Daddy not tell you   **190**
any more stories?" Her broad face looked at him through sifted light, astounded. "This is what happened, then. Roger Skunk and his mommy went home and they heard *Woo-oo, woooo-oo* and it was the choo-choo train bringing Daddy Skunk home from Boston. And they had lima beans, pork chops, celery, liver, mashed potatoes, and Pie-Oh-My for dessert. And when Roger Skunk was in bed Mommy Skunk came up and hugged him and said he smelled like her little

baby skunk again and she loved him very much. And that's
the end of the story."   200

"But Daddy."

"What?"

"Then did the other little animals run away?"

"No, because eventually they got used to the way he was
and did not mind it at all."

"What's evenshiladee?"

"In a little while."

"That was a stupid mommy."

"It was *not*," he said with rare emphasis, and believed,
from her expression, that she realized he was defending his   210
own mother to her, or something as odd. "Now I want you
to put your big heavy head in the pillow and have a good
long nap." He adjusted the shade so not even a crack of day
showed, and tiptoed to the door, in the pretense that she was
already asleep. But when he turned, she was crouching on
top of the covers and staring at him. "Hey. Get under the
covers and fall fast asleep. Bobby's asleep."

She stood up and bounced gingerly on the springs.
"Daddy."

"What?"   220

"Tomorrow, I want you to tell me the story that that
wizard took that magic wand and hit that mommy"—her
plump arms chopped fiercely—"right over the head."

"No. That's not the story. The point is that the little skunk
loved his mommy more than he loved aaalll the other little
animals and she knew what was right."

"No. Tomorrow you say he hit that mommy. Do it." She
kicked her legs up and sat down on the bed with a great
heave and complaint of springs, as she had done hundreds
of times before, except that this time she did not laugh. "Say   230
it, Daddy."

"Well, we'll see. Now at least have a rest. Stay on the bed. You're a good girl."

He closed the door and went downstairs. Clare had spread the newspapers and opened the paint can and, wearing an old shirt of his on top of her maternity smock, was stroking the chair rail with a dipped brush. Above him footsteps vibrated and he called "*Joanne*. Shall I come up there and spank you?" The footsteps hesitated.

"That was a long story," Clare said.

240

"The poor kid," he answered, and with utter weariness watched his wife labor. The woodwork, a cage of moldings and rails and baseboards all around them, was half old tan and half new ivory and he felt caught in an ugly middle position, and though he as well felt his wife's presence in the cage with him, he did not want to speak with her, work with her, touch her, anything.

EXAMPLE 8B

COOLIE MOTHER
David Dabydeen

Jasmattie live in bruk—   1
Down hut big like Bata shoe-box,
Beat clothes, weed yard, chop wood, feed fowl
For this body and that body and every blasted body,
Fetch water, all day fetch water like if the whole—
Whole slow-flowing Canje river God create
Just for *she* one own bucket.

Till she foot-bottom crack and she hand cut-up
And curse swarm from she mouth like red-ants
And she cough blood on the ground but mash it in: 10
Because Jasmattie heart hard, she mind set hard

To hustle save she one-one slow penny,
Because one-one dutty* make dam cross the Canje
And she son Harilall *got* to go school in Georgetown,
Must wear clean starch pants, or they go laugh at he,
Strap leather on he foot, and he *must* read book,
Learn talk proper, take exam, go to England university,
Not turn out like he rum-sucker chamar* dadee.

Source: From Graham House Review, No. 14, Spring 1991, Hansib Publications.
Reprinted by permission of David Dabydeen.

* *dutty:* piece of earth
* *chamar:* low-caste

EXAMPLE 8C

RAGGED SONNETS
Leonard Nathan

I.

1   "So shall I live," the poet said, "supposing
   thou art true," but he wasn't referring to you,
   who are faithful, but to another woman,
   the one whose beauty he compared to Eve's apple
   and who, I add here, must have seemed
   a cruel emblem of reality,
   the way it comes in layers—a frank face
   and what's behind that face, another creature
   thinking its own thoughts, dreaming dreams
10 that wake us with a sob. Even you
   have sat bolt upright crying your surprise.
   There's nothing for it. Apples will be eaten.
   "So shall I live, supposing thou art true."
   I do not here, of course, refer to you.

Source: From Salmagundi 90–91, Spring 1991. Reprinted by permission of the author.

EXERCISES

Discussion

1. At first John Updike's story is about a father who makes up bedtime tales to entertain his young daughter, but eventually the daughter gets upset. Why? What does the title mean? Are there some serious emotions revealed?

2. Describe the use of dialogue in Updike's story. How does the father adjust his speech for his daughter to

understand him. Does his daughter really believe what her father says is true? What is her attitude toward the wizard?

3. Is this meant to be an amusing tale or a serious story?

4. There are many dialects based on the English language. How would you describe the dialect in "Coolie Mother"? What is the poem all about?

5. Is "Ragged Sonnets" really a sonnet? What do the references to "Eve's apple" mean? And what does the final line "I do not here, of course, refer to you" mean?

Writing

1. Write a little story about several young children talking about something they saw on television.

2. Write a love story about an American girl who falls in love with a handsome singer in Italy or Spain. Use realistic dialogue.

Thoughts

Revealing the thoughts of the characters in a literary work is one of the fundamental concerns of the serious writer. Even the routine thoughts of two-dimensional characters have to be expressed in some fashion or other. There are several ways to accomplish this. In *poetry* it is often the authors who tell us directly what they think about this or that, and the material is often personal and autobiographical. In *drama* the characters reveal their thoughts by talking to each other or by thinking out loud, as in a soliloquy or a cinematic *voice-over*. Even facial expressions, especially in *close-ups*, can hint at what is going on in a character's mind.

In fiction the problem is often more complex. Characters can reveal themselves in dialogue or in a first-person narration. It is also possible for narrators using the third-person point of view to tell us what is going on in a character's mind. They can do this by presenting the character's thoughts *directly* or *indirectly* in some organized way, or they can try to capture more fully the complex processes of the human mind, before language gives more grammatical coherence to thought. Hence, we have three approaches: (1) *indirect*, (2) *direct*, (3) *stream of consciousness*.

9A   Indirect thought means a description or summary of what a character thinks.

Though indirect descriptions of the thoughts of a character occur most commonly in the third person, they can also appear in the first-person point of view. For instance:

Third person: He was thinking about what he would do in case the airplane was hijacked by terrorists.
First person: I was thinking about what I would do in case the airplane was hijacked by terrorists.

There is a good illustration of indirect thought in "Barcelona" (Example 2a). The author describes what Persis is thinking in the final paragraph:

Persis is thinking, and not for the first time, how terrible it must be to be a man, how terrifying. Men are always running, chasing something. And if you are rich and successful, like Thad, you have to hunt down anyone who wants to take away your possessions. Or if you're poor, down on your luck, you might be tempted to chase after a shabby bag that holds nothing of any real value, to snatch such a bag from a foreign woman who is wearing false gold chains that shine and glimmer in the dark.

9B   Direct thought is a literal record of what occurs in the character's mind.

1 | Direct thoughts often sound like dialogue.

The difference is that they are not spoken aloud. It is as if the character is speaking to himself or herself. Most writers do not place such thoughts in quotation marks.

direct dialogue: "What should I do in case the airplane is hijacked by terrorists?" I said.

direct thought: What should I do in case the airplane is hijacked by terrorists? I wondered.

2 | Some writers put the direct thoughts of their characters in italics.

Usage here is divided. Some users of italics reserve them for stream-of-consciousness passages; some use them for any directly expressed thoughts. The following passage from William Styron's *Set This House on Fire* is described as a thought, but it is also described as a kind of haunting memory. There are obviously thin lines between conscious thoughts, unconscious thoughts, memories, reveries, and daydreams.

A brisk wind blew toward the sea, cooling Cass' brow. For a moment he closed his eyes, the flowers' crushed scent and summer light and ruined hut commingling in one long fluid hot surge of remembrance and desire. *Siete stato molto gentile con me*, he thought. *What a thing for her to say. You have been very kind to me. As if when I kissed her, and the kiss was over, and we were standing there in the field all body and groin and belly made one and wet mouths parted this was the only thing left to say. Which meant of course I'm a virgin and maybe we shouldn't but you have been very nice to me. So—So maybe I should have took her then, with gentleness and anguish and love, right there in that field last evening when I felt her full young breasts heavy in my hands and the wild way she pressed against me and her breath hot against my cheek. . . . Siete stato molto gentile con me . . . Cass . . . Cahssio. . . .*

9C Stream of consciousness is a literary technique used to capture the random, uncensored workings of the human mind.

The intense interest in psychology in the early decades of the twentieth century stirred the curiosity and imagination of the literary world. After all, Freud and Jung and others were talking about how the human mind worked, a subject with which writers have always been preoccupied. Discussions of the subconscious levels of thought led writers to explorations of techniques that might give expression to these thoughts, which were, apparently, more primitive than language itself.

1 | Some writers try to capture inner thoughts through conventional language.

Though our deepest thoughts may not occur as well-made sentences, some writers try to give the reader a sense of what is going on by using traditional syntax and certain devices that suggest the subconscious mind at work. In Virginia Woolf's *Mrs. Dalloway*, Clarissa enters a flower shop. Her reaction is described in the third person, but the reader feels drawn directly into the character's mind:

> There were flowers: delphiniums, sweet peas, bunches of lilac; and carnations, masses of carnations. There were roses; there were irises. Ah yes—so she breathed in the earthy garden sweet smell as she stood talking to Miss Pym who owed her help, and thought her kind, for kind she had been years ago; very kind, but she looked older, this year, turning her head from side to side among the irises and roses and nodding tufts of lilac with her eyes half closed, snuffing in, after the street uproar, the delicious scent, the exquisite coolness. And then, opening her eyes, how fresh like frilled linen clean from a laundry laid in wicker trays the roses looked; and dark and prim the red carnations, holding their heads up; and all the sweet peas spreading in their bowls, tinged violet, snow white, pale—as if it were the evening and girls in muslin frocks came out to pick sweet peas and roses after the superb summer's day, with its almost blue-black sky, its delphiniums, its carnations, its arum lilies was over; and it was the moment between six

and seven when every flower—roses, carnations, irises, lilac—glows; white, violet, red, deep orange; every flower seems to burn by itself, softly, purely in the misty beds; and how she loved the grey-white moths spinning in and out, over the cherry pie, over the evening primroses!

And as she began to go with Miss Pym from jar to jar, choosing, nonsense, nonsense, she said to herself, more and more gently, as if this beauty, this scent, this colour, and Miss Pym liking her, trusting her, were a wave which she let flow over her and surmount that hatred, that monster, surmount it all; and it lifted her up and up when—oh! a pistol shot in the street outside!

"Dear, those motor cars," said Miss Pym, going to the window to look, and coming back and smiling apologetically with her hands full of sweet peas, as if those motor cars, those tyres of motor cars, were all *her* fault.

2 | Some writers violate the conventions of language to try to get at the inner thoughts of a character.

James Joyce's *Ulysses* was a bold exploration of the inner workings of the human mind. In Molly Bloom's famous internal monologue, which is forty-five pages long and un-punctuated, we are allowed to eavesdrop on her private me-anderings, which are full of free associations and uncensored memories:

I wonder what shes got like now after living with that dotty husband of hers she had her face beginning to look drawn and run down the last time I saw her she must have been just after a row with him because I saw on the moment she was edging to draw down a conversation about husbands and talk about him to run him down what was it she told me O yes that sometimes he used to go to bed with his muddy boots on when the maggot takes him just imagine having to get into bed with a thing like that that might murder you

any moment what a man well its not the one way everyone
goes mad Poldy anyway whatever he does always wipes his
feet on the mat when he comes in wet or shine and always
blacks his own boots too and he always takes off his hat when
he comes up in the street like that and now hes going about
in his slippers to look for £10000 for a postcard up up O
Sweetheart May wouldnt a thing like that simply bore you
stiff to extinction actually too stupid even to take his boots
off now what could you make of a man like that Id rather die
20 times over than marry another of their sex of course hed
never find another woman like me to put up with him the
way I do know me come sleep with me yes and he knows
that too at the bottom of his heart take that Mrs Maybrick
that poisoned her husband for what I wonder in love with
some other man yet it was found out on her wasnt she the
downright villain to go and do a thing like that of course
some men can be dreadfully aggravating drive you mad and
always the worst word in the world what do they ask us to
marry them for if were so bad as all that comes to yes because
they cant get on without us white Arsenic she put in his
tea off flypaper wasnt it I wonder why they call it that if I
asked him hed say its from the Greek leave us as wise as we
were before she must have been madly in love with the other
fellow to run the chance of being hanged O she didnt care
if that was her nature what could she do besides theyre not
brutes enough to go and hang a woman surely are they

Devices such as these can give us some idea of what is
going on in a character's mind, but it is probably impossible to capture in writing the entire phenomenon of human
thought.

EXAMPLE 9A

LETTER, LOVER
Joyce Carol Oates

I had been living in the city, in my new life, only a week before the first of the letters arrived.

Miss I see you! This is to say—and here several words had been crossed vigorously out—*you cant hide.*

The message was written in green ink, in neatly printed block letters, on a sheet of lined tablet paper. There was no stamp on the envelope: just my name and street address. Whoever had sent it had shoved it through the slot of my mailbox amid a long row of mailboxes in the foyer of my apartment house.

I had opened the envelope going upstairs, ripping it with my thumbnail, eager to see who'd written to me, but when I read these words my heart kicked in my chest and for a moment I thought I might faint.

I looked behind me, I was so frightened.

I thought, *Oh it's a joke.*

The second letter came a week later, I recognized the envelope at once, in my mailbox with legitimate mail: my name and street address, no stamp. He lived in the apartment building maybe. Or might be one of my coworkers who'd followed me home.

Girl with blond hair—slut cant hide. I SEE YOU. The sheet of paper was wrinkled, soiled. Included with it was a small swatch of cloth shot with iridescent gold threads, cheap fabric, soiled too, seemingly bloodstained.

I began to wear my hair pinned up, and a scarf over it. I removed the fingernail polish from my fingernails and never wore any again.

Other letters came for me, with stamps. I skimmed their contents quickly and set them aside. It was the plain square white envelope I looked for, in my mailbox. *High heel shoes—only sluts—*and here words were crossed out—*Dont hide from me because I see through the window & the wall BLONDIE.* Included with the third letter was a snapshot of a young woman walking with her head lowered, a young woman wearing my blue raincoat, my white scarf on her head, walking on a street close by. I recognized the graffiti-scarred brick wall. I recognized the coat and the high-heeled shoes. You couldn't see who the young woman was, her face had been destroyed by an angry barrage of pinpricks. There were pinpricks too in her breasts and crotch.

I stopped wearing high-heeled shoes, I avoided that street, that particular block. There was no point in provoking him.

We know it's unwise and to no purpose, to provoke such people.

I was having difficulty sleeping. I trusted no one.

I kept the blinds to all my windows drawn during the day, and always at night. Even in the early morning when my kitchen window was flooded with sunshine I kept that blind drawn, I knew he might be watching. No point in taking chances. That's what they would say, afterward.

I wondered if the letters were being sent to me by God's will, or just by accident.

I went to the building superintendent and told him about the letters but I hadn't any to show him, one by one I'd torn them up, thrown them away, there was no evidence. Once, after the fourth or the fifth letter came, I picked up the telephone receiver to call the police, but my hand shook so badly I couldn't dial. I went to the police precinct station but when a policeman asked, staring at me, could he help me, what did I want, I backed away, I said, No, nothing, no thank you, and fled. *You are such a liar & tramp, I can read your thoughts. Im your friend.*

How are you? How are *you*? How is everybody? That's good to hear. Are you well? You sound as if you have a cold! What's it doing there?—it's raining here. It's snowing here. Oh yes I'm feeling much better. The sun is shining here. Yes my job is going well. Yes I couldn't be happier. Yes I'm making friends. Yes but you didn't call for two weeks. Is it cold there? Is it snowing there? Is the sun shining there? When are you coming home? Yes I have many friends. Yes the sun is shining. And how are *you*?

I worked on the forty-fourth floor of a building that rose sixty floors into the sky. The upper windows were sometimes opaque with fog, sometimes the sun shone fiercely through them: this was "weather." Below, on the street, there was a different "weather."

All the inhabitants of the town I'd come from, every person I had ever known, could have been fitted into that building, all lost from one another in that space. *I watch you & see your pride but that wont help. You know what will help you—NOTHING.*

Once, reading one of the messages, I came to myself standing in a corridor on the third floor of my apartment house instead of the second floor, where I lived. My eyes were flooded with tears of shame and confusion. In the distance, a baby was crying. At first I thought it was myself.

As the letters came, one by one in their plain square white envelopes, I tore them up, letters and envelopes both, and threw them away. A sickness like nausea rose in me and I worried I might show the shame of it in my face.

Then, one day, searching for a pair of stockings, I discovered the letters in one of my bureau drawers, five or six of them, or seven, intact!—in their original envelopes, neatly folded and preserved. So I saw that it was meant for me to keep them after all, despite my disgust.

I thought, This is evidence. Should I ever be required to provide evidence.

I thought, Of course I must move away.
How obvious: I must return home.

It was Christmas. The first letter had come in the early autumn, and now strips of cheap glittering tinsel and colored Christmas ornaments were strung about the foyer of the apartment house when, unlocking my mailbox, I saw another of the plain square white envelopes inside. This time I could not bear to touch it. I stood for some minutes, unmoving. My eyes spilled tears. A fellow tenant, unlocking his mailbox close by, noticed me, and asked politely, "Is something wrong, miss?"

I did not know this man's name but I knew his face for I'd been aware of him as a fellow tenant, as one is aware of an object hovering in the periphery of one's vision that might, or might not, advance; an object that might, or might not, possess its own identity and volition. I saw my trembling fingers snatch up the envelope and hand it to the man, I heard my voice thin as frayed cloth—"I can't open it!"

Hesitating only a fraction of an instant, the man took the envelope from me.

This man whose name I did not know was a few years older than I, yet still young, with a frowning face, a somber manner. I knew, or believed I knew, that he lived on the floor above me, and that he lived alone.

He turned the envelope in his fingers, examining it.

Then he opened it, and unfolded the sheet of tablet paper, and read the message, standing very still as he read, and silent. Out of the envelope there fell something, not a snapshot but a clipping, from a glossy magazine perhaps, I was never to see this clipping but supposed it might have been a photograph of a woman modeling lingerie, the young man picked it up and crumpled it in his fingers to save me the embarrassment of seeing. I was saying, "I don't know who it is who sends me these things, he doesn't let me rest, he won't ever let me go, he wants to drive me away and I've been so happy here," words that tumbled out without my understanding where they might lead, words that surprised me with their vehemence and boldness, "I went to the building superintendent, I went to the police, nobody can stop him, nobody can "help"? me. . . ."

The young man reread the letter, his cheeks visibly reddening. I could hear his outraged breath.

Then he lifted his eyes to my face, it was the first time we exchanged that look which we would, over the course of weeks, then months, exchange many times, and he frowned, and said, "—I'll keep this: you don't want to see this," and I whispered, "Thank you," and he said, "—No, you don't want to see this, it isn't very nice," and he folded up both the letter and the envelope, thoughtfully, and put them away in an inside pocket of his coat.

EXAMPLE 9B

RUBY TELLS ALL
Miller Williams

When I was told, as Delta children were,
that crops don't grow unless you sweat at night,
I thought that it was my own sweat they meant.
I have never felt as important again
as on those early mornings, waking up,   5
my body slick, the moon full on the fields.
That was before air conditioning.
Farm girls sleep cool now and wake up dry,
but still the cotton overflows the fields.
We lose everything that's grand and foolish;   10
it all becomes something else. One by one,
butterflies turn into caterpillars
and we grow up, or more or less we do,
and, Lord, we do lie then. We lie so much
the truth has a false ring and it's hard to tell.   15

I wouldn't take crap off anybody
if I just knew that I was getting crap
in time not to take it. I could have won
a small one now and then if I was smarter,
but I've poured coffee here too many years   20
for men who rolled in in Peterbilts,
and I have gotten into bed with some
if they could talk and seemed to be in pain.
I never asked for anything myself;
giving is more blessed and leaves you free.   25
There was a man, married and fond of whiskey.
Given the limitations of men, he loved me.

Lord, we laid concern upon our bodies
but then he left. Everything has its time.
We used to dance. He made me feel the way   30
a human wants to feel and fears to.
He was a slow man and didn't expect.
I would get off work and find him waiting.
We'd have a drink or two and kiss awhile.
Then a bird-loud morning late one April   35
we woke up naked. We had made a child.
She's grown up now and gone though god
        knows where.
She ought to write, for I do love her dearly
who raised her carefully and dressed her well.   40
Everything has its time. For thirty years
I never had a thought about time.
Now, turning through newspapers, I pause
to see if anyone who passed away
was younger than I am. If one was   45
I feel hollow for a little while
but then it passes. Nothing matters enough
to stay bent down about. You have to see
that some things matter slightly and some don't.
Dying matters a little. So does pain.   50
So does being old. Men do not.
Men live by negatives, like don't give up,
don't be a coward, don't call me a liar,
don't ever tell me don't. If I could live
two hundred years and had to be a man   55
I'd take my grave. What's a man but a match,
a little stick to start a fire with?
My daughter knows this, if she's alive.
What could I tell her now, to bring her close,

something she doesn't know, if we met somewhere?   **60**
Maybe that I think about her father,
maybe that my fingers hurt at night,
maybe that against appearances
there is love, constancy, and kindness,
that I have dresses I have never worn.   **65**

Source: "Ruby Tells All," reprinted by permission of Louisiana State University Press from Imperfect Love by Miller Williams. Copyright © 1985 by Miller Williams.

EXAMPLE 9C

COAL TRAIN
Jay Parini

Three times a night it woke you
in middle summer, the Erie Lackawanna,
running to the north on thin, loud rails.
You could feel it coming a long way off:
at first, a tremble in your belly,
a wire trilling in your veins, then diesel
rising to a froth beneath your skin.
You could see the cowcatcher,
wide as a mouth and eating ties,
the headlight blowing a dust of flies.
There was no way to stop it.
You lay there, fastened to the tracks
and waiting, breathing like a bull,
your fingers lit at the tips like matches.
You waited for the thunder of wheel and bone,
the axles sparking, fire in your spine.
Each passing was a kind of death,
the whistle dwindling to a ghost in air,
the engine losing itself in trees.
In a while, your heart was the loudest thing,
your bed was a pool of night.

EXERCISES

Discussion

1. In "Letter, Lover" what is going through the narrator's mind? She gets a letter from a man who lives in the same building as she does. Or is this just her imagination? How can you tell what is real from what is imagination? Is the man who reads one of the letters to her the man who has been sending obscene mail to her? Does she finally get attracted to the man upstairs who is real and protective?

2. In "Ruby Tells All" Miller Williams uses a very direct device for revealing the thoughts of the main character. What is it? Are we supposed to assume that Ruby is writing these things, saying them, or just thinking them? Is this a monologue, a soliloquy, or just a narrative in the first person?

3. What are some of the more important thoughts that pass through Ruby's mind when she thinks about her life or life in general?

4. In "Coal Train" what runs through the writer's mind? When he says *you*, does he mean *himself*?

Writing

1. Using a different character, write a poem in the style of "Ruby Tells All."

2. Write a story that uses indirect descriptions of what your characters are thinking.

3. Write a stream-of-consciousness monologue made up entirely of the unpunctuated, free association thoughts of one person, as in the passage from Joyce's *Ulysses*.

4. Write a poem about jealousy. Try to capture the thoughts and feelings of the jealous person.

Time

When readers begin a literary work they want to know: (1) what is happening; (2) to whom it is happening; (3) where it is happening; and (4) when it is happening. This is all fundamental information that orients readers, so that they can follow the story or drama or poem. In the simple fairy-tale opening we are given all this information in a swift and general way: "Once upon a time in the land of Sumeria there lived a king who had three daughters and no sons." Since many fairy tales and folktales take place in some indefinite and remote past and in an equally remote or imaginary land, it is not necessary to go into any greater detail about *where* and *when*. More realistic and more modern stories usually take place in more definite places and in periods of time that are more precisely defined. When the artistic situation calls for it, a writer should be able to: (1) establish clearly the *period* in which the work takes place; (2) describe the *immediate action* as it unfolds; (3) look back at *past actions* that preceded the immediate action; (4) indicate the *duration* of the action; and (5) use *transitions* to make clear how much time has passed between major scenes and to introduce flashbacks.

10A **Every literary work has a time frame.**

1 | A literary work can be set in any time period.

The period can be historically specific or merely within the scope of human conjecture, including the very remote past and the very distant future. For example, consider a movie called *One Million B.C.*, made first in 1939 and then remade in 1966. There are novels such as *The Time Machine* by H. G. Wells and *Last and First Men* by Olaf Stapledon that take us as far into the future as we can possibly imagine. Between these extremes there are endless possibilities.

There are many popular historical periods. For example, the remote past of the Old Testament, used in such novels as Thomas Mann's *Joseph and His Brothers*; the less remote past of the New Testament, used in such works as *The Robe* by Lloyd C. Douglas; ancient Rome, the setting for such novels as Robert Graves' *I, Claudius*; the Renaissance, which is the background for Shakespeare's *Romeo and Juliet*; the early American colonial period, which Hawthorne used so well in *The Scarlet Letter*; and the Civil War period, made memorable in Margaret Mitchell's *Gone with the Wind*.

2 | It is sometimes difficult to draw a clear line between what is considered historical and what is considered contemporary.

For older writers who lived through the war years, World War II may seem contemporary. For younger writers who were born twenty years after the war was over, it all seems a matter of history, as does the Vietnam War. In general, we think of contemporary times as those that are part of the experience of people who are now alive. But the present keeps slipping away into the past, and, finally, it is buried along with the last eyewitnesses and becomes history.

3 | It is difficult to bring history back to life.

Though many a good writer has been able to make history live again, in some sense it is always dead, and it is therefore difficult for the living to identify with times that are past.

The truly important business of literature seems to be to interpret the experiences of one's own times. Most readers prefer a contemporary setting, though there remains a certain fascination with historical fiction, and young writers should not be discouraged from trying their hand at re-creating an earlier period than their own. Sometimes the past is merely romanticized; sometimes it is recreated accurately. It is important in serious historical fiction to be accurate, but not to swamp the plot with history and lose track of the story.

4 | The contemporary period can be divided into more specific decades.

Unless a specific time is indicated in a literary work, the reader will probably assume that the period is "today," or approximately the year in which the work is written. However, since the term *contemporary* can cover several decades, it may be important to know exactly what the period is, especially if the drama is linked with social or political events. Each modern period is associated with certain events, styles, and ideas. Looking back at our recent history, for instance, we often refer to the Beat Generation, the Cold War era, the Vietnam years, and the post-Soviet world. We try to characterize each decade as it slips into history.

10B Distinguishing present action from past action contributes to the clarity of the work.

1 | Present action refers to what happens in the main time frame established for the story.

There may be flashbacks or other references to prior action, but these are distinguished from the present action. The basic tense chosen by the writer has nothing to do with present action. In most stories the past tense is used, but even if the present tense is used, we know that the events have already taken place and that the writer is only trying to make them sound more immediate. When he says, for instance, "I jump into my car and drive like a madman to the nearest farmhouse," we don't assume that he is writing as he drives.

In Paul Ruffin's "The Fox" (Example 5a), the main time frame is very simple. A woman in a rural setting is baking a pie in the kitchen. Her husband comes in and says he saw a fox with a wounded leg, possibly from a trap he had once set for coons. He goes on in detail about the incident as she continues her work, but she is thinking about how much she hates this man. It is clear that there is a parallel between the wounded fox and the trapped woman. All this is *present time*. Then there is a break and we hear about their past in two paragraphs that are inserted outside the main time frame of the action. We return to the main action. The man gets his shotgun and says he's going out to finish off the fox. The woman, who has tried to protect herself from this man with cold indifference, remains in the kitchen. Suddenly, she plunges her hand into the center of the hot pie and leaves it there "until the burning stopped and there was no feeling left at all."

2 | In all action some things have to be *omitted*, some have to be *summarized*, and some have to be *dramatized*.

Any sequence of events in real life can involve hundreds of details. In a literary work it is impossible to include everything, and it is impossible to dramatize everything that *is* included. Some action has to be summarized, especially in works that cover a lot of events over a long period of time. A summarized action is one that is simply *told* to the reader and not acted out. In "The Fox," for instance, we are told: "Their relationship, from her intense hatred of him when they were in grade school together through an infatuation in high school that was consummated in her father's hayloft one Sunday afternoon, had come finally full circle, back to something that she thought at times was hate, at other times mere indifference." In contrast to this summarized action, we have the shocking ending of the story, which is dramatized action.

10C Past action refers to anything that has already taken place prior to the main time frame of the literary work.

1 | Most past action is summarized.

The easiest and most concise way to bring past events into the current action of a literary work is to make a brief summarized reference to them. This can be done in several ways:

1. The omniscient narrator can simply tell us what happened;
2. Past events can be referred to in dialogue;
3. A character can recall past events in a monologue or soliloquy; and
4. A character can think about the past.

2 | Past action can be dramatized in a flashback.

Most literary works with a plot have a chronological order. They start at the beginning and end at the end. Occasionally, however, the events are not revealed in a chronological order. This does not necessarily upset the main time frame. Sometimes, it is more effective to tell a story by beginning at the end or in the middle.

A *flashback* is a dramatized incident that has already taken place prior to the current sequence of events that constitutes the story, play, or narrative poem. Usually, a flashback is a subjective device, something we witness through the mind of one of the characters in a vivid reverie, memory, or dream. In the movie *Casablanca*, Rick's dialogue dissolves into a flashback to happier days in Paris, when he and Ilsa were first in love, and when the Germans were marching into the city. The scene is dramatized and is wonderfully romantic. But things did not work out, and suddenly we are back in Casablanca, back within the framework of present action.

The flashback technique has often been used in films, partly because it is easy to accomplish. All one needs is a simple transition. On stage, it is not often used, because the live theater lacks the technology available to film and television. In fiction, it is used, but requires a good deal of skill to avoid confusion and the awkwardness of moving back and forth in time. It is even used in poetry. In "Digging" by Seamus Heaney (Chapter 7) the poet's mind rushes back twenty years to a scene from his boyhood, when he hears his father digging in the garden.

10D Duration refers to the amount of time that passes in the whole work or any part of it.

Writers must not only indicate *when* the action takes place, but they must also indicate *how long* it lasts.

1 | There is a difference between objective and subjective time.

There are, in a sense, two different kinds of time: (1) *objective time*, the sort that ticks away on a clock in what we call "the real world," and (2) *subjective time*, a strictly human experience of duration. We have all waited for minutes that seemed like hours when something important was at stake, and we have all heard the old cliché that time passes quickly when you're having fun.

Subjective writers have always been fascinated with the discrepancy between external and internal time, with the idea that a moment that ticks away on a clock can actually be expanded almost infinitely in a person's mind. In a story called "Moments of Being" by Virginia Woolf, all that happens is that a rose pinned to Fanny Wilmot's dress falls to the floor. Fanny looks for the pin on the floor, finds it, and pins the rose back in place. What goes through her mind in that moment takes eight pages to describe.

2 | The duration of the action can be indicated in a variety of ways.

The handling of subjective time is closely linked to those techniques by which writers reveal the thoughts of their characters (see Chapter 9). Objective time can be indicated in many ways. In drama, whether on stage or screen, time can appear to be passing pretty much as it does in real life, but usually there is careful selection and even distillation. There is no way that all of reality can be captured in any art form.

In fiction, the duration of the action can be indicated, first of all, in some simple, direct way. For instance, the narrator can tell us that John and Mary spent an hour together, or that the flight to London took six hours. Novels that use a diary form usually indicate the date at the beginning of each section. Epistolary novels usually include dates on the letters. Many of the indicators of duration in an ordinary first-person or third-person narrative are woven into the story in an incidental way without being intrusive. In strictly chronological narratives it is easier to keep duration clear. In narratives that move back and forth in time, things can sometimes get confused.

10E Transitions are devices for linking episodes.

1 | Transitions are usually used between dramatized scenes.

Since literary works have to be selective and often consist of a sequence of important scenes, there must be transitions to guide the reader from one scene to another. The transition must indicate two important things: how much *time* has elapsed since the last major scene and *where* the new scene is located. These items are always included in a playscript, but, unfortunately, the audience does not usually have a copy of the script. The information has to be indicated in the set, the action, or the dialogue. A character might glance at his watch and say to his wife: "It's eleven o'clock. Where have you been for the last six hours?" Some transitions in drama are purely technical and can be indicated by lighting or by a curtain. Daylight dims to darkness. Dawn blossoms beyond shaded windows. In crude theatrical productions and early films, it was not uncommon to be shown a literal notice on a card or on the screen: "Two years later," or whatever information was required.

2 | Transitions in fiction can be frequent and varied.

Without the benefit of stage or screen devices, fiction has to rely on the written word. This sometimes makes things easier and sometimes more difficult. A writer can always begin a new scene by saying: "The next day Mary was up by six and ready to leave for New York by seven." On the other hand, there are usually more scenes in fiction, and sometimes there are elaborate transitions full of explanations and summarized action. For instance: "Mary spent the next six months looking after her dying father in a dreary farmhouse in Vermont, an experience that plunged her into a profound depression that did not end with his death. It was not until she met John in April that she began to recover from the ordeal. She was sitting on a bench in Washington Square Park."

In fiction, as in films, transitions are necessary to introduce flashbacks. Some of these have become conventional, even trite. Since the flashback is a dramatized memory of something in the past, we have to make the transition through the point of view of the character, who might stare into a mirror or into a lake, who might look through a photo album or at the portrait of a woman (as in the film *Laura*), or who might listen to a special piece of music and fall into a reverie. In the movies the lake can shimmer, the camera can go out of focus, the music can fade in or out. Comparable things can be used in fiction, but they have to be described instead of staged. Above all, it is important to make a clear distinction between a flashback and current action. There has to be a transition at both ends. Flashbacks often end abruptly—someone calling the character's name, a knock at the door, the telephone ringing, some kind of intrusion from present reality. Flashbacks should be used with caution. They should not be used too frequently and they should not be too long. The material should be especially significant in some way.

EXAMPLE 10A

WHAT SHE'S SAYING NOW
Lee K. Abbott

The whole story, as Trudy told it, was supposedly   1
about the common themes of this age: love and
the hurt of it. She liked to point out that love was
life itself—fearsome and double-edged, like a fillet
knife. Briefly, the plot was this: a woman named
Trudy Louise Weaver of Deming, New Mexico,
marries a wild youth named Bobby "Cooter" Brown
of Lordsburg, Texas. Childless, they live together for
nearly nine years, blissful as fairy tale couples, and
then—this is one suffering part—they split up. There   10
are other parts, too, some fetching as youth itself; but,
in the main, she wants you to know, hers was a story
with the smell and shape of a rotted fruit.

    Like many folks who were getting divorced a few
years ago, Trudy was born in that big explosion of
fertility after WW II. Her parents, Earl and Mildred,
had a fair-sized cotton farm south of town and from
it, as Trudy grew up, the world looked to her like
miracle and romance—big enough to delight, small
enough to manage. She was an A student, gifted   20
in algebra and plane geometry, a pom-pom girl for
the Wildcats, a candy striper at the Mimbres Valley
Hospital, and, though she never made much of it,
the kind of Protestant open-minded enough to read,
say, D.H. Lawrence and not get slack-witted about
it. She had a dark side as well—moments of fluster
and mood such as, she believed, you found among
otherwise stable monarchs. "I am not a—what?—a
Tartar," she would say to herself when overcome by

gloom. "I am aloft and beautiful as a princess but,   30
alas, depressed." In 1966, the story goes, she won
a drama scholarship to SMU where, at an October
Deke mixer, she met a sophomore named Cooter. He
liked to snort Buckhorn beer through his nose and in
Composition class the year before had carved himself a tattoo on his forearm. It was supposed to be a
complete sentence—"about the crazed and genuinely
goofy," he said—but she could only make out a few
words, namely, Time and Fear.

   As seems now inevitable—in such love and story as   40
this—they became a pair, inseparable as bird and song.
Yes, Trudy tried to explain to her roommate, Cooter
was creepy—no more attractive than hair on a woman's lip. His nails were dirty, he liked to chew Redman
tobacco, but—and here she'd get misty-eyed—he was,
well, exciting. A force, she said. A spirit which might
lead to rampage or eternal laughter. In addition, he
could play guitar and sing as well as any you heard
on KDFW. She particularly liked the song he made
up in her honor, "A Woman at Her Window," which   50
had in it, by virtue of its lilt and flutter, something she
thought of as melty and fine as the sort of beauty she
was keen for.

   On the night they became engaged (she was a
sophomore now), Cooter tried to feel her up. They
were parked in his Ford pick-up at Lake Dallas and
for an instant, beguiled by the twinkling stars and
blossom-heavy April breeze, she had no idea Cooter's
hand was up her skirt.

   "Hey," she said, "what do you think you're doing?"   60
   Cooter had the expression of a slow-footed night
beast caught in the glare of a headlamp. "Aw, c'mon,
Trudy, we're almost—you know."

They were nothing, she said. And they would be nothing until the I do's were uttered. This was a point of pride, she said. Like another's belief in the hereafter.

"Well, I'll be damned." Cooter sounded wounded as a duck. "What can it hurt?"

Whereupon, if you believe the version most oft-told, she slugged him near the earhole and pitched herself out of his truck, saying "We're finished, Robert Brown. Say goodbye to me!"

There now pass several months—through summer and almost to Thanksgiving—during which Trudy tries to forget about that old peckerwood. There is some talk that she saw, at least twice, a French major named Eliot and that she went to a Cowboys game once with a graduate assistant in that branch of physics you need heavy, thick glasses to know; but, for the most part, these months, as she recalls now, were lived in books and the library and her room. She was taking a new curriculum now, Accounting, and she set herself to it as she imagined Hercules had set himself to the stable-clearing parts of the Seven Labors. Yet, she had to admit, she was heartbroken. Something had gone out of her. Something that brought to mind such language as "tingle" and "tremor." She had felt her heart, she believed, sink, shrink and harden.

And then one day by accident, she bumped into Cooter in the bookstore. He was buying a sweatshirt which said "Be Free, Die Young." His face was ruined and loose.

"You can take me now," she said. "Let's go to your place and be frolicsome."

All the versions of what happened next are contrary and troubled as dark waters, a few nearly obscene with joy; but all agree that in May, after Cooter's graduation, they were married, honeymooned in New Orleans, and then, because of his father's connection with Sinclair Oil, they took up residence in Midland where Cooter worked as a petroleum geologist. It was a time, Trudy says, which seemed to have the density and texture of oil itself—slow and not lovely.

Not much evidence from this period in their lives exists—a period, Trudy believes, tense as that between earthquakes; all that survives are two letters.

In the first, this to her roommate, Trudy writes of ragged wings and an epic thirst for wonderland. "Cooter has a beard now," she said, "which brings out the Rasputin in him. Plus he has a gang of buddies with names like Poot and Billy Boy. They smoke that red-dirt marijuana and go off, Cooter says, into the hinterlands. I am happy, mostly, though swamped sometimes by heartpangs and the urge to be elsewhere—including the moon." In the next paragraph, she says that Cooter thinks her too tender for this world, that he's tired of her weep-bouts and related downwardness, but what does he know? Men are an irksome breed, led about largely by their glands and ancient brains. "P.S., we shall be here awhile as Cooter's heart murmur and flat feet will keep him from the jungle troubles pursued by Mr. Nixon."

The second letter, discovered only recently, was written around the time of Cooter's twenty-sixth birthday party, which was held at the Hitching Post and brought the sheriff to end it. "Dear Mr. Brown," it began, "you don't know me as I am the underhalf

of that female you live with. I am more fire than ice   130
and am spoken to by wondrous spirits—who say we
are bored, our finer reaches dry as ditch weeds. There
is trouble here, and inside your Trudy where I live is
only dust and smoke and such blazes as you will find
when the world ends."

Then, in 1974, Cooter Brown was fired.

And Trudy bought a Toronado demonstrator with
their savings.

And Cooter, except for one tune about mirth and
omens, stopped playing the guitar.   140

And Trudy began an affair.

There's not much to know about this last event,
Trudy says, except that in the context of her dismay
something like sex with a stranger seemed itself golden,
a pleasure for the A student still in her. O.T. LeDuc
wasn't so much nicer as he was different; for he, too,
as she imagines it now, was equally tragic and thrown
about by life. They used to take her car into the desert
and flop naked into the back seat. He was an English
teacher, skinny as a pencil, and seemed full of mastery   150
and order. He used to beat his chest and holler about
the bombs in his head—those that went Boom-Boom
when she, herself sweaty and thrashful, cast light on
the dim places his species had crawled from. "I am
touching your stingy heart," she'd whisper and there,
in the desert twilight, his howl sounded as lonesome
and perfect as the music she imagined made by this
planet spinning in space.

"Robert Brown," she said one night to her husband, "do you know what love is?"   160

He was collapsed by the TV and had the eye-
balls of a fish. She had told him about O.T. and for

a time, his face mashed as any she'd ever seen, he'd tried choking her.

"I think love's a mystery," she said, "devastating as death—but meant for few."

Which produced in him an outcry such as you find today in violent comic books—bold, big enough to be read across the room: "Aaarrrggghhh!"

To be true, Trudy says, a reconciliation of sorts   170
followed and after they moved to El Paso—Cooter's father had put in a good word with Texaco—the subject of her infidelity became the first thing they mentioned to their new friends. One night, at the Cavern of Music in Juarez, Cooter made her tell the whole story again.

"Ain't that a bitch?" Cooter said.

"I was much pleased," Trudy said. "I made this noise—Ya-Ya-Ya-Ya—and flew the same flight my lover was on."   180

"Listen to that," Cooter said. "Doesn't that bring out the shithead in you?"

And then, one day, she knew the marriage was over. Her hands were wet and everything—furniture to flatware—seemed impersonal as age. It was an insight, she remembers, which struck her with the same force Cooter had, years before, when he'd told her he had no higher ambition than to be rich or mildly famous. She was standing in the bathroom and it seemed to her that the creature in the mirror was not   190
she at all, but a joke of a woman dragged into the present moment by want and dashed expectation.

"Cooter," she said, "you are not the tempest I deserve."

He was in the garage, a piece of his car in his greasy hands.

"You know what's in here?" She was pointing at her breast.

She tried telling him about the girl she'd been— that one who'd seen life as a pleasant march from one achievement to the next. She wanted to go home, she said, climb on that old bed of hers and sleep for ten thousand years. She wanted to stand on her daddy's porch again and watch the sun go down without the noise it was making now. "I believe in the yonder worlds, don't you?"

"Who was it?" Cooter said. "I bet I know the sumbitch. It's Worm Foody, ain't it?"

There was no one, she said. This was not a man-woman thing. This was another relation being addressed: her to herself.

"You give me fifteen minutes," she said. "I'll be out of here."

It is always here that she mentions her abiding fondness for Cooter. She likes to point to his virtues, such as no concern for money. That she was leaving, she insists, was not really his fault; he'd just been, it appeared, the vehicle which conveyed her through this vale of tears and brought her to a crossroads where the future opened wide as the horizon and said to her, in a voice wise and breathless, "Let's dream now, little darling. We are grown now and hope to live forever."

On her last trip to that dusty, well-dinged Toronado, he grabbed her by the shoulders, shook her some.

"I could get me someone too," he said. "I got my eye right now on a lady named Brenda."

Yes, she said. Her heart, once hard as stone, seemed soft now and able to soar.

And then, as she always is in this part, she is driving away, unburdened as God, certain that what lurks out here in the big world has a name and substance and gives reward to those who believe in passionate, wistful dreams.

Source: From Witness Vol. 1–2, Summer 1987. Reprinted by permission of the author.

EXAMPLE 10B

MONTAGE
Robert DeMaria

We see Betty born sticky-eyed, gasping,
Sucking, growing, howling, falling,
Leaping across the schoolyard
Into her high-school lover's arms
After the big game, and landing in
The church all in white, squeezing out
Babies, a girl, a boy, a girl, a boy.
And shopping at Shop-Rite and Finast,
Pushing her wire cart, feeding the dogs
And the cats, weeping over the broken crockery
And a sick mother, a dead father,
A child's bloody nose, combing her hair,
Brushing her teeth, consulting her doctor,
Her dentist, husband, lawyer, broker,
Rotor-rooter man, and piano tuner,
Wondering how to get the money
To send the children to college,
And what to do when her spouse is dead,
Putting out the dried-up Christmas tree
With bits of tinsel still clinging to it,
And turning to see in a mirror an old woman
With lines in her face, who proves to be
Her very own personal self
Shortly before the diagnosis
Declares her unfit to linger any longer
In this consumer's paradise,
And she is consumed.

EXAMPLE 10C

THE SPEED OF LIGHT
Judith Kroll

1   sometime, someone is writing of this

her hair good brown, she looks out a train window
and notices again how it frames an etching

the innocent greens of the fields
and the dark farmer
in his eye-white headcloth and loincloth, under the sky

and what becomes of our friends?
they blow by us like leaves

as we move in life
10   into the past and the future

we decide where to send our parents to school
we wake up younger than our children

EXERCISES

Discussion

1. In "What She's Saying Now" by Lee K. Abbott the passage of time is important. Why is it important? How does the author handle time in this story? Would it have been better to have the main character telling her own story?

2. "Montage" is a poem that covers a lifetime of a woman at high speed. What is the effect of this device? What is a *montage* in movie making?

3. In "The Speed of Light," Judith Kroll is also dealing with the passage of time. What is her message? Does she contradict herself when she says "as we move in life/into the past and the future"?

Writing

1. Write a short story or poem in which an incident that occurs in a few moments is expanded through a *subjective sense of time*.

2. Write a short story, poem, or play that contains at least one *flashback*.

3. Write a story or film script in which events that occurred over a long period of time are condensed in a *montage*.

4. Write a one-act play with an historical setting (for instance, a lonely encounter between a Confederate and a Union soldier in the Civil War).

5. A young man sits beside his unconscious and terminally ill father in a hospital. They have never gotten along well, and the young man had to be persuaded by his mother to make this visit. Create a *flashback* that will help to explain the bad relationship, but also describe the *present* feelings of the young man.

6. A young woman who ran away from home at sixteen and was disowned by her parents is now on her way back at the age of twenty-one. Capture *past* events while she is on the road. Then describe *present* events, her arrival, and her confrontation with her parents.

Images and Sounds

Words are the medium of the art of writing. A piece of writing, therefore, is limited to the effects the words can achieve. Fortunately, words can do a great deal. For example, with words writers can convey ideas, create images, and create sounds and patterns of sounds. Writers do not necessarily do these things separately. In a single powerful passage a writer can accomplish all three. Consider the *ideas*, *images*, and *sounds* in this song by Shakespeare (from *The Tempest*):

> Full fathom five thy father lies;
>   Of his bones are coral made;
> Those are pearls that were his eyes;
>   Nothing of him that doth fade,
> But doth suffer a sea change
> Into something rich and strange.
> Sea nymphs hourly ring his knell:
>   Ding-dong.
> Hark! now I hear them—Ding-dong bell.

Language is always associated with ideas, but in the literary recreation of human experience images and sounds are very important, especially in poetry. A consideration of *imagery* can be conveniently divided into three categories: (1) metaphors and similes, (2) allusions, and (3) symbols. *Sounds* in literature can be considered in the following categories: (1) rhyme, (2) rhythm, and (3) patterns and form.

IMAGES

Imagery is a broad term that encompasses all kinds of pictures in the mind and all the literary devices that put them there. Images tend to be visual, but, as in dreams, they appeal to all the senses. Literal description contains certain literary devices that are specifically designed to evoke images. We think of imagery in connection with poetry, but it is also an effective device in prose, as we can see in this very brief story by Sandra Cisneros:

SALVADOR LATE OR EARLY

Salvador with eyes the color of caterpillar, Salvador of the crooked hair and crooked teeth, Salvador whose name the teacher cannot remember, is a boy who is no one's friend, runs along somewhere in that vague direction where homes are the color of bad weather, lives behind a raw wood doorway, shakes the sleepy brothers awake, ties their shoes, combs their hair with water, feeds them milk and corn flakes from a tin cup in the dim dark of the morning.

Salvador, late or early, sooner or later arrives with the string of younger brothers ready. Helps his mama, who is busy with the business of the baby. Tugs the arms of Cecilio, Arturito, makes them hurry, because today, like yesterday, Arturito has dropped the cigar box of crayons, has let go the hundred little fingers of red, green, yellow, blue, and nub of black sticks that tumble and spill over and beyond the asphalt puddles until the crossing-guard lady holds back the blur of traffic for Salvador to collect them again.

Salvador inside that wrinkled shirt, inside the throat that must clear itself and apologize each time it speaks, inside that forty-pound body of boy with its geography of scars, its history of hurt, limbs stuffed with feathers and rags, in what part of the eyes, in what part of the heart, in that cage of the chest where something throbs with both fists and knows only what Salvador knows, inside that body too small to contain the hundred balloons of happiness, the single guitar of grief, is a boy like any other disappearing out the door, beside the schoolyard gate, where he has told his brothers they must wait. Collects the hands of Cecilio and Arturito, scuttles off dodging the many schoolyard colors, the elbows and wrists criss-crossing, the several shoes running. Grows small and smaller to the eye, dissolves into the bright horizon, flutters in the air before disappearing like a memory of kites.

Source: From WOMAN HOLLERING CREEK. Copyright © 1991 by Sandra Cisneros. Published by Vintage Books, a division of Random House Inc., and originally in hardcover by Random House Inc. By permission of Susan Bergholz Literary Services, New York, NY and Lamy, NM. All rights reserved.

11A Metaphors and similes make nonliteral comparisons.

Some comparisons cannot be taken literally. If you say "Terry looks like Donna," you are making a *literal* comparison. If you say "Terry looks like a beautiful blossom," you are not making a literal comparison, but you are evoking an *image* that will help to describe Terry. Nonliteral comparisons are also called figures of speech. Obviously, a person is not literally a flower, but a person and a flower might both have a certain attractive quality that makes the comparison possible.

1 | A simile says that one thing is *like* another (nonliterally).

Similes and metaphors both evoke images. The only difference is that a simile uses the words "as" or "like" ("Terry is as beautiful as a blossom"), and a metaphor says that one thing *is* another ("Terry is a beautiful blossom").

A simile can be a simple comparison, as in Robert Burns' famous line: "Oh, my love is like a red, red, rose . . ." A simile can also be extended and elaborate, perhaps even the basis of a whole poem. In "Sonnet 97" Shakespeare uses an elaborate simile, which compares the absence of the lover from his loved one to a winter:

How like a winter hath my absence been
From thee, the pleasure of the fleeting year!

What freezings have I felt, what dark days seen!
What old December's bareness everywhere!
And yet this time removed was summer's time,   5
The teeming autumn, big with rich increase,
Bearing the wanton burthen of the prime,
Like widowed wombs after their lord's decease;
Yet this abundant issue seemed to me
But hope of orphans and unfathered fruit;   10
For summer and his pleasures wait on thee,
And, thou away, the very birds are mute;
Or, if they sing, 'tis with so dull a cheer
That leaves look pale, dreading the winter's near.

Similes are not used only in poetry of the past. They are probably as commonly used in contemporary poetry as they were in Shakespeare's day. "New Snow" by Reg Saner provides some good examples:

NEW SNOW

Because it has fallen all night
like some vague mother of dreams
unlocking us from ourselves,
I rise before dawn and go out—
under elms, black trunk, black branch,   5
each involved with its beautiful spook—
between power poles where the light
travels by rope, into the open field.
Below, our dark town draws its soft
stone breath. Along this slope,   10
boulders like curds, and clumped gorse
nodding heavy as cauliflower—
great empty-handed donors
grown in weightless air. A mile off
through last week's frozen ruts   15
a car crunches away, as over the boards

of an old bridge. Walking slowly
among weeds whose stalks
like forgetful birds
are still taking weather in   20
through delicate bones, I pause.
The low clouds pause with us.
Everything speechless.

2 | A metaphor asserts the identity of the things compared.

At times it may strengthen a comparison to leave out *like* or *as*
and simply say that, figuratively speaking, one thing *is* another, as
in "War is hell!" At other times a simile might be more suitable.

A metaphor can be incidental or it can be elaborate.
In "Ode to a Nightingale" Keats uses the phrase "the view-
less wings of Poesy." A more modern poet, Eamon Grennan,
makes use of more elaborate metaphors in the following poem:

LYING LOW

The dead rabbit's
Raspberry belly
Gapes like a mouth;

Bees and gilded flies
Make the pulpy flesh   5
Hum and squirm:

O love, they sing
In their nail-file voices,
We are becoming one another.

His head intact, tranquil,   **10**
As if he's dreaming
The mesmerised love of strangers

Who inhabit the red tent
Of his ribs, the radiant
Open house of his heart,   **15**

Source: Eamon Grennan, "Lying Low" from *Out of Sight: New and Selected Poems.* Copyright © 1998, 2010 by Eamon Grennan. Reprinted with the permission of The Permissions Company, Inc., on behalf of Graywolf Press, Minneapolis, Minnesota, www.graywolfpress.org.

In the following poem by Jimmy Santiago Baca there is a coherent pattern of metaphors:

FALL

Somber hue diffused on everything.
　　　　Each creature, each emptied corn stalk,
　　　　　is richly bundled in mellow light.
In that open unharvested field of my own life,
I have fathered small joys and memories.
My heart was once a lover's swing that creaked in wind
of these calm fall days.
Autumn chants my visions to sleep,
and travels me back into a night
when I could touch stars and believe in myself . . .
Along the way, grief broke me,
　　　　my faith became hardened dirt
　　　　walked over by too many people.
My heart now, as I walk down this dirt road,
on this calm fall day,
　　　　is a dented
　　　　tin bucket
　　　　filled with fruits
　　　　picked long ago.

It's getting harder
to lug the heavy bucket.
I spill a memory on the ground,
it gleams,
rain on hot embers
of yellow grass.

Source: By Jimmy Santiago Baca, from BLACK MESA POEMS, copyright ©1989 by Jimmy Santiago Baca. Reprinted by permission of New Directions Publishing Corp.

3 | Personification means giving human qualities to ideas and things.

There is a natural tendency in literature to translate abstractions and inanimate objects into human terms, because those are the terms we can all experience. Hence, the breeze *whispers*, we are *stalked* by death, ideas *leap* into our minds, the peacock *struts*, and the lion is a *king*. A brilliant example of the use of personification can be found in *Jitterbug Perfume*, a novel by Tom Robbins:

The beet is the most intense of vegetables. The radish, admittedly, is more feverish, but the fire of the radish is a cold fire, the fire of discontent not of passion. Tomatoes are lusty enough, yet there runs through tomatoes an undercurrent of frivolity. Beets are deadly serious.

Slavic peoples get their physical characteristics from potatoes, their smoldering inquietude from radishes, their seriousness from beets.

The beet is the melancholy vegetable, the one most willing to suffer. You can't squeeze blood out of a *turnip* . . .

The beet is the murderer returned to the scene of the crime. The beet is what happens when the cherry finishes with the carrot. The beet is the ancient ancestor of the autumn moon, bearded, buried, all but fossilized; the dark green sails of the grounded moon-boat stitched with veins of primordial plasma; the kite string that once connected the moon to the Earth now a muddy whisker drilling desperately for rubies.

The beet was Rasputin's favorite vegetable. You could see it in his eyes.

11B Allusions depend upon a common body of knowledge.

1 | An allusion is a reference to a specific person, place, or thing.

Allusions are often used in similes or metaphors, as in, "Like Sisyphus, he found his work endless and futile." (In Greek mythology Sisyphus was punished in Hades by having to roll a boulder uphill forever, only to have it roll down again as soon as it reached the top.) Allusions expand a writer's ability to use nonliteral comparisons and to evoke images. They are drawn from a common body of knowledge in a given culture. Unless they have broad recognition they might be too specialized or obscure to be effective. Many allusions are drawn from Greek mythology, the Bible, familiar literature, well-known events and figures in history, and popular culture, including movies, music, cartoons, and even television commercials. For instance:

- He was the Michael Jordan of the playground league.
- Her Mona Lisa smile gave her an air of mystery.
- Her life was like Schubert's unfinished symphony.
- Her Madonna style is very popular.
- Like Paul Revere, he tried to warn the public.
- He met his Waterloo at Watergate.

Some allusions are extended and elaborate. Good examples can be found in "Daddy" by Sylvia Plath (Example 3b). In this poem there are extended allusions to Naziism, the Holocaust, Aryanism, and German military equipment.

11C **Symbols are tangible representations of things that are complex, general, or abstract.**

A symbol, whether it appears in literature or anywhere else, is something tangible that stands for something abstract, or something very specific that stands for something very general. Flags are symbols of the countries they represent. The Statue of Liberty symbolizes the democratic ideal. The cross represents the crucifixion and perhaps the whole Christian faith. In a sense, all of language is symbolic, since it is a system of signs that refer to things in the real world. What concerns us for the moment is how symbols function in literature.

1 | There is a connection between symbols in dreams and symbols in literature.

Both dreams and literature use symbols to give expression to feelings that come from the subconscious mind, and both depend, to some extent, on certain basic ways of representing these hidden feelings. In other words, there is a kind of dream language that is also used in literature. There is a private dimension in dreams, however. The same objects may have different connotations for different people. On the other hand, because we all share human nature and some kind of social context, there are certain consistencies in the language of dreams.

2 | In literature, symbols must have some public meaning.

Without a shared context of meaning there wouldn't be any communication between the writer and the reader. Edgar Allan Poe's raven was not exclusively his own nightmare. The raven, the crow, and the owl have long been associated with death. The Indians of the Northwest say that when you hear the owl call your name you will die. In the Freudian system, objects of an appropriate shape, such as towers or guns, are considered phallic symbols; and objects such as houses and staircases and caves refer to the female, often the mother.

3 | Symbols are not comparisons in the same way that metaphors, similes, and allusions are.

Symbols are objects or actions or even people that actually appear in a literary work and bring with them certain connotations.

One of our most famous literary symbols is Melville's white whale, Moby Dick. It is impossible to read this novel as just another adventure story. There are obviously symbols in the novel, and they are not easy to interpret. What does the white whale stand for? Is he good or evil? Is he the inscrutable, godlike mystery, that power in the universe that is not to be questioned? He is called Job's whale. Job's problem was that he questioned God's treatment of him, instead of accepting with absolute humility whatever seemed to be God's Will. The debate about this famous symbol goes on, but the drama is magnificent and moving. Some important and fundamental truth has been captured here, even if we can't force it into more ordinary language. That is precisely what symbols are for. They accomplish things that ordinary language cannot.

Another well-known symbol is found in Virginia Woolf's *To the Lighthouse*. The setting of the novel is the summer house of Mr. and Mrs. Ramsay, somewhere on the British coast, probably in the Hebrides. Offshore, there is a lighthouse with three beams of light. Every summer the Ramsay family and their guests gather at the house. There are artists, poets, and professors. And there are the children. There is much talk of sailing to the lighthouse. It seems at times mysterious and unreachable. An elusive, distant source of light, it is a tangible and suggestive symbol of many things. It suggests something mystical, something beyond human grasp or comprehension, perhaps death or eternity or a cold indifferent universe. Mrs. Ramsay finds it comforting at times, and, at other times, terrifying. Mr. Ramsay is afraid that logic will never get him to the lighthouse, to ultimate truth. Lily, the painter friend of Mrs. Ramsay, can complete her painting only when, after many years, Mr. Ramsay and his children finally sail to the lighthouse. The moment they land, she has a kind of vision.

In Joseph Conrad's *Victory*, set in the East Indies, the hero runs off to a deserted island with a woman. He is a disenchanted European. She is a lost soul, playing in a hotel orchestra in one of those exotic places Conrad was so fond of (now Malaysia or Indonesia). Their love affair on this deserted island suggests the Garden of Eden. It is a return to purity and innocence, before the Fall. But evil lurks in the wings. A satanic figure, Mr. Jones, imagines that there is a treasure on the island and arrives there to get it. He is accompanied by two henchmen, Ricardo the killer and Pedro the brute. The struggle is full of suspense, but, the ending is, inevitably, tragic.

There has been much discussion of the Marabar Caves in E. M. Forster's *A Passage to India*. This excerpt will serve as a good illustration of how a symbol is described:

They are dark caves. Even when they open towards the sun, very little light penetrates down the entrance tunnel into the circular chamber. There is little to see, and no eye to see it, until the visitor arrives for his five minutes, and strikes a match. Immediately another flame rises in the depths of the rock and moves towards the surface like an imprisoned spirit: the walls of the circular chamber have been most marvellously polished. The two flames approach and strive to unite, but cannot, because one of them breathes air, the other stone. A mirror inlaid with lovely colours divides the lovers, delicate stars of pink and grey interpose, exquisite nebulae, shadings fainter than the tail of a comet or the midday moon, all the evanescent life of the granite, only here visible. Fists and fingers thrust above the advancing soil—here at last is their skin, finer than any covering acquired by the animals, smoother than windless water, more voluptuous than love. The radiance increases, the flames touch one another, kiss, expire. The cave is dark again, like all the caves.

Symbols expand human expression and make it possible to grasp certain complexities that cannot be described in a literal fashion.

The Scarlet Letter by Nathaniel Hawthorne is full of symbolism. The novel takes place in Puritan seventeenth-century Massachusetts. Hester Prynne bears an illegitimate child and is branded with an embroidered letter "A" as her punishment. The A is for adultery, since she has a husband, even though he has been away long enough to be considered dead. She refuses to name her lover, who is Arthur Dimmesdale, a young minister. The whole fabric of the novel is made of symbols. The scarlet letter itself is open to many interpretations. Is Hester ashamed of it or proud of it? Does it stand for her sin or her rebellion? She names her daughter Pearl, because she was purchased at such a dear price. Chillingworth, the secretly returned husband, is a satanic figure who seeks revenge. Dimmesdale is a saintly figure, whom Chillingworth tries to destroy with guilt. Much of the symbolism deals with the struggle between good and evil and the struggle between nature and the repressive forces of religion and society.

One of the most effective symbols in drama can be found in Tennessee Williams' *The Glass Menagerie.* Laura, a fragile character, has a collection of equally fragile glass animals, one of which is a unicorn. Laura's attachment to the unicorn indicates her preference for fantasy and her rejection of reality. The unicorn in some cultures has also symbolized virginity, the Virgin Mary, and even Christ. In any case, when Jim, the "gentleman caller," accidentally knocks over the unicorn and it falls to the floor, the horn breaks off. Laura calls it a blessing in disguise, because now the unicorn will look like all the other horses. In other words, the loss of the unicorn's horn symbolizes Laura's return to reality. After her encounter with Jim she will no longer feel unattractive and "freakish," as she puts it, because of her limp and sensitivity. She will feel less different from other people.

4 | Allegory is related to symbolism.

In allegorical works, characters and objects usually represent something more complex than they themselves appear to be. For instance, the rose has been a popular symbol in Western literature. It has been used mostly as a symbol of love, as in the medieval poem "The Romance of the Rose." In this allegory, a lover is admitted to a beautiful park by Idleness. The whole thing takes place in a dream. In the park the lover finds such characters as Pleasure, Delight, Cupid, and, finally, the Rose. After he kisses the Rose, he is driven away by other allegorical figures, such as Danger, Shame, Scandal, and Jealousy. Two French authors were involved in its creation and the poem is much too long to summarize completely. It is a classical allegory and clearly contains symbolic elements.

SOUNDS

11D Rhyme involves an arrangement of similar sounds.

We usually associate the manipulation of sounds with poetry, but it occurs, of course, in all of literature. The language in the plays of Tennessee Williams is often poetic, as is the language in the novels of Virginia Woolf. Here, for instance, is a passage from her *Between the Acts*:

> Fly then follow, she hummed, the dappled herds in the cedar grove, who, sporting play, the red with the roe, the stag with the doe. Fly away. I grieving stay. Alone I linger, I pluck the bitter herb by the ruined wall, the churchyard wall, and press its sour, its sweet, its sour, long grey leaf, so twixt thumb and finger.

1 | The word *rhyme* has several meanings.

A *rhyme* can refer to a poem that has rhyming lines. It can mean, in general, the similarity in sound that certain words have. Specifically, it can mean *end rhyme*. Hence, when we say *rhyming couplets* we mean two lines that end in the same sound:

> Say what strange motive, Goddess! could compel
> A well-bred lord to assault a gentle belle?
> **(Alexander Pope, "The Rape of the Lock")**

2 | End rhyme means using similar sounds at the end of lines of poetry.

The sounds that rhyme are the accented syllables and all that follows. The rhyming, therefore, can involve just one syllable or two or three or even more, though the more syllables that are involved the more difficult the rhyming possibilities. End rhymes usually involve one or two syllables and, occasionally, three:

hair-fair	mother-brother	readily-steadily
cold-bold	writer-fighter	imitate-intimate
blood-flood	beauty-duty	slippery-frippery
kill-thrill	flying-crying	flowering-towering

3 | Feminine rhymes are rhymes of two or more syllables in which the final syllable is unstressed.

All of the previous examples, except those in the first column, are examples of feminine rhyme. In the second column there are *double feminine rhymes*, and in the third column there are *triple feminine rhymes*, the stressed syllable plus two.

4 | Masculine rhymes end in a stressed syllable.

Masculine rhymes include all single-syllable rhymes, as in the first column above, beginning with *hair-fair*. In masculine polysyllabic rhymes the unstressed syllables precede the final stressed syllable: *compel-dispel*.

IMPECCABLE CONCEPTION

Maya Angelou

I met a Lady Poet
who took for inspiration
colored birds, and whispered words,
a lover's hesitation.

A falling leaf could stir her.   5
A wilting, dying rose
would make her write, both day and night,
the most rewarding prose.

She'd find a hidden meaning   10
in every pair of pants,
then hurry home to be alone
and write about romance.

5 | Off rhyme (near rhyme, slant rhyme) is the use of sounds that are close but not exactly the same.

Consider the following examples of off rhyme.

> herd-beard (Shakespeare)
> sound-wound (Wordsworth)
> good-blood (Dryden)
> love-prove (Marlowe)

Since pronunciation changes with time, it is possible that some of the off rhymes mentioned once had the same sound.

In the following poem by Emily Dickinson the second and fourth lines of each stanza are off-rhymed:

> Remorse—is Memory—awake—
> Her parties all astir—
> A Presence of Departed Acts—
> At window—and at Door—
>
> It's Past—set down before the Soul   5
> And lighted with a Match—
> Perusal—to facilitate—
> And help Belief to stretch—
>
> Remorse is cureless—the Disease
> Not even God—can heal—   10
> For 'tis His institution—and
> The Adequate of Hell—

6 | Internal rhyme involves similar sounds within a given line of poetry.

Not all rhymes are end rhymes. Within a given line of poetry similar sounds may be used. The main devices involved are:

Alliteration: the repetition of sounds at the beginning of two or more words in the same line of poetry.

> Had we but world enough, and time,
> This coyness, lady, were no crime.
> We would sit down, and think which way
> To walk, and pass our long love's day.
> **Andrew Marvell**

Assonance: the repetition of vowel sounds within a line of poetry or even throughout a group of lines or the whole poem.

> I wake and feel the fell of dark, not day.
> **G. M. Hopkins**

Consonance: the repetition of consonant sounds, especially at the end of a word, within a line of poetry or throughout a group of lines or the whole poem.

> The Devil is dead, good people all!
> Who are the bearers that bear the pall?
>
> One of them thinks he has slain God too,
> With the self-same sword that Satan slew.
> **Mary Elizabeth Coleridge**

Notice all the alliteration, assonance, consonance, and outright repetition of words in this poem by Gerard Manley Hopkins:

[I WAKE AND FEEL THE FELL OF DARK, NOT DAY.]

I wake and feel the fell of dark, not day.
What hours, O what black hours we have spent
This night! what sights you, heart, saw; ways you went!
And more must, in yet longer light's delay.

With witness I speak this. But where I say   5
Hours I mean years, mean life. And my lament
Is cries countless, cries like dead letters sent
To dearest him that lives alas! away.

I am gall, I am heartburn. God's most deep decree
Bitter would have me taste: my taste was me;   10
Bones built in me, flesh filled, blood brimmed the curse.

Selfyeast of spirit a dull dough sours. I see
The lost are like this, and their scourge to be
As I am mine, their sweating selves, but worse.

11E Rhythm involves an arrangement of sounds with regular intervals and beats.

It is part of human nature to respond to rhythms. After all, they are inside of us as well as outside of us. We have a heartbeat. We breathe rhythmically. Even the simple act of walking has a rhythm to it. We have an inner clock that measures out time (our circadian rhythm). The world we live in is full of rhythms to which we respond: night and day, the seasons, the tides, the sounds that animals make, from the birds at dawn to crickets at night. The chirps of the snowy tree cricket are so precise that if you add the number forty to the number of chirps per fifteen-second interval, you get the exact temperature in Fahrenheit.

Rhythm is obvious in music and dance, but there are also natural rhythms in language. There are *stressed* and *unstressed* syllables. There is *pause* and *pitch* and the *length* of a phrase or clause. Ordinary speech in English tends to be *iambic*. An "iamb" is a metrical unit made up of two syllables, the first one unstressed, the second one stressed. The following ordinary sentence contains four iambs:

Ĭ came tŏ school ălóne tŏdáy.
  1   2   3   4

Though there are some natural rhythms in ordinary speech, there is not always a clear pattern. In literature we can manipulate language to create clearer patterns and more pleasing sounds. Rhythm can be varied to suit the material. It can be slower or faster. It can flow smoothly or it can be choppy and full of pauses. It can be a rising rhythm or a falling rhythm. There are subtleties and variations to suit all poetic occasions from love and death to awe-inspiring nature; from the mysteries of the universe to the microcosmic incidents in a moment as small as a raindrop.

1 | Pauses are used in a variety of ways in poetry.

The pause in poetry, as in music, is very important. It is a fundamental tool of the poet. There can be slight pauses and long pauses and anything in between. There are so many combinations of sounds that can be "poetic" that prosody can hardly be considered an exact science. However, three terms are often used in the discussion of pauses in poetry.

(A) Caesura (indicated in diagramming by //)

A clear pause or break that can occur anywhere within a line of poetry. Old English poetry, the main example of which is

Beowulf, is written in lines that are divided into two parts by a strong caesura. This kind of pause remains a useful device. An effective use of the caesura can be found in the following sixteenth-century poem by George Peele:

HOT SUN, COOL FIRE

Hot sun, cool fire, tempered with sweet air,
Black shade, fair nurse, shadow my white hair.
Shine, sun; burn, fire; breathe, air, and ease me;
Black shade, fair nurse, shroud me and please me.
Shadow, my sweet nurse, keep me from burning;   5
Make not my glad cause cause of mourning.
    Let not my beauty's fire
    Inflame unstaid desire,
    Nor pierce any bright eye
    That wandereth lightly.   **10**

(B) End-stopped lines

Though the rules of grammar still apply in most poems, poetry is basically constructed by lines, and there is a natural tendency to pause at the end of each line when you read a poem. If the meaning or rhythm or construction of a line invites a full pause, the line is described as *end-stopped.* A series of full pauses has a clear effect on the overall rhythm. This anonymous poem was written in the early seventeenth century:

THE SILVER SWAN

The silver swan, who living had no note,
When death approached, unlocked her silent throat;
Leaning her breast against the reedy shore,
Thus sung her first and last, and sung no more:
"Farewell, all joys; Oh death, come close mine eyes;   5
More geese than swans now live, more fools than wise."

(C) Run-on lines

When the meaning or construction of a line carries it quickly into the next line, allowing only a minimal pause, the effect on the overall rhythm is quite different. The run-on lines may contribute to the feeling of exhilaration in this poem by Robert Graves:

TO BE IN LOVE

To spring impetuously in air and remain
Treading on air for three heart-beats or four,
Thence to descend at leisure; or else to climb
A forward-tilted crag with no hand-holds;
5   Or, disembodied, to carry jasmine back
From a Queen's garden—this is being in love,
Armed with *agilitas* and *subtilitas*,
At which few famous lovers even guessed,
Though children may foreknow it, deep in dreams,
10   And ghosts may mourn it, haunting their own tombs,
And peacocks cry it, in default of speech.

Source: Complete Poems In One Volume by Robert Graves, Ed. Patrick Quinn. Copyright © Carcanet Press Limited, December 2000. Reprinted by permission.

2 | Cadence is a general term that refers to sequences of sound and arrangements of accents.

In free verse, cadence refers to a kind of rhythm that is not measurable in stressed and unstressed syllables but in sequences of sound, emphasis, and accent. Even in poetry free of conventional meter, there must be an element of music. In the following poem there may not be standard patterns of sound, but the sounds are certainly being arranged to provide a suitable cadence for the content:

BALL GAME
Richard Eberhart

Caught off first, he leaped to run to second, but
Then struggled back to first.
He left first because of a natural desire
To leap, to get on with the game.
When you jerk to run to second   5
You do not necessarily think of a home run.
You want to go on. You want to get to the next stage,
The entire soul is bent on second base.
The fact is that the mind flashes
Faster in action than the muscles can move.   10
Dramatic! Off first, taut, heading for second,
In a split second, total realization,
Heading for first. Head first! Legs follow fast.
You struggle back to first with victor effort
As, even, after a life of effort and chill,   15
One flashes back to the safety of childhood,
To that strange place where one had first begun.

Source: "The Ball Game," from Collected Poems, 1930–1976 by Richard Eberhart.
Copyright © 1976 by Richard Eberhart. Reprinted by permission of Oxford
University Press, USA.

3 | Scansion is a way of analyzing meter in poetry.

Scanning a poem means diagramming the lines according to
stressed (´) and unstressed (˘) syllables.

When Í dŏ coúnt thĕ clóck thăt télls thĕ tíme . . .
Shakespeare

Diagramming can help to clarify poetic structure.

4 | Meter is the pattern of stressed and unstressed syllables in a line or group of lines or whole poem.

Meter is measured in feet. A foot is usually a stressed syllable with one or more unstressed syllables. The most common meters in English are:

(A) Iambic (˘ ´)

Iambic meters are made of feet or units with an unstressed syllable followed by a stressed syllable (*iambs*). This is the most widely used meter in poetry written in English, perhaps because it seems natural in ordinary speech. These lines are from an anonymous seventeenth-century poem:

> There is a lady sweet and kind,
> Was never face so pleased my mind;
> I did but see her passing by,
> And yet I love her till I die.

(B) Anapestic (˘ ˘ ´)

Anapestic meters are made of units with two unstressed syllables followed by a stressed syllable (*anapests*).

> Oh, the flowers are blooming in England today,
> But her soldiers are dying in lands far away.

(C) Trochaic (´ ˘)

Trochaic meters are made of units with a stressed syllable followed by an unstressed syllable (*trochees*).

> Take me now in midnight darkness.
> Tell me how the morning's brightness
> Robs our love of peaceful lightness.

(D) Dactylic (´ ˇ ˇ)

Dactylic meters are made of units with a stressed syllable followed by two unstressed syllables (*dactyls*).

> Cannon to right of them,
> Cannon to left of them,
> Cannon in front of them
> > Volleyed and thundered . . .
> > **Tennyson, "The Charge of the Light Brigade"**

5 | At times poets make use of five less common kinds of meter.

(A) Monosyllabic rhythm (´)

A single stressed syllable does not meet the conventional definition of a metric foot since it is not accompanied by any unstressed syllables, but lines made up entirely of such syllables do occur occasionally in poetry. They do not occur very often since they would sound like the unrelieved dripping of a faucet. They may be more suitable for chants and cheers, such as the one that begins: "Two, four, six, eight. . . ." On the other hand, some well-known poets have used such lines. Tennyson wrote, "Break, break, break . . ." And in T. S. Eliot's "The Waste Land" we find "Twit twit twit" and "Jug jug jug jug jug." In the following little poem considerable use is made of monosyllabic rhythm:

P.O.P.
Robert DeMaria

> P.O.P.
> Perfectly
> Ordinary
> People.

P.O.P.
pop, POP,
Pop, p.o.p.
popopopopop.
Population.

(B) Spondaic rhythm (´´)

A spondee does not meet the conventional definition of a metric foot, since it is made up of two stressed syllables and no unstressed syllables. A line made up entirely of spondees is rare, but can occasionally be found. An example is Emily Dickinson's "Wild Nights! Wild Nights!" (See Chapter 2.) Spondees are more often used to vary other meters.

(C) Accentual rhythm

In poems that are like songs the accents are very strong and can carry along a lot of miscellaneous unstressed syllables.

Frănkiĕ sh̆e wăs ă goŏd wómăn, Jŏhnnÿ h̆e wăs h̆er mán . . .

The cadence of free verse depends a good deal on accents.

(D) Rising rhythm

Iambic and anapestic meter are considered *rising*, since each foot ends in a stressed syllable.

(E) Falling rhythm

Trochaic and dactylic meter are considered *falling*, since trochees and dactyls begin with a stressed syllable and fall away into unstressed syllables.

6 | The length of a line is measured in metrical units.

The length of a line of poetry can be described in terms of the number of metrical units (feet) used in that line. The conventional terminology follows:

monometer (one unit)
dimeter (two units)
trimeter (three units)
tetrameter (four units)
pentameter (five units)
hexameter (six units)
heptameter (seven units)
octameter (eight units)

Rarely does a line of poetry have more than eight feet. There are certain practical and natural limitations, such as the way we breathe, and the fact that rhyme works better with lines of a reasonable length. Trimeter, tetrameter, and pentameter are the most commonly used line lengths.

7 | Metrical line patterns are determined by the type and number of metrical units.

A full description of a measured line of poetry includes the term that describes the units employed, as well as the term that describes the number of units employed. Many combinations are possible. Here are just a few examples:

(A) Iambic tetrameter

Come líve wǐth me aňd bé my lóve (Marlowe)

(B) Iambic pentameter

Whěn Í do coúnt thě clóck thǎt télls thě tíme (Shakespeare)

(C) Anapestic trimeter

Thĕre wás ă yoŭng gírl ŏf Pĕrú
Who hăd nóthiňg whătévĕr tŏ dó (anonymous)

(D) Anapestic tetrameter

Oh, thĕ flówĕrs ăre bloómiňg iň Eńglaňd tŏdáy (anonymous)

(E) Trochaic pentameter

Névĕr, névĕr, névĕr, névĕr, névĕr! (Shakespeare)

(F) Dactylic dimeter

Cánnŏn tŏ right ŏf thĕm,
Cánnŏn tŏ léft ŏf thĕm, (Tennyson)

8 | Varying the pattern avoids monotony and gives the poet greater freedom.

Poetry is a work of art, not a metronome. A poem that sticks perfectly to its basic meter is in danger of sounding monotonous. Most poems, therefore, have pleasant variations woven into their fabric. These variations also provide poets with the flexibility they need to create a wide range of sounds. A sudden spondee or anapest in a poem of iambic pentameter can introduce some interesting shades and subtleties. This poem is written basically in *iambic tetrameter*, but notice the occasional variations (for example, the monosyllabic stresses in lines three and four and the trochee at the beginning of line six).

THE PASSIONATE SHEPHERD TO HIS LOVE
Christopher Marlowe

Come live with me and be my love,
And we will all the pleasures prove
That valleys, groves, hills, and fields,
Woods, or steepy mountain yields.

And we will sit upon the rocks,   5
Seeing the shepherds feed their flocks,
By shallow rivers to whose falls
Melodious birds sing madrigals.

And I will make thee beds of roses
And a thousand fragrant posies,   10
A cap of flowers, and a kirtle
Embroidered all with leaves of myrtle;

A gown made of the finest wool
Which from our pretty lambs we pull;
Fair lined slippers for the cold,   15
With buckles of the purest gold;

A belt of straw and ivy buds,
With coral clasps and amber studs:
And if these pleasures may thee move,
Come live with me, and be my love.   20

The shepherds' swains shall dance and sing
For thy delight each May morning:
If these delights thy mind may move,
Then live with me and be my love.

11F Patterns and form are essential in literature.

The nature of literary form is complex and controversial. Scholarly wars have been fought over the definition of form, and whole schools of critical thought have been built on a way of defining it.

1 | *Form* and *genre* are sometimes used as synonyms.

Genre is a French word that means *genus*, *type*, or *kind*. It can be used very loosely to classify literary works that have various kinds of things in common. It can be used to refer to works that are grouped by content or by structure. Poetry can be considered a genre, but so can specific kinds of poetry, such as the lyric. The novel might be considered a genre, but so might the epistolary novel or the historical novel. In this sense of the word, drama is a *form* of literature. Comedy, in turn, is a form of drama, and farce is a form of comedy. Some critics may object to using the word form this way, and some may object merely to the looseness with which it is used, but the real controversy has to do with mechanical versus organic form, especially in poetry.

2 | *Mechanical form* suggests that the content of a work can be separated from the techniques by which it is presented.

In such an approach form refers exclusively to those techniques, to structures, and patterns. In poetry, for instance, form is seen as something "external," as a container into which the contents are poured. That form is usually created out of arrangements of rhyme and rhythm. Formalists believe that "form is everything," and that a poem can be judged strictly in terms of its language, style, and structure.

3 | *Organic form* suggests that content cannot be separated from modes of expression.

In this approach the form of a literary work is to be found in the whole work. It is that "internal" force that makes the work cohere, that which unifies it. Content, language, style, structure—all are interrelated. There is no separation between content and container. The artistic vision requires a fusion of all the ingredients. It is simpler to describe mechanical form than it is to describe organic form, but perhaps this is because mechanical form is simplistic. This is why some instructors prefer teaching the mechanical approach over the organic approach. Most modern scholars, however, seem brave enough to pursue all the implications of the concept of form as organic. One of these implications is that the grouping of works by genre and mechanics is not a very significant exercise and not a very valid way to understand a work of art. On the other hand, from our point of view, it might be useful to be aware, at least, of some of the conventional patterns and forms in literature, especially in poetry. (See Chapter 11—f, 6, for a discussion of open form.) The concept of organic form might be applied to the following poem:

MOVING THE CHAIR
Diane Wakoski

I forget how differently
men do things, from women.
At least in the world I prefer. So,
it surprises me to see him move the chair
away from, yes the rather awkward   5
    genteel place where
I've put it. He swings it comfortably over his
tall body, around to the other side

of the table, negotiating in a very small space
with perfect control. Puts the chair in a place   10
where he can lean his elbows on the table,
concentrate.

It surprises me
in the way it might surprise me
if he had suddenly put his arms around me,   15
if I were walking without noticing,
as I often do, and a door were about to hit me.

It surprises me to realize
this physical control. I know I love it
when I watch dancers, and I think I know this   20
when I think about sex,
but what I always forget
is its daily force in certain men.
They are there to hold you
when you might fall. They can   25
make the world more comfortable
just by being able to swing a chair over
their heads and place it perfectly
in a spot you hadn't realized
was even there.   30

Source: "Moving the Chair." From The Archaeology of Movies & Books: Jason
the Sailor by Diane Wakoski. Reprinted by permission of Black Sparrow Books,
an imprint of David R. Godine, Publisher, Inc. Copyright © by Diane Wakoski.

4 | There are certain conventional forms in fiction and drama.

There was a time when certain forces in society, especially in
literary circles, kept poetry very conventional. Today, poetry
has been liberated from these restraints, but, for the most
part, fiction and drama have not. The marketplace may have
a lot to do with it. There's not much money in poetry today

and not much of an audience. The same cannot be said for fiction and drama. Million-dollar deals in mass-market publishing have become commonplace, and television has provided a huge and hungry audience for drama. A large audience tends to create conventions more easily, since there are substantial rewards for those who cater to the general taste, instead of exploring new ways of doing things. The only outlets for experimental work are usually small literary magazines. Such publications have proliferated, but they rarely achieve much circulation.

Formula writing has become widespread in television, film, and fiction. Certain forms dominate these fields. Situation comedies and adventure series, soaps and made-for-television movies have become rigid in format, content, and style. It is hardly necessary to describe the typical sitcom or soap opera. We are all sufficiently familiar with the forms. The same is true of mass-market paperback novels, which are carefully classified according to what the publishers call *genres*, such as romance, science-fiction, fantasy, adventure, mystery, and family saga.

Serious fiction and drama are more daring when it comes to form, but they are still influenced by certain conventions. Most short stories adhere to the conflict-development-resolution sequence. Most narratives are chronological. A few manipulate past and present or objective and subjective elements. Shorter fiction is usually written without major breaks or sections. Longer fiction may be divided into numbered parts. In the novel, the chapter is still the dominant subdivision.

Plays are divided into acts and scenes—usually three acts. Shakespeare preferred five, a convention of *his* time. One-act plays tend to adhere to unity of time and place and employ a single set and very few characters.

Of course, there are refreshing exceptions to these conventions, but they rarely attract sufficient attention to become widely known. This should not discourage the serious writer, whose real satisfaction must come from artistic success rather than financial reward. However, it is not a happy situation, and literary history is full of stories of great authors who spent their lives in misery and poverty only to be recognized posthumously. In an age of mass communication and pandemic materialism the idealism necessary for honest artistic achievement becomes more and more difficult.

5 | There are certain conventional patterns in poetry.

When we talk about conventional patterns in poetry we are usually referring to mechanical form. Since contemporary poetry has become so dominated by free verse (free-form, open-form verse), there are some instructors who feel that it is not even worthwhile reviewing the conventional patterns. Some even feel that there is some risk of restraining or stifling the young poet. These extreme views, fortunately, do not prevent most workshops from discussing certain traditional patterns of rhyme and rhythm. Let us consider, then, some of the conventional ways in which the lines of a poem have been organized or grouped.

(A) The stanza

In measured poems a stanza is a grouping of lines that tends to have a well-defined form in terms of rhythm and usually rhyme. When a poem has more than one stanza, the pattern is usually repeated throughout. Stanzas can be as simple as the two-line couplet or as complex as the nine-line Spenserian stanza or the stanzaic sonnet of fourteen lines. The following terminology is used to describe the length of a stanza:

> couplet (two lines)
> tercet (three lines)

quatrain (four lines)
pentastich or cinquain (five lines)
sestet (six lines)
septet (seven lines)
octave (eight lines)

(B) Couplets, tercets, and quatrains

These groupings of lines have often been called the building blocks of poetry, since, more often than not, they serve as stanzas in longer poems, though they can stand alone as complete poems. Any meter can be used in these basic line groupings, but the rhyming possibilities are rather limited.

A couplet can only use *aa*. Tercets generally use *aaa* or *aba*. Quatrains often use *abab*, but sometimes *abba* or some other configuration, especially if the rhyming runs on into the next stanza.

(C) Couplets

Two-liners are often used in epitaphs, such as this one from Kipling's "Epitaphs of the War":

> If any question why we died,
> Tell them, because our fathers lied.

Aside from epitaphs there aren't too many two-line poems, but here is one by Ben Jonson called "To Fool or Knave":

> Thy praise or dispraise is to me alike;
> One doth not stroke me, nor the other strike.

The *heroic couplet* is two rhyming lines in iambic pentameter. It was once a popular form used in epic poetry and poetic drama, but it is not found very often in modern verse. There are plenty of examples in the work of Alexander Pope

(1688–1744)—these often quoted lines from "An Essay on Criticism," for instance:

> A little learning is a dangerous thing;
> Drink deep, or taste not the Pierian spring:

There is an unusual use of couplets with repeated sounds and an overall pattern in "For Virginia Kidd" by Ursula K. Le Guin:

FOR VIRGINIA KIDD
Ursula K. Le Guin

> The patience of women
> is stupid and beautiful as the patience of donkeys.
>
> The impatience of men
> is stupid and terrible as the impatience of horses.
>
> 5　The impatience of women
> is like thunderstorms among mountains.
>
> The patience of men
> is like streams in the valleys.

Source: "For Virginia Kidd," copyright © 1988 by Ursula K LeGuin. From Wild Oats and Firewood. Reprinted by permission of the author and the author's agent, Virginia Kidd.

(D) Tercets

Stanzas of three lines with a rhyming pattern that is sometimes linked to subsequent stanzas, as in *terza rima* ("third rhyme"), an Italian form that rhymes the middle line of each tercet with the first and third lines of the following tercet. One of the most famous examples in English literature is Shelley's "Ode to the West Wind," which begins:

Oh wild West Wind, thou breath of Autumn's being,
Thou, from whose unseen presence the leaves dead
Are driven, like ghosts from an enchanter fleeing,

Another well-known poem written in tercets rhymes all three lines in each stanza (*aaa*) and uses iambic tetrameter. It is "Upon Julia's Clothes," by Robert Herrick (1591–1674):

UPON JULIA'S CLOTHES

Whenas in silks my Julia goes,
Then, then, methinks, how sweetly flows
That liquefaction of her clothes.

Next, when I cast mine eyes, and see
5   That brave vibration, each way free,
O, how that glittering taketh me!

Poems consisting of just one tercet are fairly rare, but Ben Jonson has given us this:

ON SPIES

Spies, you are lights in state, but of base stuff,
Who, when you've burnt yourselves down to the snuff,
Stink and are thrown away. End fair enough.

(E) Quatrains

The four-line stanza with a rhyme scheme is the workhorse of poetry. It is long enough to produce a complete and viable poem, but is more commonly used as a building block in longer poems. Quatrains lend themselves either to long lines or to lines that are brief and swift-moving. They are as appropriate for light verse as they are for serious themes. This example from Lord Byron is on the amusing side:

[WHEN A MAN HATH NO FREEDOM TO FIGHT FOR AT HOME]

When a man hath no freedom to fight for at home,
  Let him combat for that of his neighbors;
Let him think of the glories of Greece and of Rome,
  And get knocked on his head for his labors.

5   To do good to mankind is the chivalrous plan,
  And is always as nobly requited;
Then battle for freedom wherever you can,
  And, if not shot or hanged, you'll get knighted.

(F) More complex stanzas

A brief mention here of some of the longer and more complex stanzas should be sufficient to indicate just how long and complex they can be:

  Rhyme royal: seven lines of iambic pentameter (*ababbcc*)
  Ottava rima: eight lines of iambic pentameter (*abababcc*)
  Spenserian stanza: nine lines, eight of them iambic pentameter, one of them iambic hexameter (*ababbcbcc*)

Some of our complete poetic forms have been around for a long time and are very conventional. Some of us forget, because we are living in a free-verse era, that for thousands of years and in cultures all over the world, poetry was full of conventions. Not only did tradition fix the forms of poetry, but it often determined the content and even the very wording.

The ancient Greeks brought formal poetry to a high level of sophistication that covered a wide range from the lyric to the epic to the poetic drama. The word *lyric*, in fact, comes from the Greek. Originally it meant a poem accompanied by a musical instrument, usually a lyre. Formalism was dominant throughout the development of English poetry. It has only been in the decades since World War I that there has been a widespread break with traditional forms, a natural reflection of the rebellion against *all* traditional forms, political, moral, and aesthetic. This modern artistic freedom is the main characteristic of contemporary poetry, but some of the sturdier conventional forms still survive, among them *sonnets*, *ballads*, and *limericks*.

(G) Sonnets

The sonnet was imported to England in the sixteenth century from Italy, where it was developed during the Renaissance. It has fourteen lines and a rhyme scheme. The meter is usually iambic pentameter. The sonnet has survived for five hundred years because it is a useful form for the development of a single idea. The most famous collection of sonnets (154 of them) was written by Shakespeare, but almost every major poet has been drawn to the form, from Spenser to Donne to Edna St. Vincent Millay and more contemporary poets.

The Shakespearean sonnet, though it is a complete stanza in itself, has within it three quatrains in which alternate lines rhyme (*abab*) and a rhyming couplet that usually contains a concluding thought. The Petrarchan sonnet, which is not nearly as popular, is made of an octave (*abbaabba*) and a sestet (*cdcdcd*, or some other variation). The Petrarchan sonnet is also known as the Italian sonnet. Here is an example of each of these types of sonnets. Notice that the rhyme scheme in Donne's Petrarchan sonnet is *abbaabbacddcee*.

SONNET 94
William Shakespeare

They that have power to hurt and will do none,
That do not do the thing they most do show,
Who, moving others, are themselves as stone,
Unmoved, cold, and to temptation slow;
They rightly do inherit heaven's graces   5
And husband nature's riches from expense;
They are the lords and owners of their faces,
Others but stewards of their excellence.
The summer's flower is to the summer sweet,
Though to itself it only live and die,   10
But if that flower with base infection meet,
The basest weed outbraves his dignity:
For sweetest things turn sourest by their deeds;
Lilies that fester smell far worse than weeds.

SONNET 10
John Donne

Death, be not proud, though some have
    calléd thee
Mighty and dreadful, for thou are not so;
For those whom thou think'st thou dost
    overthrow
                                                          5
Die not, poor Death, nor yet canst thou kill me.
From rest and sleep, which but thy pictures be,
Much pleasure; then from thee much more
    must flow,
And soonest our best men with thee do go,   10
Rest of their bones, and soul's delivery.
Thou'art slave to fate, chance, kings,
    and desperate men,
And dost with poison, war, and sickness dwell,

And poppy' or charms can make us sleep as well   15
And better than thy stroke; why swell'st
    thou then?
One short sleep past, we wake eternally
And death shall be no more; Death, thou
    shalt die.   20

(H) Ballads

A ballad is a narrative poem easily remembered because of
its simple stanza construction: four lines rhyming *abab* or
abcb, with four accented syllables in the first and third lines
and three in the second and fourth lines. Sometimes a refrain is added to each stanza. Ballads are often anonymous.
Since they are handed down orally, there may be many variations of the same tale.

FRANKIE AND JOHNNY
Anonymous

Frankie and Johnny were lovers,
    Lordy, how they could love,
Swore to be true to each other,
    True as the stars up above,
        He was her man, but he done her wrong.   5

Frankie went down to the corner,
    To buy her a bucket of beer,
Frankie says "Mister Bartender,
    Has my lovin' Johnny been here?
        He is my man, but he's doing me wrong."   10

"I don't want to cause you no trouble
    Don't want to tell you no lie,

I saw your Johnny half-an-hour ago
   Making love to Nelly Bly.
      He is your man, but he's doing you wrong."   **15**

Frankie went down to the hotel
   Looked over the transom so high,
There she saw her lovin Johnny
   Making love to Nelly Bly.
      He was her man; he was doing her wrong.   **20**

Frankie threw back her kimono,
   Pulled out her big forty-four;
Rooty-toot-toot: three times she shot
   Right through that hotel door,
      She shot her man, who was doing her wrong. **25**

"Roll me over gently,
   Roll me over slow,
Roll me over on my right side,
   'Cause these bullets hurt me so,
      I was your man, but I done you wrong."   **30**

Bring all your rubber-tired hearses
   Bring all your rubber-tired hacks,
They're carrying poor Johnny to the burying ground
   And they ain't gonna bring him back,
      He was her man, but he done her wrong.   **35**

Frankie says to the sheriff,
   "What are they going to do?"
The sheriff he said to Frankie,
   "It's the 'lectric chair for you.
      He was your man, and he done you wrong."   **40**

"Put me in that dungeon,
    Put me in that cell,
Put me where the northeast wind
    Blows from the southeast corner of hell,
        I shot my man, 'cause he done me wrong."   **45**

(I) Limericks

Limerick is a county in Ireland, and legend has it that this light and amusing and sometimes naughty poetic form originated there. A limerick consists of five lines that rhyme *aabba*. There are three stresses in the first, second, and fifth lines, and there are two stresses in the third and fourth lines. Limericks are often anonymous.

There was a young girl of Peru
Who had nothing whatever to do,
    So she sat on the stairs
    And counted her hairs—
Six thousand, four hundred, and two.   **5**

(J) Other forms

There are many other traditional forms, one of which is worth mentioning here, partly because it is used by Dylan Thomas in his widely appreciated poem, "Do Not Go Gentle into That Good Night." This poem is a *villanelle*, which consists of six stanzas—five tercets and a quatrain. There are only two rhymes: *aba, aba, aba, aba, aba, abaa*. The lines tend to have five stresses and to be iambic.

DO NOT GO GENTLE INTO THAT GOOD NIGHT

Do not go gentle into that good night,
Old age should burn and rave at close of day;
Rage, rage against the dying of the light.

Though wise men at their end know dark is right,
5 Because their words had forked no lightning they
Do not go gentle into that good night.

Good men, the last wave by, crying how bright
Their frail deeds might have danced in a green bay,
Rage, rage against the dying of the light.

10 Wild men who caught and sang the sun in flight,
And learn, too late, they grieved it on its way,
Do not go gentle into that good night.

Grave men, near death, who see with blinding sight
Blind eyes could blaze like meteors and be gay,
15 Rage, rage against the dying of the light,

And you, my father, there on the sad height,
Curse, bless, me now with your fierce tears, I pray.

Do not go gentle into that good night.
Rage, rage against the dying of the light.

(K) Blank verse

Any poetry written in unrhymed lines of iambic pentameter is called *blank verse*. These lines can be arranged in stanzas or they can go on indefinitely, as in poetic drama, where they have proven extremely effective, especially in Shakespeare's plays. Blank verse appeared in England in the sixteenth century. Though some minor authors first made use of it in drama, it was Christopher Marlowe, born the same year as Shakespeare, who first used it brilliantly. One of his most famous passages is from *Doctor Faustus*:

> Was this the face that launched a thousand ships,
> And burnt the topless towers of Ilium?
> Sweet Helen, make me immortal with a kiss.
> Her lips suck forth my soul: see where it flies.
> Come, Helen, come give me my soul again.
> Here will I dwell, for heaven is in those lips,
> And all is dross that is not Helena.

(Act V, scene i)

(L) Graphic forms

Poems designed for the eye can be considered along the same lines as those that have mechanical requirements, though they can also be considered with free verse because they are not subject to the usual conventions of rhyme and rhythm. Many poems have a visual dimension, but some poems depend *primarily* on the visual. The author actually draws a picture or design with his words, as in the case of this famous mouse's tale (tail) in *Alice's Adventures in Wonderland*:

Fury said to a
mouse, That he
met in the
house,
"Let us
both go
to law:
I will
prosecute
you. Come, I'll
take no denial;
We must
have a trial:
For really
this morning
I've nothing
to do."
Said the
mouse to the
cur, "Such a
trial,
dear Sir,
With no
jury or
judge,
would be
wasting
our breath."
"I'll be judge,
I'll be jury,"
Said
cunning
old Fury:
"I'll
try the
whole
cause,
and
condemn
you
to
death."

(6) Free verse (open form) has no rigid patterns of rhyme and rhythm.

Robert Frost said that free verse is "like playing tennis with the net down." The remark suggests that it is not only easier to write free verse but also unfair, not playing the game according to the rules. The formalists would applaud him; the believers in organic form would not. Furthermore, they might even object to the term *free verse* on the grounds that it suggests freedom from form. They tend to prefer the terms *free form* or *open form.*

The use of free verse in the twentieth century has a good deal to do with the search for a more natural way of using the English language. Poets such as Ezra Pound and William Carlos Williams objected to the artificiality and awkwardness created by the attempt to stay within traditional principles that we inherited from ancient Greece and Rome via literary giants such as Milton. A rapidly changing and democratic society such as America could not put up with the rigidity of formal poetry for long. Inevitably, American poetry found its own voice in a freer approach, a more natural language. The frontier country that embraced Huckleberry Finn could hardly feel at home with the rigid formalness of Milton.

Since all poetry has *some* form, "free form" is a bit misleading. By free verse we mean a way of making effective sounds without counting accents and syllables systematically. In addition, free-form verse does not depend on strict rhyming; it depends more on diction, cadence, and tone for its "music." The chief characteristic of free verse is "infinite variety," but the bottom line is a verbal creation that pleases the ear, the mind, and even the eye, whether it is achieved with free form or closed form.

With so much variety it is difficult to categorize free verse. The only approach that makes sense is to discuss each poem individually, to explore its language, its imagery, its cadence, and especially that central mystery that holds it all together and gives it unity and significance.

In the following poem what we have is a visual image that captures a boy's reaction to the death of his father. The simple language is part of the whole effect. The cadence, too, is simple and childlike.

UPON LEARNING OF HIS FATHER'S DEATH
Fred Byrnes

> A sandy-haired boy
> in a flannel shirt
> stands on a dirt road
> with dust swirling
> 5   Hands in blue-jean pockets
> fingering a fifty-cent piece
> Wishing he could come home

Here is another free-form poem, this one about a mother. Notice how the title becomes part of the poem. There is no conventional structure here, no rhyme scheme or pattern of accents, though the general cadence of the first stanza seems echoed in the second stanza. It might have been written as prose, but something would have been lost. There is a visual dimension as the poem stands, and each line emphasizes something. The concise language sharpens the sustained image—the mother as protector and predator, as hawk and owl.

MY RIGHT EYE
Siv Cedering Fox

is a hawk
that circles all night
looking for the small mice
of dreams
to run out from under   5
my pillow.

My left eye is an owl
alert in its hollow
waiting for nightmares to come
on the wings   10
of bats.
In the morning

I am the predator
returning from my hunt,
the gatherer come back   15
to my nest.
My family is fed.
My eyes ache.

7 | Technique is not enough to create a good poem; the statement or vision is also important.

In 1991 *The Mississippi Review* invited poets to respond to the following observation: *It has sometimes been said that contemporary poetry, however technically brilliant, lacks statement or vision.* Here are a few quotations from the responses:

> *At present, poetry suffers from the curse of mere competence. Many poets string words skillfully together, but the results lack soul, passion, and inspiration.*

Jack Anderson

What the reader wants to know is how he really feels and how the poet really feels.

R. P. Dickey

Most American poetry isn't about anything.

Stephen Dobyns

Poets obsessed with form and little else are easy to forget.

Dave Etter

The problem with contemporary poetry is that it is afflicted with all too much vision and statement and all too little technical brilliance.

William Logan

I prefer poetry that knows what it has to say only after the poem is written.

Paul Hoover

All poets write from some personal vision of our world, and American poets often address our society's concerns clearly and directly . . .

Peter Meinke

There is more to poetry than mere truth.

Bin Ramke

. . . contemporary poetry is no model of technical brilliance. And neither does it possess large statements or visions . . .

Peter Wild

EXAMPLE 11A

WHAT LIPS MY LIPS HAVE KISSED
Edna St. Vincent Millay

What lips my lips have kissed, and where, and why,
I have forgotten, and what arms have lain
Under my head till morning; but the rain
Is full of ghosts tonight, that tap and sigh
Upon the glass and listen for reply,   5
And in my heart there stirs a quiet pain
For unremembered lads that not again
Will turn to me at midnight with a cry.
Nor knows what birds have vanished one by one,
Thus in the winter stands the lonely tree,   10
Yet knows its boughs more silent than before:
I cannot say what loves have come and gone;
I only know that summer sang in me
A little while, that in me sings no more.

EXAMPLE 11B

ASHES IN JULY
Laura Albrecht

He sits on the stairs
Half a flight above me,
Flipping through
A shiny magazine,
5   Humming a saxophone
Solo like a nursery
Rhyme melody.
The back of my head,
Hair blowing
10   In the hot south
Wind, reflects
In the silver lenses
Of his sunglasses,
Superimposed over
15   Flash reflections
Of blue jean
And vodka ads
From the moving pages
Of his magazine.
20   He brings a lit
Cigarette to his mouth
And inhales,
Taste of sweat
Salt on his lips.
25   He tilts his head
Back to stare
At the swollen sun,
To feel its white
Warmth on his chin,

30   His cheekbones and ears.
    His ashes slip
    And blow down
    Into my dark hair,
    Dot the back
35   Of my bare arm,
    cling to my damp
    Fingers like soft
    Dissolving flakes
    Of his singed magazine,
40   Of his burnt skin.
    I notice his humming
    Has quieted
    And tilt my head back.
    The sun seems larger
45   And there isn't
    One white cloud in sight.

Source: "Ashes in July," by Laura Albrecht. From The Ledge, No. 12, 1991.
Reprinted by permission of The Ledge Magazine & Press.

EXAMPLE 11C

ACTS OF GOD
Howard Nemerov

Are exhibitions of bad taste on a scale
Beyond belief, filling your living room
With mud or lava, blowing the schoolhouse roof
Down on the parking lot, tossing the boats
5   Out of the marina and smashing them across
The highway's back, piquantly fixing for
The earthquake to catch his people on their knees
Good Friday morning; if Attila the Hun
Had done the hundredth part of what God does
10   You wouldn't ask him to dinner at your house.
But God gets away with it time and time again
And gets adored for doing it as well
As lest he do it to us another time.
The hope is our prayers will make Him nicer, but
15   It don't look likely, and to make it worse
An Act of God is anything at all
That lets the insurance people off the hook.

EXAMPLE 11D

USES OF THE IMPERATIVE
Mary Baine Campbell

Stop grieving. Try on rage.
See how the wind of it
Explodes among the clouds
Announcing blue. Listen.
To the fast new song of smithereens.
Let fire loose in the trash.
Hose down the mold of grief
Till your skin burns.
Grief colonized you like a virus.
Go swimming in blood.
Destroy what you can.

Does winter fester with the lost
Love of summer? No.
It kills everything in sight.
On the other side of the world
Enormous flowers rage
Into an opposing bloom.

Source: "Uses of the Imperative," from The World, the Flesh and Angels by
Mary Baine Campbell. Copyright © 1989 by Mary Baine Campbell. Reprinted
by permission of the author.

EXAMPLE 11E

OCTOBER OBSERVED, HUDSON FALLS IN BILL'S BACKYARD

(for William Bronk)
Richard Elman

The whole afternoon glistening
on a string-bean pole. The beans
toughening to that light
are big hard gray
green beans,
dirty fingers reaching
toward this light
above the rotten melon heads,
half-gnawed tomatoes,
and cucumber scars,
a last spray of cornflowers,
almost as pale as
this cold cloudless sky.
The cat's learning to fly—
to feed 3 baby birds
on the roof of
his mouth. The enormity
of their tiny separate
gaping needs
and his fiercely furred shadows.

Source: "October Observed, Hudson Falls, In Bill's Backyard," from Cathedral-Tree-Train (Junction Press, NY, 1992). Reprinted by permission.

EXAMPLE 11F

LEGACY

(For Blues People)
Imamu Amiri Baraka

In the south, sleeping against
the drugstore, growling under
the trucks and stoves, stumbling
through and over the cluttered eyes
of early mysterious night. Frowning
drunk waving moving a hand or lash.
Dancing kneeling reaching out, letting
a hand rest in shadows. Squatting
to drink or pee. Stretching to climb
pulling themselves onto horses near
where there was sea (the old songs
lead you to believe). Riding out
from this town, to another, where
it is also black. Down a road
where people are asleep. Towards
the moon or the shadows of houses.
Towards the songs' pretended sea.

Source: "Legacy," from Black Magic. Copyright © 1969 by Amiri Baraka. Reprinted by permission of SLL/Sterling Lord Literistic, Inc.

EXERCISES

Discussion

1. Describe the structure of "What Lips My Lips Have Kissed" (Example 11a) by Edna St. Vincent Millay. Is it a Shakespearean sonnet? Comment on the imagery and the meaning.

2. Discuss the form of "Ashes in July" (Example 11b) by Laura Albrecht. Would you call this a narrative poem? Is there any suspense? Comment on the descriptive details.

3. Is "Acts of God" (Example 11c) by Howard Nemerov a poem that has open or closed form? What central idea does it deal with?

4. Comment on the form of "Uses of the Imperative" (Example 11d) by Mary Baine Campbell. What does the title mean? Describe the tone, imagery, and language of the poem.

5. In Example 11e Richard Elman captures a certain moment in time. How does he fix this moment in the reader's mind? Comment on the setting.

Writing

1. Write a sonnet in either the Petrarchan or Shakespearean fashion.

2. Write a poem about some aspect of nature, using as many images as possible.

3. Write a poem in which you make *allusions* to at least *four* of the following: Venus, Prometheus, Job, Adam and Eve, the Apocalypse, Atlantis, Caesar, Napoleon, the Crusades, Babylon, Watergate, Woodstock, Disneyland, Hollywood, Dracula, Frankenstein.

4. Write a quatrain in iambic tetrameter that rhymes *abab*.

5. Complete a poem in *anapestic tetrameter* that begins: Oh, the flowers are blooming in summer today, But our soldiers are dying in lands far away.

6. Write three limericks.

7. Write a ballad, with or without a refrain.

8. Write a free-verse poem about something one of the following titles might suggest:

> Going to the Mall
> The Winter Solstice
> Children of the Night
> The Graveyard Shift at Seven Eleven
> Discovering Old Toys in Dark Places
> Falling in Love with Faraway Places
> Eyes that Smile and Lips that Lie

The Performance Factor: Plays and Film Scripts

Literary works that are intended for some kind of production have to take into account the advantages and limitations of "the performance factor." In a sense, such works of art are not complete until the vision in the writer's mind is translated into a live or electronic medium. It is the job of the writer to indicate as clearly as possible what that vision is. But it is the job of the director to make that vision come alive on stage or screen. The final result is a collaboration, just as a concert is a collaboration between the composer and the musicians who perform the work. Although play-writing for any medium (stage, film, or television) has much in common with poetry and fiction, it is often taken up separately in writing workshops because of production technicalities and because a somewhat different relationship exists between the work and its audience. Poetry and fiction are usually read privately, though there are times when they are read aloud to an audience. Plays are very rarely written simply to be read. They are intended for an audience of some kind or another, either the theater audience that gathers for a collective experience, or the scattered and anonymous audience that watches television under a variety of circumstances. These work-and-viewer differences have to be taken into account by the writer.

12A Plays for the stage.

1 | Stage plays involve an interaction between the performers and the audience.

The stage play is still generally considered the most effective way to present a drama. On the stage we can see real people acting out human dramas, crying and laughing, loving and hating. No two- or even three-dimensional arrangement of light particles on a screen can bring an audience closer to reality, in spite of the current claims made for "virtual reality." What is it, exactly, that happens in the theater? The audience sits in the dark. The stage is lit up. The actors wear costumes and makeup. It is all like a dream. The audience slips into the shadows. The stage becomes reality. Vicariously, we experience what goes on there. Aristotle knew this and described it in his *Poetics* two thousand four hundred years ago. There's a kind of magic in the whole experience. We feel the "pity and fear" and other intense emotions in a tragedy, and we emerge from the drama purified in some way, relieved of certain anxieties, at least for the moment. Aristotle called it *catharsis*, and the term has survived as a way of describing the dramatic experience. And the survival of live drama in a hi-tech world is evidence that it has something special to offer.

Writing for the stage is not the same as writing for film or television. The writer has to keep in mind certain important things.

2 | The live stage has its physical limitations.

Students who are writing plays for the first time and have been drenched in television occasionally forget that a live play has its limitations. Not everything can be shown. A character cannot leap on his or her horse and gallop across the desert in pursuit of his or her enemy. Car chases are also out. Realistic battle scenes are virtually impossible. Quick cuts, montages, and fantastic special effects all belong to other media. Students accustomed to the flexibility of film and television often feel restrained and frustrated when they have to write for a real stage, but it is very important to work within these limitations. With imagination a great deal can be done, but it is not a good idea to get too ambitious. When Shakespeare needed a battle scene he usually put a few armed men on a knoll and allowed them to talk about what they saw in the distance, which is, of course, offstage. Sometimes reports of major actions came through messengers, who delivered eloquent descriptions of important events. In modern times, the messenger has been replaced by the telephone or perhaps a radio or television news report.

3 | Settings are usually simple, especially in one-act plays.

Even the most elaborate stage settings cannot compete with what can be done on film or on television. Stage designers over the years have devised numerous means to suggest more than what can actually be seen on stage. A partially framed structure can suggest a house in which several rooms are visible. A few sticks of furniture can suggest a bedroom or living room. A painted backdrop can suggest the great outdoors. Too many scene changes can present problems. Props have to be moved around. The curtain has to come down. There are delays that break the tension of the play. Many successful, long-running plays have relied on a single set, and almost all one-act plays use a single uncomplicated set. Since most one-act plays only run about fifteen to thirty minutes, there really isn't enough time for scene changes. The action is usually limited to one location.

4 | It is an advantage to have a limited cast of characters in a stage play.

Old epic movies used to promise "a cast of thousands." That sort of promise could never be made about stage plays. There simply isn't room enough. It would also be too expensive, even if it could be done. The revenues from stage plays are not nearly as high as the revenues from films and television productions. In any case, it is more practical to have a limited cast for a lot of other reasons. Characters have to be introduced. We have to get to know them. The fewer the characters, the more we get to know about them. Most full-length plays rarely have more than half a dozen significant characters, and one-act plays often have only two or three. The ideal range seems to be two to five. Some plays have only one character, but these plays turn into monologues. Dialogue is, by definition, impossible unless there are at least two characters involved.

5 | There are various ways to show how time passes on stage.

In plays with several acts a significant passage of time might logically occur between the acts. Sometimes a new scene means a new time frame. If a lot of time passes, we are usually informed about it in the dialogue. Sometimes the costuming and set can also be used for this purpose. Incidental passages of time, such as from night to morning, can be shown by traditional devices, such as lighting—a darkened window that gradually grows lighter, for instance, as the sun rises. A momentary darkening of the stage has also been used to show time passing. This is almost like the brief closing of the curtain, but less cumbersome. Most one-act plays avoid the problem of passing time. They take place in a unified period, just as they take place in a single location.

6 | Dialogue has many functions in a stage play.

In a novel a writer can tell us as much as he or she wants us to know about his or her characters and the events they are involved in. A play, on the other hand, is not a story told to us, but a story *acted out*. There is usually no narrator to provide us with background information and explanations, though such a device is not unknown in the theater. The Greek chorus, in fact, sometimes served this function in antiquity, and, more recently, Thornton Wilder used a commentator who talked directly to the audience in *Our Town*. More commonly, the burden falls on the characters, and the principal device for revealing information is dialogue. The characters can talk about the past, present, and future. They can talk to each other about characters who are not present. They can speculate about who the murderer is in a mystery. They can make confessions of love. They can tell us in monologues or dialogues about how they feel. Shakespeare was fond of the formal soliloquy ("To be or not to be . . .") and that device still appears at times in contemporary drama. In dialogue, characters can tell us where they are, what time period they are in, and what's going on in the rest of the world ("News, lads, our wars are done," says a messenger in *Othello*).

It's no wonder, then, that some people think that a play is merely a handful of people standing around talking to one another. In most film and television dramas there is a lot less talk because more can be shown.

7 | Action is necessary to keep a drama from being static.

If all that a play needed was dialogue, there would be no point in asking the audience to sit still with their eyes glued on the stage. They need more than a couple of people talking to each other to keep their attention. There has to be some action. Sometimes the action is minor. The characters get up and sit down, walk across the stage, open a door, answer the phone, and so on. Sometimes it is major, even violent (Othello smothers Desdemona). The visual element is as important in comedy as it is in tragedy. There are pratfalls and disguises and all sort of amusing entrances and exits. One-act plays often run the risk of being all talk, since the plot is usually very limited. It is up to both the writer and the director to make sure that the audience has something interesting to look at.

8 | Proper script form is necessary to guide the actors and the director.

A manuscript for a play written for the stage must take into account certain practical considerations.

(A) Characters

The names of the characters must be clearly indicated, so that the actors can see at a glance who speaks the lines. The names of the characters sometimes appear in capital letters at the left-hand margin and are followed by a colon, while the rest of the script is indented. Some writers prefer to indent the names of the characters and bring everything else back to the margin.

(B) Dialogue

The dialogue must be clearly separated from all other notations. It begins immediately after the colon, unless there are some intervening stage directions. If the dialogue continues for more than one line, all subsequent lines are indented, using the standard paragraph indentation of five spaces.

(C) Stage directions

The stage directions must appear in a form that distinguishes them from the dialogue. They are italicized (underlined) and often placed in parentheses.

(D) Notations

Notations about how the character is to deliver certain lines (for example, *angrily, playfully*) can be distinguished from ordinary stage directions by being italicized and placed in parentheses after the character's name and before the colon.

There is obviously some flexibility in the above form, and you will find considerable variety in published play-scripts. Some writers indent the characters' names and bring everything else back to the left-hand margin. Some use italics for stage directions, but not parentheses. In anthologies the publisher usually selects a format that is consistent throughout the collection.

In addition to using a clear manuscript form, the playwright must provide some introductory information: a *cast of characters* and an indication of *time* and *place* (scene). Some writers are very concise about this information; others are quite detailed. G. B. Shaw's introductory material, for instance, was often very elaborate.

Here is a brief example of the most commonly used playscript form. It is the beginning of a one-act play (or possibly a longer play) created merely as an illustration. You may want to try your hand at completing it.

INTIMATE STRANGERS

CHARACTERS

LAURA HOLMAN, *an attractive young woman, 21, from Boston.*
PAUL CONRAD, *a handsome, experienced man of 30 or so.*

TIME

The present, mid-summer

PLACE

A hotel room in the Berkshire Mountains of Massachusetts

(The stage grows light as someone draws open the curtains of the sliding glass doors that lead to a narrow terrace. The room is done in a typical modern resort style. It is neat and functional. LAURA wakes up. She is scantily dressed and looks confused. When her eyes settle on PAUL, who is silhouetted against the window, she is startled.)

PAUL Good morning, Mrs. Conrad!

LAURA (*holding her head and squinting her eyes because of the sunlight*). Mrs. Conrad? (*She looks around, as though there might be another woman in the room.*) Who's Mrs. Conrad?

PAUL (*smiling*). You are, sweetheart. (*He advances toward the bed.*)

LAURA (*holding a sheet to her breast and shrinking away*). Now, wait a minute. Let me think. This is all a dream, right?

PAUL (*as though he assumes she is joking*). Right! And I hope we never wake up.

LAURA (*frowning*). I remember a lot of champagne bottles.

PAUL We had a party.

LAURA Who was there?

PAUL Just me and you, darling. (*He sits on the bed.*)

LAURA What was the occasion?

PAUL The anniversary of our first meeting.

LAURA But that was just a week ago at the Beacon. I remember that. I had had a big fight with my mother and step-father and told them I was moving out. I called Mary, my college roommate, and she said she'd put me up for a while. Then I guess I went to the Beacon for a drink. I was upset, naturally.

PAUL There were tears in your eyes when I saw you sitting alone. I couldn't resist asking you what was wrong. We had a long talk. Later, you said you loved me. I felt the same way. It was all very sudden—love at first sight, I guess.

LAURA (*beginning to remember*). That's what it felt like at the time.

PAUL I called you up the next day and asked you to marry me.

LAURA I thought it was a joke.

PAUL But you said *yes*.

LAURA You said something about spending the weekend together.

PAUL Well, we did—I mean, we are. Only it's not an ordinary weekend; it's our honeymoon.

LAURA (*shaking her head.*) I must have really been out of it!

PAUL You were very happy.

LAURA It must have been the champagne.

PAUL You mean, you don't remember?

LAURA I do and I don't. The details are a little fuzzy. (*She looks at her left hand and sees a wedding ring there.*)

PAUL We drove across the border and found a justice of the peace.

LAURA A white house with green shutters?

PAUL Yes.

LAURA Next to a church and a graveyard?

PAUL That's right!

LAURA Oh, my God!

PAUL You're not sorry, are you?

LAURA No! Yes! I mean, I don't know. It's all sort of crazy. We hardly know each other.

PAUL When you fall in love, nothing else is worth knowing.

LAURA Why didn't we wait?

PAUL If we had waited, you might have changed your mind. When we first met you told me how much you hated the way your head ruled your heart, and how you have never allowed yourself to fall in love.

LAURA If I had been sober, I guess I'd never be here.

PAUL (*moving closer and becoming amorous*). That's right. Now, aren't you glad we *are* here?

LAURA (*holding him off*). Actually, I don't even know where we are, and—and, don't be offended, Paul, but I don't know anything about you. Where do you live? What do you do?

PAUL What difference does it make? I'll take good care of you. We'll be very happy.

LAURA (*charmed by his handsomeness and manner, but frightened by his evasiveness*). I need some coffee or something. I don't feel very well.

PAUL I'm not surprised. We've been to the moon and back. This is the planet Earth, darling. Welcome back to reality.

(to be continued)

12B Scripts for film and television.

A screenplay for film or television is not just a stage play put on film or tape and shown on a screen. It is a drama written and produced for an entirely different medium. And that medium is fairly recent, compared to the antiquity of live drama. It dates back merely decades, not centuries or millennia. The writer of screenplays has to be fully aware of how this medium works—its technological advantages and its theatrical limitations. Only a few points can be touched on here. Workshops in writing for film and television usually require specialized textbooks.

1 | Plays for the screen have no interaction between players and audience.

Characters on a screen may give wonderful performances, but they are not really there. They do not hear the applause, if there is any. They do not hear the laughter or sense the tears. And the performance they give is always exactly the same, since it's merely on film or tape. This makes the experience of going to the movies or watching television very different from the experience of going to the theater to see a live play. It is true, however, that going to the movies is still a collective experience, since people actually leave their homes and gather in a theater to watch, simultaneously, a play on a large screen. Though this audience cannot have any effect on what is happening on the screen, they can have some effect on one another. Most people prefer to be part of a large enthusiastic audience rather than a small and scattered group. It is probably for this reason that movie houses still survive. Technologically, television has almost made them obsolete, especially as the television screens get larger and larger. But a distinction remains and the writer has to keep it in mind. Going to the movies is a communal experience with a larger-than-life screen, and watching television is something that happens in the privacy of one's home and involves a much smaller screen and often an audience of only one or two people. While watching television, people can move around, eat and drink and even fall asleep. Video tapes allow them to schedule their own shows and to stop the action anytime they want. They can also rewind, repeat, go fast forward, turn off the sound, and so on. And for some people television is just a private dream-machine for insomniacs. Ironically, however, while people are watching a major event alone in their homes, they may very well be part of a vast audience of twenty million people or more. All of this the writer of screenplays has to keep in mind. Some kinds of screenplays work better in the movie theater and some kinds are more suitable for television. An epic film with a large cast, such as *Lawrence of Arabia*, is certainly more effective on a movie screen.

2 | Technology provides great flexibility for screenplays.

There may not be any *interaction* between the audience and screen, but there is certainly audience *reaction* to the fantastic things that can be done on a flat surface. Each year the technology gets better, but that doesn't mean that the screenplays get any better. In fact, some film critics have complained that hi-tech special effects are taking over, and that the most profitable box office attractions are those that thrill, chill, and shock the audience through the use of new and sophisticated techniques. *Terminator II* was talked about largely in terms of special effects. It has been common knowledge for a long time that the larger the audience the lower the intellectual level must be.

Though more artistic film and television ventures cannot command mind-boggling budgets or appeal to vast audiences, they still have available to them the basic advantages of the medium. Mobility is, perhaps, the greatest advantage that screenplays have over stage plays. Through this medium "the stage" has been liberated from the restraints of space and time. A mere *cut* can switch the action from New York to Hong Kong. The action can take place on the ground, in the air, at sea, under the sea, or in outer space. Time changes are a cinch. Montages, fades, flashbacks, and slow-motion are just a few of the devices used to indicate and manipulate the passage of time. And viewing the drama through the eye of the camera is infinitely more flexible than seeing it from a seat in a theater. The camera can zoom in on a distant object. It can move alongside a speeding automobile. It can see things from any character's point of view. And it can give us close-ups that allow us to read the emotions in an actor's eyes or feel the intimate passions of lovers.

3 | Dialogue has fewer functions in a screenplay than it has in a stage play.

Because of all the things that can be accomplished visually on the screen, less has to be explained or described through dialogue. A battle scene can be shown, not merely talked about. A past event can be shown in a flashback; it does not have to be narrated. Human emotions can be revealed in close-ups; they do not have to be as fully explored verbally as they are in stage plays. That doesn't mean that dialogue is not important. It remains a vital part of the screenplay as a work of art. Think of all the wonderful lines that are quoted from *Casablanca* or the films of Woody Allen.

4 | A screenplay is visualized in terms of master scenes and cuts.

A stage play writer thinks in terms of a few large blocks of action known as acts or scenes. A screenplay writer thinks in terms of a continuous flow of action, in which any change of time or location can be accomplished in a split second. The *master scene* in a screenplay is not the same as the concept of the *act* or *scene* in a stage play. It is merely a way of indicating that there has been a shift in location and that a new setup has to be arranged for the camera. The shift may only be as simple as going from the interior of a house to the exterior of the same house. A simple dramatic episode might require a number of master scenes in a film script.

5 | A standard manuscript form has evolved to deal with the requirements of film and television.

(A) Title

Use capital letters for the title. For scripts intended for submission a complete title page is necessary. It should include the title, author's name and address, or author's agent's name and address, and a brief indication of the type of script it is: an episode in a television series, an original screenplay, an adaptation of a novel or short story, and so on.

(B) Cast of characters

The cast of characters should be listed with a brief description of each character. There should be a heading for this list, and the heading and names of the characters should be capitalized. The descriptions should be in upper and lower case. Use a double-space between characters.

(C) Master scenes

The line for master scenes begins at the left-hand margin and is entirely capitalized. Three elements are included: interior (INT.) or exterior (EXT.), location (WASHINGTON SQUARE PARK), and time (DAY or NIGHT). Use a dash between location and time.

Example:

EXT. WASHINGTON SQUARE PARK—DAY

A master scene is any scene that requires a set shift, even if it is from one room to another of the same house, or from outside the front door to inside the front door, or from outside of an automobile to inside of an automobile. Filming cannot be continuous when a new set is required, even though in the finished product there is an illusion of continuity.

(D) Stage directions

Stage directions include descriptions of action, places, and people. They are single-spaced and use upper and lower case. They begin at the left-hand margin. There is a double-space before and after. Characters and camera notations are capitalized.

(E) Dialogue

Dialogue is centered, fifteen spaces from each margin, right and left. It is single-spaced. The speaker's name is centered and fully capitalized and followed by a double-space. A passage of dialogue is also followed by a double-space.

(F) Dialogue notations

Notations about how the words are spoken should be placed in parentheses one space under the character's name. Do not overuse such notations. Such notations, such as O.S. (off stage) or V.O. (voice over) are placed in parentheses beside the character's name.

(G) Camera notations

Camera notations are to be used only when absolutely necessary to describe the desired effect. Detailed camera notations are the business of the director, not the writer. They are fully capitalized. The most common notations are:

FADE IN Capitalized and followed by a colon, this notation begins at the left-hand margin and is used at the beginning of every script and at the beginning of each act, if there are several. It is followed by a double-space.

FADE OUT Capitalized and used with a period at the very end of the script, it appears flush with the right-hand margin, and is preceded by a double-space.

CUT TO Used with caps and colon, flush with the right-hand margin, it indicates a major shift in scene, not just minor set shifts. It is preceded by a double-space and followed by a new master scene line.

POV Indicates a shot from the *point of view* of one of the characters.

CLOSE UP A close view of a portion of the shot, usually a face, perhaps just the eyes or hands or an object, such as a knife or a gun.

INSERT Used in master scene lines in capitals for such items as a letter or newspaper story or clock. Inserts are isolated in the script because they are shot separately and inserted later.

ESTABLISHING SHOT A form of insert, usually a stock shot of a location to let the viewer know where we are. For instance, a shot of the New York skyline, or the White House, or the Eiffel Tower in Paris. Used in master scene lines.

Example:

EXT. ESTABLISHING SHOT OF NEW YORK SKYLINE—DAY

STOCK SHOT Any shot taken from the files and inserted to indicate place or action, such as an airliner taking off or landing, a train arriving or leaving. Used in master-scene lines.

MONTAGE A series of rapid cuts showing a process or the passage of time or any series of related actions. For instance, a character thinking of her father might have a brief vision of the various stages of her childhood. Shot separately and inserted. Used in master scene lines.

Example:

MONTAGE. MEMORIES OF CHILDHOOD
KIM riding a tricycle with her father nearby. KIM as a scout. Kim graduating from high school, her father in the audience, looking proud.

FULL SHOT (or WIDE SHOT) A full view of the set.

TWO SHOT A close shot, usually just full enough for two people.

REVERSE SHOT A shift in POV from one person to another, usually used in conversations between two people.

OVER THE SHOULDER SHOT The camera's eye is behind the character and takes in the back of the character and beyond.

HIGH ANGLE A shot that looks down at the action and has the effect of diminishing and distancing the characters and the action as though the POV were godlike.

LOW ANGLE A shot from a POV that looks up at the action, so that the characters seem to loom and grow larger.

MOVING SHOT A shot that follows a moving object, usually a person or a vehicle. The camera seems to stand still.

FOLLOWING SHOT A shot that follows the action, but with a camera that moves along with the object.

For a sample script see Example 12b.

EXAMPLE 12A

AM I BLUE
Beth Henley

CHARACTERS

JOHN POLK, *Seventeen.*
ASHBE, *Sixteen.*
HILDA, *Thirty-five, a waitress.*
STREET CHARACTERS: BARKER, WHORE, BUM, CLAREECE

SETTINGS
A bar, the street, the living room of a run-down apartment

TIME
Fall 1968

The scene opens on a street in the New Orleans French Quarter on a rainy blue bourbon night. Various people: a whore, bum, street barker, CLAREECE appear and disappear along the street. The scene then focuses on a bar where a piano is heard from the back room playing softly and indistinctly "Am I Blue?" The lights go up on JOHN POLK, who sits alone at a table. He is seventeen, a bit overweight and awkward. He wears nice clothes, perhaps a navy sweater with large white monograms. His navy raincoat is slung over an empty chair. While drinking, JOHN POLK concentrates on the red-and-black card that he holds in his hand. As soon as the scene is established, ASHBE enters from the street. She is sixteen, wears a flowered plastic rain cap, red galoshes, a butterfly barrette, and jeweled cat eyeglasses. She is carrying a bag full of stolen goods. Her hair is very curly. ASHBE makes her way cautiously to JOHN POLK'S table. As he sees her coming, he puts the card into his pocket. She sits in the empty chair and pulls his raincoat over her head.

ASHBE Excuse me . . . do you mind if I sit here, please?

JOHN POLK (*Looks up at her—then down into his glass.*) What are you doing hiding under my raincoat? You're getting it all wet.

ASHBE Well, I'm very sorry, but after all, it is a raincoat. (*He tries to pull off coat.*) It was rude of me, I know, but look, I just don't want them to recognize me.

JOHN POLK (*Looking about.*) Who to recognize you?

ASHBE Well, I stole these two ashtrays from the Screw Inn, ya know, right down the street. (*She pulls out two glass commercial ashtrays from her white plastic bag.*) Anyway, I'm scared the manager saw me. They'll be after me, I'm afraid.

JOHN POLK Well, they should be. Look, do you mind giving me back my raincoat? I don't want to be found protecting any thief.

ASHBE (*Coming out from under coat.*) Thief—would you call Robin Hood a thief?

JOHN POLK Christ.

ASHBE (*Back under coat.*) No, you wouldn't. He was valiant—all the time stealing from the rich and giving to the poor.

JOHN POLK But your case isn't exactly the same, is it? You're stealing from some crummy little bar and keeping the ashtrays for yourself. Now give me back my coat.

ASHBE (*Throws coat at him.*) Sure, take your old coat. I suppose I should have explained—about Miss Marcey. (*Silence.*) Miss Marcey, this cute old lady with a little hump in her back. I always see her in her sun hat and blue print dress. Miss Marcey lives in the apartment building next to ours. I leave all the stolen goods as gifts on her front steps.

JOHN POLK Are you one of those kleptomaniacs? (*He starts checking his wallet.*)

ASHBE You mean when people all the time steal and they can't help it?

JOHN POLK Yeah.

ASHBE Oh, no. I'm not a bit careless. Take my job tonight, my very first night job, if you want to know. Anyway, I've been planning it for two months, trying to decipher which bar most deserved to be stolen from. I finally decided on the Screw Inn. Mainly because of the way they're so mean to Mr. Groves. He works at the magazine rack at Diver's Drugstore and is really very sweet, but he has a drinking problem. I don't think that's fair to be mean to people simply because they have a drinking problem—and, well, anyway, you see I'm not just stealing for personal gain. I mean, I don't even smoke.

JOHN POLK Yeah, well, most infants don't, but then again, most infants don't hang around bars.

ASHBE I don't see why not, Toulouse Lautrec did.

JOHN POLK They'd throw me out.

ASHBE Oh, they throw me out, too, but I don't accept defeat. (*Slowly moves into him.*) Why it's the very same with my pick-pocketing.

(*JOHN POLK sneers, turns away.*)

It's a very hard art to master. Why, every time I've done it I've been caught.

JOHN POLK That's all I need is to have some slum kid tell me how good it is to steal. Everyone knows it's not.

ASHBE (*About his drink.*) That looks good. What is it?

JOHN POLK Hey, would you mind leaving me alone—I just wanted to be alone.

ASHBE Okay. I'm sorry. How about if I'm quiet?

(*JOHN POLK shrugs. He sips drink, looks around, catches her eye; she smiles and sighs.*)

I was just looking at your pin. What fraternity are you in?

JOHN POLK SAE.

ASHBE Is it a good fraternity?

JOHN POLK Sure, it's the greatest.

ASHBE I bet you have lots of friends.

JOHN POLK Tons.

ASHBE Are you being serious?

JOHN POLK Yes.

ASHBE Hmm. Do they have parties and all that?

JOHN POLK Yeah, lots of parties, booze, honking horns; it's exactly what you would expect.

ASHBE I wouldn't expect anything. Why did you join?

JOHN POLK I don't know. Well, my brother—I guess it was my brother—he told me how great it was, how the fraternity was supposed to get you dates, make you study, solve all your problems.

ASHBE Gee, does it?

JOHN POLK Doesn't help you study.

ASHBE How about dates? Do they get you a lot of dates?

JOHN POLK Some.

ASHBE What were the girls like?

JOHN POLK I don't know—they were like girls.

ASHBE Did you have a good time?

JOHN POLK I had a pretty good time.

ASHBE Did you make love to any of them?

JOHN POLK (*To self.*) Oh, Christ—

ASHBE I'm sorry—I just figured that's why you had the appointment with the whore—'cause you didn't have anyone else—to make love to.

JOHN POLK How did you know I had the, ah, the appointment?

ASHBE I saw you put the red card in your pocket when I came up. Those red cards are pretty familiar around here. The house is only about a block or so away.

It's one of the best, though, really very plush. Only two murders and a knifing in its whole history. Do you go there often?

JOHN POLK Yeah, I like to give myself a treat.

ASHBE Who do you have?

JOHN POLK What do you mean?

ASHBE I mean which girl.

(JOHN POLK gazes into his drink.)

LOOK, I just thought I might know her is all.

JOHN POLK Know her, ah, how would you know her?

ASHBE Well, some of the girls from my high school go there to work when they get out.

JOHN POLK G.G., her name is G.G.

ASHBE G.G.—Hmm, well, how does she look?

JOHN POLK I don't know.

ASHBE Oh, you've never been with her before?

JOHN POLK No.

ASHBE (*Confidentially.*) Are you one of those kinds that likes a lot of variety?

JOHN POLK Variety? Sure, I guess I like variety.

ASHBE Oh, yes, now I remember.

JOHN POLK What?

ASHBE G.G., that's just her working name. Her real name is Myrtle Reims; she's Kay Reims's older sister. Kay is in my grade at school.

JOHN POLK Myrtle? Her name is Myrtle?

ASHBE I never liked the name, either.

JOHN POLK Myrtle, oh, Christ. Is she pretty?

ASHBE (*Matter-of-fact.*) Pretty, no she's not real pretty.

JOHN POLK What does she look like?

ASHBE Let's see . . . she's, ah, well, Myrtle had acne, and there are a few scars left. It's not bad. I think they sort of give her character. Her hair's red, only I don't think it's really red.

It sort of fizzles out all over her head. She's got a pretty good figure—big top—but the rest of her is kind of skinny.

JOHN POLK I wonder if she has a good personality.

ASHBE Well, she was a senior when I was a freshman; so I never really knew her. I remember she used to paint her fingernails lots of different colors—pink, orange, purple. I don't know, but she kind of scares me. About the only time I ever saw her true personality was around a year ago. I was over at Kay's making a health poster for school. Anyway, Myrtle comes busting in screaming about how she can't find her spangled bra anywhere. Kay and I just sat on the floor cutting pictures of food out of magazines while she was storming about slamming drawers and swearing. Finally, she found it. It was pretty garish—red with black and gold-sequined G's on each cup. That's how I remember the name—G.G.

(*As ASHBE illustrates the placement of the G's she spots HILDA, the waitress, approaching. ASHBE pulls the raincoat over her head and hides on the floor. HILDA enters through the beaded curtains spilling her tray. HILDA is a woman of few words.*)

HILDA Shit, damn curtain. 'Nuther drink?

JOHN POLK Ma'am?

HILDA (*Points to drink.*) Vodka Coke?

JOHN POLK No, thank you. I'm not quite finished yet.

HILDA Napkins clean.

(*ASHBE pulls her bag off the table. HILDA looks at ASHBE, then to JOHN POLK. She walks around the table, as ASHBE is crawling along the floor to escape. ASHBE runs into HILDA'S toes.*)

ASHBE Are those real gold?

HILDA You again. Out.

ASHBE She wants me to leave. Why should a paying customer leave? (*Back to HILDA.*) Now I'll have a mint julep and easy on the mint.

HILDA This preteen with you?

JOHN POLK Well—I—No—I—

HILDA IDs.

ASHBE Certainly, I always try to cooperate with the management.

HILDA (*Looking at JOHN POLK'S ID.*) ID, 11-12-50. Date 11-11-68.

JOHN POLK Yes, but—well, 11-12 is less than two hours away.

HILDA Back in two hours.

ASHBE I seem to have left my identification in my gold lamé bag.

HILDA Well, boo hoo. (*Motions for ASHBE to leave with a minimum of effort. She goes back to table.*) No tip.

ASHBE You didn't tip her?

JOHN POLK I figured the drinks were so expensive—I just didn't—

HILDA No tip!

JOHN POLK Look, miss, I'm sorry. (*Going through his pockets.*) Here, would you like a—a nickel—wait, wait here's a quarter.

HILDA Just move ass, sonny. You, too, Barbie.

ASHBE Ugh, I hate public rudeness. I'm sure I'll refrain from ever coming here again.

HILDA Think I'll go in the back room and cry. (*ASHBE and JOHN POLK exit. HILDA picks up tray and exits through the curtain, tripping again.*) Shit. Damn curtain.

(*ASHBE and JOHN Polk are now standing outside under the awning of the bar.*)

ASHBE Gee, I didn't know it was your birthday tomorrow. Happy birthday! Don't be mad. I thought you were at least twenty or twenty-one, really.

JOHN POLK It's okay. Forget it.

ASHBE (*As they begin walking, various blues are heard coming from the nearby bars.*) It's raining.

JOHN POLK I know.

ASHBE Are you going over to the house now?

JOHN POLK No, not till twelve.

ASHBE Yeah, the pink-and-black cards—they mean all night. Midnight till morning. (*At this point a street barker beckons the couple into his establishment. Perhaps he is accompanied by a whore.*)

BARKER Hey, mister, bring your baby on in, buy her a few drinks, maybe tonight ya get lucky.

ASHBE Keep walking.

JOHN POLK What's wrong with the place?

ASHBE The drinks are watery rotgut, and the show girls are boys.

BARKER Up yours, punk!

JOHN POLK (*Who has now sat down on a street bench.*) Look, just tell me where a cheap bar is. I've got to stay drunk, but I don't have much money left.

ASHBE Yikes, there aren't too many cheap bars around here, and a lot of them check IDs.

JOHN POLK Well, do you know of any that don't?

ASHBE No, not for sure.

JOHN POLK Oh, God, I need to get drunk.

ASHBE Aren't you?

JOHN POLK Some, but I'm losing ground fast. (*By this time a bum who has been traveling drunkenly down the street falls near the couple and begins throwing up.*)

ASHBE Oh, I know! You can come to my apartment. It's just down the block. We keep one bottle of rum around. I'll serve you a grand drink, three or four if you like.

JOHN POLK (*Fretfully.*) No, thanks.

ASHBE But look, we're getting all wet.

JOHN POLK Sober, too, wet and sober.

Ashbe Oh, come on! Rain's blurring my glasses.

John Polk Well, how about your parents? What would they say?

Ashbe Daddy's out of town and Mama lives in Atlanta; so I'm sure they won't mind. I think we have some cute little marshmallows. (*Pulling on him.*) Won't you really come?

John Polk You've probably got some gang of muggers waiting to kill me. Oh, all right—what the hell, let's go.

Ashbe Hurrah! Come on. It's this way. (*She starts across the stage, stops, and picks up an old hat.*) Hey look at this hat. Isn't it something! Here, wear it to keep off the rain.

John Polk (*Throwing hat back onto street.*) No, thanks, you don't know who's worn it before.

Ashbe (*Picking hat back up.*) That makes it all the more exciting. Maybe it was a butcher's who slaughtered his wife or a silver pirate with a black bird on his throat. Who do you guess?

John Polk I don't know. Anyway, what's the good of guessing? I mean, you'll never really know.

Ashbe (*Trying the hat on.*) Yeah, probably not. (*At this point, Ashbe and John Polk reach the front door.*) Here we are. (*Ashbe begins fumbling for her key. Clareece, a teeny-bopper, walks up to John Polk.*)

Clareece Hey, man, got any spare change?

John Polk (*Looking through his pockets.*) Let me see—I—

Ashbe (*Coming up between them, giving Clareece a shove.*) Beat it, Clareece. He's my company.

Clareece (*Walks away and sneers.*) Oh, shove it, Frizzels.

Ashbe A lot of jerks live around here. Come on in. (*She opens the door. Lights go up on the living room of a rundown apartment in a run-down apartment house. Besides being merely run-down, the room is a malicious pigsty with colors, paper hats, paper dolls, masks, torn-up stuffed animals, dead flowers and leaves, dress-up clothes, etc., thrown all about.*) My bones are cold. Do you want a towel to dry off?

JOHN POLK Yes, thank you.

ASHBE (*She picks a towel up off of the floor and tosses it to him.*) Here. (*He begins drying off as she takes off her rain things; then she begins raking things off the sofa.*) Please do sit down. (*He sits.*) I'm sorry the place is disheveled, but my father's been out of town. I always try to pick up and all before he gets in. Of course he's pretty used to messes. My mother never was too good at keeping things clean.

JOHN POLK When's he coming back?

ASHBE Sunday, I believe. Oh, I've been meaning to say—

JOHN POLK What?

ASHBE My name's Ashbe Williams.

JOHN POLK Ashbe?

ASHBE Yeah, Ashbe.

JOHN POLK My name's John Polk Richards.

ASHBE John Polk? They call you John Polk?

JOHN POLK It's family.

ASHBE (*Putting on socks.*) These are my favorite socks, the red furry ones. Well, here's some books and magazines to look at while I fix you something to drink. What do you want in your rum?

JOHN POLK Coke's fine.

ASHBE I'll see do we have any. I think I'll take some hot Kool-Aid myself. (*She exits to the kitchen.*)

JOHN POLK Hot Kool-Aid?

ASHBE It's just Kool-Aid that's been heated, like hot chocolate or hot tea.

JOHN POLK Sounds great.

ASHBE Well, I'm used to it. You get so much for your dime it makes it worth your while. I don't buy presweetened, of course, it's better to sugar your own.

JOHN POLK I remember once I threw up a lot of grape Kool-Aid when I was a kid. I've hated it ever since. Hey, would you check on the time?

ASHBE (*She enters carrying a tray with several bottles of food coloring, a bottle of rum, and a huge glass.*) I'm sorry we don't have Cokes. I wonder if rum and Kool-Aid is good? Oh, we don't have a clock, either. (*She pours a large amount of rum into the large glass.*)

JOHN POLK I'll just have it with water, then.

ASHBE (*She finds an almost empty glass of water somewhere in the room and dumps it in with the rum.*) Would you like food coloring in the water? It makes a drink all the more aesthetic. Of course, some people don't care for aesthetics.

JOHN POLK No, thank you, just plain water.

ASHBE Are you sure? The taste is entirely the same. I put it in all my water.

JOHN POLK Well—

ASHBE What color do you want?

JOHN POLK I don't know.

ASHBE What's your favorite color?

JOHN POLK Blue, I guess. (*She puts a few blue drops into the glass—as she has nothing to stir with, she blows into the glass, turning the water blue.*) Thanks.

ASHBE (*Exits. She screams from kitchen.*) Come on, say come on, cat, eat your fresh good milk.

JOHN POLK You have a cat?

ASHBE (*Off.*) No.

JOHN POLK Oh.

ASHBE (*She enters carrying a tray with a cup of hot Kool-Aid and Cheerios and colored marshmallows.*) Here are some Cheerios and some cute little colored marshmallows to eat with your drink.

JOHN POLK Thanks.

ASHBE I one time smashed all the big white marshmallows in the plastic bag at the grocery store.

JOHN POLK Why did you do that?

ASHBE I was angry. Do you like ceramics?

JOHN POLK Yes.

ASHBE My mother makes them. It's sort of her hobby. She is very talented.

JOHN POLK My mother never does anything. Well, I guess she can shuffle the bridge deck okay.

ASHBE Actually, my mother is a dancer. She teaches at a school in Atlanta. She's really very talented.

JOHN POLK (*Indicates ceramics.*) She must be to do all these.

ASHBE Well, Madeline, my older sister, did the blue one. Madeline gets to live with Mama.

JOHN POLK And you live with your father.

ASHBE Yeah, but I get to go visit them sometimes.

JOHN POLK You do ceramics, too?

ASHBE No, I never learned . . . but I have this great pot holder set. (*Gets up to show him.*) See I make lots of multicolored pot holders and sent them to Mama and Madeline. I also make paper hats. (*Gets material to show him.*) I guess they're more creative, but making pot holders is more relaxing. Here, would you like to make a hat?

JOHN POLK I don't know, I'm a little drunk.

ASHBE It's not hard a bit. (*Hands him material.*) Just draw a real pretty design on the paper. It really doesn't have to be pretty, just whatever you want.

JOHN POLK It's kind of you to give my creative drives such freedom.

ASHBE Ha, ha, ha, I'll work on my pot holder set a bit.

JOHN POLK What time is it? I've really got to check on the time.

ASHBE I know. I'll call the time operator. (*She goes to the phone.*)

JOHN POLK How do you get along without a clock?

ASHBE Well, I've been late for school a lot. Daddy has a watch. It's 11:03.

JOHN POLK I've got a while yet.

ASHBE (*Twirls back to her chair, drops, and sighs.*)

JOHN POLK Are you a dancer, too?

ASHBE (*Delighted.*) I can't dance a bit, really. I practice a lot is all, at home in the afternoon. I imagine you go to a lot of dances.

JOHN POLK Not really, I'm a terrible dancer. I usually get bored or drunk.

ASHBE You probably drink too much.

JOHN POLK No, it's just since I've come to college. All you do there is drink more beer and write more papers.

ASHBE What are you studying for to be?

JOHN POLK I don't know.

ASHBE Why don't you become a rancher?

JOHN POLK Dad wants me to help run his soybean farm.

ASHBE Soybean farm. Yikes, that's really something. Where is it?

JOHN POLK Well, I live in the Delta, Hollybluff, Mississippi. Anyway, Dad feels I should go to business school first; you know, so I'll become, well, management minded. Pass the blue.

ASHBE Is that what you really want to do?

JOHN POLK I don't know. It would probably be as good as anything else I could do. Dad makes good money. He can take vacations whenever he wants. Sure it'll be a ball.

ASHBE I'd hate to have to be management minded. (*JOHN POLK shrugs.*) I don't mean to hurt your feelings, but I would really hate to be a management mind. (*She starts walking on her knees, twisting her fists in front of her eyes, and making clicking sounds as a management mind would make.*)

JOHN POLK Cut it out. Just forget it. The farm could burn down and I wouldn't even have to think about it.

ASHBE (*After a pause.*) Well, what do you want to talk about?

JOHN POLK I don't know.

ASHBE When was the last dance you went to?

JOHN POLK Dances. That's a great subject. Let's see, oh, I don't really remember. It was probably some blind date. God, I hate dates.

ASHBE Why?

JOHN POLK Well, they always say that they don't want popcorn and they wind up eating all of yours.

ASHBE You mean, you hate dates just because they eat your popcorn? Don't you think that's kind of stingy?

JOHN POLK It's the principle of the thing. Why can't they just say, yes, I'd like some popcorn when you ask them. But, no, they're always so damn coy.

ASHBE I'd tell my date if I wanted popcorn. I'm not that immature.

JOHN POLK Anyway, it's not only the popcorn. It's a lot of little things. I've finished coloring. What do I do now?

ASHBE Now you have to fold it. Here . . . like this. (*She explains the process with relish.*) Say, that's really something.

JOHN POLK It's kind of funny looking. (*Putting the hat on.*) Yeah, I like it, but you could never wear it anywhere.

ASHBE Well, like what, anyway?

JOHN POLK Huh?

ASHBE The things dates do to you that you don't like, the little things.

JOHN POLK Oh, well just the way they wear those false eyelashes and put their hand on your knee when you're trying to parallel park and keep on giggling and going off to the bathroom with their girlfriends. It's obvious they don't want to go out with me. They just want to go out so that they can wear their new clothes and won't have to sit on their ass in the dormitory. They never want to go out with me. I can never even talk to them.

ASHBE Well, you can talk to me and I'm a girl.

JOHN POLK Well, I'm really kind of drunk and you're a stranger . . . Well, I probably wouldn't be able to talk to you tomorrow. That makes a difference.

ASHBE Maybe it does. (*A bit of a pause, and then, extremely pleased by the idea, she says.*) You know we're alike because I don't like dances, either.

JOHN POLK I thought you said you practiced . . . in the afternoons.

ASHBE Well, I like dancing. I just don't like dances. At least not like—well, not like the one our school was having tonight. . . . They're so corny.

JOHN POLK Yeah, most dances are.

ASHBE All they serve is potato chips and fruit punch, and then this stupid baby band plays and everybody dances around thinking they're so hot. I frankly wouldn't dance there. I would prefer to wait till I am invited to an exclusive ball. It doesn't really matter which ball, just one where they have huge golden chandeliers and silver fountains and serve delicacies of all sorts and bubble blue champagne. I'll arrive in a pink silk cape. (*Laughing.*) I want to dance in pink!

JOHN POLK You're mixed up. You're probably one of those people that live in a fantasy world.

ASHBE I do not. I accept reality as well as anyone. Anyway, you can talk to me, remember. I know what you mean by the kind of girls it's hard to talk to. There are girls a lot that way in the small clique at my school. Really tacky and mean. They expect everyone to be as stylish as they are, and they won't even speak to you in the hall. I don't mind if they don't speak to me, but I really love the orphans, and it hurts my feelings when they are so mean to them.

JOHN POLK What do you mean—they're mean to the orpheens? (*Notices pun and giggles to self.*)

ASHBE Oh, well, they sometimes snicker at the orphans' dresses. The orphans usually have hand-me-down, drab, ugly dresses. Once Shelly Maxwell wouldn't let Glinda borrow her pencil, even though she had two. It hurt her feelings.

JOHN POLK Are you best friends with these orphans?

ASHBE I hardly know them at all. They're really shy. I just like them a lot. They're the reason I put spells on the girls in the clique.

JOHN POLK Spells, what do you mean, witch spells?

ASHBE Witch spells? Not really, mostly just voodoo.

JOHN POLK Are you kidding? Do you really do voodoo?

ASHBE Sure, here I'll show you my doll. (*Goes to get doll, comes back with straw voodoo doll. Her air as she returns is one of frightening mystery.*) I know a lot about the subject. Cora she used to wash dishes in the Moonlight Café, told me all about voodoo. She's a real expert on the subject, went to all the meetings and everything. Once she caused a man's throat to rot away and turn almost totally black. She's moved to Chicago now.

JOHN POLK It doesn't really work. Does it?

ASHBE Well, not always. The thing about voodoo is that both parties have to believe in it for it to work.

JOHN POLK Do the girls in school believe in it?

ASHBE Not really; I don't think. That's where my main problem comes in. I have to make the clique believe in it, yet I have to be very subtle. Mainly, I give reports in English class or Speech.

JOHN POLK Reports?

ASHBE On voodoo.

JOHN POLK That's really kind of sick, you know.

ASHBE Not really. I don't cast spells that'll do any real harm. Mainly, just the kind of thing to make them think—to keep them on their toes. (*Blue drink intoxication begins to take over and JOHN POLK begins laughing.*) What's so funny?

JOHN POLK Nothing. I was just thinking what a mean little person you are.

ASHBE Mean! I'm not mean a bit.

JOHN POLK Yes, you are mean—(*Picking up color.*) and green, too.

ASHBE Green?

JOHN POLK Yes, green with envy of those other girls; so you play all those mean little tricks.

ASHBE Envious of those other girls, that stupid, close-minded little clique!

JOHN POLK Green as this marshmallow. (*Eats marshmallow.*)

ASHBE You think I want to be in some group . . . a sheep like you? A little sheep like you that does everything when he's supposed to do it!

JOHN POLK Me a sheep—I do what I want!

ASHBE Ha! I've known you for an hour and already I see you for the sheep you are!

JOHN POLK Don't take your green meanness out on me.

ASHBE Not only are you a sheep, you are a *normal* sheep. Give me back my colors! (*Begins snatching colors away.*)

JOHN POLK (*Pushing colors at her.*) Green and mean! Green and mean! Green and mean! Et cetera.

ASHBE (*Throwing marshmallows at him.*) That's the reason you're in a fraternity and the reason you're going to manage your mind, and dates—you go out on dates merely because it's expected of you even though you have a terrible time. That's the reason you go to the whorehouse to prove you're a normal man. Well, you're much too normal for me.

JOHN POLK Infant bitch. You think you're really cute.

ASHBE That really wasn't food coloring in your drink, it was poison! (*She laughs, he picks up his coat to go, and she stops throwing marshmallows at him.*) Are you going? I was only kidding. For Christ sake, it wasn't really poison. Come on, don't go. Can't you take a little friendly criticism?

JOHN POLK Look, did you have to bother me tonight? I had enough problems without—(*Phone rings. Both look at phone; it rings for the third time. He stands undecided.*)

ASHBE Look, wait, we'll make it up. (*She goes to answer phone.*) Hello—Daddy. How are you? . . . I'm fine . . . Dad, you sound funny . . . what? . . . Come on, Daddy, you know she's not here. (*Pause.*) Look, I told you I wouldn't call anymore. You've got her number in Atlanta. (*Pause, as she sinks to the floor.*) Why have you started again? . . . Don't say that. I can tell it. I can. Hey, I have to go to bed now, I don't want to talk anymore, okay? (*Hangs up phone, softly to self.*) Goddamnit.

JOHN POLK (*He has heard the conversation and is taking off his coat.*) Hey, Ashbe— (*She looks at him blankly, her mind far away.*) You want to talk?

ASHBE No. (*Slight pause.*) Why don't you look at my shell collection? I have this special shell collection. (*She shows him collection.*)

JOHN POLK They're beautiful, I've never seen colors like this. (*ASHBE is silent, he continues to himself.*) I used to go to Biloxi a lot when I was a kid . . . one time my brother and I, we camped out on the beach. The sky was purple. I remember it was really purple. We ate pork and beans out of a can. I'd always kinda wanted to do that. Every night for about a week after I got home, I dreamt about these waves foaming over my head and face. It was funny. Did you find these shells or buy them?

ASHBE Some I found, some I bought. I've been trying to decipher their meaning. Here, listen, do you hear that?

JOHN POLK Yes.

ASHBE That's the soul of the sea. (*She listens.*) I'm pretty sure it's the soul of the sea. Just imagine when I decipher the language. I'll know all the secrets of the world.

JOHN POLK Yeah, probably you will. (*Looking into the shell.*) You know, you were right.

ASHBE What do you mean?

JOHN POLK About me, you were right. I am a sheep, a normal one. I've been trying to get out of it, but now I'm as big a sheep as ever.

ASHBE Oh, it doesn't matter. You're company. It was rude of me to say.

JOHN POLK No, because it was true. I really didn't want to go into a fraternity, I didn't even want to go to college, and I sure as hell don't want to go back to Hollybluff and work the soybean farm till I'm eighty.

ASHBE I still say you could work on a ranch.

JOHN POLK I don't know. I wanted to be a minister or something good, but I don't even know if I believe in God.

ASHBE Yeah.

JOHN POLK I never used to worry about being a failure. Now I think about it all the time. It's just I need to do something that's—fulfilling.

ASHBE Fulfilling, yes, I see what you mean. Well, how about college? Isn't it fulfilling? I mean, you take all those wonderful classes, and you have all your very good friends.

JOHN POLK Friends, yeah, I have some friends.

ASHBE What do you mean?

JOHN POLK Nothing—well, I do mean something. What the hell, let me try to explain. You see it was my "friends," the fraternity guys that set me up with G.G., excuse me, Myrtle, as a gift for my eighteenth birthday.

ASHBE You mean, you didn't want the appointment?

JOHN POLK No, I didn't want it. Hey, ah, where did my blue drink go?

ASHBE (*As she hands him the drink.*) They probably thought you really wanted to go.

JOHN POLK Yeah, I'm sure they gave a damn what I wanted. They never even asked me. Hell, I would have told them a handkerchief, a pair of argyle socks, but, no, they have to get me a whore just because it's a cool-ass thing to do. They make me sick. I couldn't even stay at the party they gave. All the sweaty T-shirts and moron sex stories—I just couldn't take it.

ASHBE Is that why you were at the Blue Angel so early?

JOHN POLK Yeah, I needed to get drunk, but not with them. They're such creeps.

ASHBE Gosh, so you really don't want to go to Myrtle's?

JOHN POLK No, I guess not.

ASHBE Then are you going?

JOHN POLK (*Pause.*) Yes.

ASHBE That's wrong. You shouldn't go just to please them.

JOHN POLK Oh, that's not the point anymore; maybe at first it was, but it's not anymore. Now I have to go for myself—to prove to myself that I'm not afraid.

ASHBE Afraid? (*Slowly, as she begins to grasp his meaning.*) You mean, you've never slept with a girl before?

JOHN POLK Well, I've never been in love.

ASHBE (*In amazement.*) You're a virgin?

JOHN POLK Oh, God.

ASHBE No, don't feel bad, I am, too.

JOHN POLK I thought I should be in love—

ASHBE Well, you're certainly not in love with Myrtle. I mean, you haven't even met her.

JOHN POLK I know, but, God, I thought maybe I'd never fall in love. What then? You should experience everything—shouldn't you? Oh, what's it matter, everything's so screwed.

ASHBE Screwed? Yeah, I guess it is. I mean, I always thought it would be fun to have a lot of friends who gave parties and go to dances all dressed up. Like the dance tonight—it might have been fun.

John Polk Well, why didn't you go?

Ashbe I don't know. I'm not sure it would have been fun. Anyway, you can't go—alone.

John Polk Oh, you need a date?

Ashbe Yeah, or something.

John Polk Say, Ashbe, ya wanna dance here?

Ashbe No, I think we'd better discuss your dilemma.

John Polk What dilemma?

Ashbe Myrtle. It doesn't seem right you should—

John Polk Let's forget Myrtle for now. I've got a while yet. Here, have some more of this blue-moon drink.

Ashbe You're only trying to escape through artificial means.

John Polk Yeah, you got it. Now, come on. Would you like to dance? Hey, you said you liked to dance.

Ashbe You're being ridiculous.

John Polk (*Winking at her.*) Dance?

Ashbe John Polk, I just thought—

John Polk Hmm?

Ashbe How to solve your problem—

John Polk Well—

Ashbe Make love to me!

John Polk What?!

Ashbe It all seems logical to me. It would prove you weren't scared, and you wouldn't be doing it just to impress others.

John Polk Look, I—I mean I hardly know you—

Ashbe But we've talked. It's better this way, really. I won't be so apt to point out your mistakes.

John Polk I'd feel great stripping a twelve-year-old of her virginity.

Ashbe I'm sixteen! Anyway, I'd be stripping you of yours just as well. I'll go put on some Tiger Claw perfume. (*She runs out.*)

JOHN POLK Hey, come back! Tiger Claw perfume, Christ.

ASHBE (*Entering.*) I think one should have different scents for different moods.

JOHN POLK Hey, stop spraying that! You know I'm not going to—well, you'd get neurotic or pregnant or some damn thing. Stop spraying, will you!

ASHBE Pregnant? You really think I could get pregnant?

JOHN POLK Sure, it'd be a delightful possibility.

ASHBE It really wouldn't be bad. Maybe I would get to go to Tokyo for an abortion. I've never been to the Orient.

JOHN POLK Sure, getting cut on is always a real treat.

ASHBE Anyway, I might just want to have my dear baby. I could move to Atlanta with Mama and Madeline. It'd be wonderful fun. Why, I could take him to the supermarket, put him in one of those little baby seats to stroll him about. I'd buy peach baby food and feed it to him with a tiny golden spoon. Why, I could take colored pictures of him and send them to you through the mail. Come on—(*Starts putting pillows onto the couch.*) Well, I guess you should kiss me for a start. It's only etiquette; everyone begins with it.

JOHN POLK I don't think I could even kiss you with a clear conscience. I mean, you're so small, with those little cat-eye glasses and curly hair—I couldn't even kiss you.

ASHBE You couldn't even kiss me? I can't help it if I have to wear glasses. I got the prettiest ones I could find.

JOHN POLK Your glasses are fine. Let's forget it, okay?

ASHBE I know, my lips are too purple, but if I eat carrots, the dye'll come off and they'll be orange.

JOHN POLK I didn't say anything about your lips being too purple.

ASHBE Well, what is it? You're just plain chicken, I suppose—

JOHN POLK Sure, right, I'm chicken, totally chicken. Let's forget it. I don't know how, but somehow this is probably all my fault.

ASHBE You're darn right it's all your fault! I want to have my dear baby or at least get to Japan. I'm so sick of school I could smash every marshmallow in sight! (*She starts smashing.*) Go on to your skinny pimple whore. I hope the skinny whore laughs in your face, which she probably will because you have an easy face to laugh in.

JOHN POLK You're absolutely right; she'll probably hoot and howl her damn fizzle red head off. Maybe you can wait outside the door and hear her, give you lots of pleasure, you sadistic little thief.

ASHBE Thief—was Robin Hood— Oh, what's wrong with this world? I just wasn't made for it is all. I've probably been put in the wrong world, I can see that now.

JOHN POLK You're fine in this world.

ASHBE Sure, everyone just views me as an undesirable lump.

JOHN POLK Who?

ASHBE You for one.

JOHN POLK (*Pause.*) You mean because I wouldn't make love to you?

ASHBE It seems clear to me.

JOHN POLK But you're wrong, you know.

ASHBE (*To self, softly.*) Don't pity me.

JOHN POLK The reason I wouldn't wasn't that—it's just that—well, I like you too much to.

ASHBE You like me?

JOHN POLK Undesirable lump, Jesus. Your cheeks, they're—they're—

ASHBE My cheeks? They're what?

JOHN POLK They're rosy.

ASHBE My cheeks are rosy?

JOHN POLK Yeah, your cheeks, they're really rosy.

ASHBE Well, they're natural, you know. Say, would you like to dance?

JOHN POLK Yes.

ASHBE I'll turn on the radio. (*She turns on radio. Ethel Waters is heard singing "Honey in the Honeycomb." ASHBE begins snapping her fingers.*) Yikes, let's jazz it out. (*They dance.*)

JOHN POLK Hey, I'm not good or anything—

ASHBE John Polk.

JOHN POLK Yeah?

ASHBE Baby, I think you dance fine! (*They dance on, laughing, saying what they want till end of song. Then a radio announcer comes on and says the 12:00 news will be in five minutes. Billie Holiday or Terry Pierce begins singing, "Am I Blue?"*)

JOHN POLK Dance?

ASHBE News in five minutes.

JOHN POLK Yeah.

ASHBE That means five minutes till midnight.

JOHN POLK Yeah, I know.

ASHBE Then you're not—

JOHN POLK Ashbe, I've never danced all night. Wouldn't it be something to—to dance all night and watch the rats come out of the gutter?

ASHBE Rats?

JOHN POLK Don't they come out at night? I hear New Orleans has lots of rats.

ASHBE Yeah, yeah, it's got lots of rats.

JOHN POLK Then let's dance all night and wait for them to come out.

ASHBE All right—but, but how about our feet?

JOHN POLK Feet?

ASHBE They'll hurt.

JOHN POLK Yeah.

Ashbe (*Smiling.*) Okay, then let's dance. (*He takes her hand, and they dance as lights black out and the music soars and continues to play.*)

EXAMPLE 12B

APPOINTMENT IN SAMARRA
W. Somerset Maugham

There was a merchant in Bagdad who sent his servant to market to buy provisions, and in a little while the servant came back, white and trembling, and said, "Master, just now when I was in the market-place I was jostled by a woman in the crowd and when I turned I saw it was Death that jostled me. She looked at me and made a threatening gesture; now, lend me your horse, and I will ride away from this city and avoid my fate. I will go to Samarra and there Death will not find me."

The merchant lent him his horse, and the servant mounted it, and he dug his spurs in its flanks and as fast as the horse could gallop he went. Then the merchant went down to the market-place and he saw Death standing in the crowd and he came to Death and said, "Why did you make a threatening gesture to my servant when you saw him this morning?"

"That was not a threatening gesture," Death said. "It was only a start of surprise. I was astonished to see him in Bagdad, for I have an appointment with him tonight in Samarra."

The following adaptation of the tale by Maugham illustrates basic filmscript form:

APPOINTMENT IN SAMARRA

CHARACTERS

SERVANT, *a simple, uneducated man*
MASTER, *a wealthy merchant of Bagdad*
DEATH, *in the spectral form of an old woman*

FADE IN:

EXT. ESTABLISHING SCENE OF ANCIENT BAGDAD—
DAY A walled city of many mosques, narrow streets and crowds.

EXT. THE MARKETPLACE IN BAGDAD—DAY
A noisy series of stalls and shops where buyers bargain loudly
with peddlers. FULL SHOT of the whole market. Then CLOSE
UP of the SERVANT, *who is shopping for fruit and vegetables at*
a stall where he must compete with many women. A woman
behind him jostles him. He turns to her with an annoyed look,
which turns quickly to a look of horror. What he sees is a skele-
ton-like face framed in a black shawl. It is DEATH *in the form*
of an old woman. He runs away, pushing everyone aside.

INT. MASTER'S HOUSE IN BAGDAD—DAY
The home of a wealthy man. Typical old Arab style. Arches and
tiles and rugs. The MASTER *is seated at the table, having a light*
lunch. Another servant, a woman, attends him. The SERVANT
comes rushing in.

SERVANT
(breathless)

Master! Master! You must help me. My life is in
danger.

MASTER

Now, now, what is this all about?
Can't you see that I am eating?

SERVANT

Please, master, listen to me. I was
in the marketplace, getting the
provisions you asked for when I was

nudged by a ghostly creature who was
the very spectre of death. I am
afraid that she has come for me.
She made a threatening gesture at
me. I am sure I am going to die.
I must get away. I must escape
this fate.

MASTER

But if it is your fate, there is no
escaping it.

SERVANT

Yes, yes, I must try. I must flee
this city. I will go to Samarra,
where I am not known, where no one
will find me. Please, sir, lend me
your horse. Let me make my escape.

MASTER

If you insist, you may take the
horse, but I think perhaps you have
made a mistake. I will go myself
to the marketplace and find out
what this is all about. You are too
young to die. Perhaps the figure of
Death mistook you for someone else.

SERVANT

Oh, thank you, Master. Thank you!

He exits hastily.

EXT. STABLE OF MASTER'S HOUSE IN BAGDAD—DAY

SERVANT takes horse from stable and mounts. He rides off at a gallop. MOVING SHOT lingers on his retreat.

EXT. MARKETPLACE IN BAGDAD—DAY

The MASTER makes his way through the crowd, pushing aside lower-class people, who show their humility when they see he is a rich man. MEDIUM SHOT of MASTER looking here and there. PAN of market stalls and crowd. CLOSE UP of MASTER spotting the person he is looking for. He makes his way toward DEATH, the old woman.

> MASTER
> (calling out)
>
> You! You there!

DEATH turns to look at him. CLOSE UP of horrible face in a black shawl.

> DEATH
>
> What is it, sir?

> MASTER
>
> My servant was here this morning and said
> that you made a threatening gesture towards
> him. I want to know why.

> DEATH
>
> I'm sorry, sir. That was not a
> threatening gesture. It was only
> a start of surprise. I was astonished

to see him here in Bagdad, for I
have an appointment with him tonight
in Samarra.

FADE OUT.

EXERCISES

Discussion

1. In *Am I Blue* (Example 12a) by Beth Henley, there
   are three settings indicated, but could they all be
   accommodated by a simple imaginative stage setup?
2. Discuss the passage of time in Henley's play.
3. How much do we learn about the plot through the
   dialogue in this play? What exactly is going on here? Is
   there any *stage business* or action to keep this play from
   being all dialogue?
4. What are we supposed to think about these characters?
   How are they developed? Do they seem to be typical
   teenagers?
5. Discuss the humor in this play. Would you call it a
   comedy?
6. "Appointment in Samarra" (Example 12b) by
   W. Somerset Maugham is a very short story. In what
   ways does the screenplay version make it a longer
   work? Could it be made even longer?
7. Does the folktale quality of the story get lost in the
   film version? What is the central point of the story?
   Would it be believable as a realistic drama?

Writing

1. Write a screenplay based on a short folktale. Dramatize the action that is usually merely summarized in such stories.

2. Write a screenplay that is based on one of the stories included in this book.

3. Write a one-act play in which all the characters are teenagers. Limit the cast to two to five characters, and use only one set and a single time frame.

4. Write a one-act play in which a man and a woman are discussing their romantic relationship, which, at the moment involves a problem. Find ways to introduce action in order to avoid a static dialogue.

5. Write a one-act play, humorous or serious, in which three people are in a lifeboat in the South Pacific, adrift after the freighter on which they were passengers sank suddenly. They are a white man, an African-American man, and a white woman. They are the only survivors and may face starvation or the prospect of reaching a small uninhabited island, where they might have to spend the rest of their lives.

Fundamentals of Writing

This chapter will help you with the most common problems in the fundamentals of writing. It has been put together with creative writing students in mind and is not intended as a comprehensive guide to college composition, which is usually a prerequisite for any more advanced work in writing.

13A Grammar

In creative writing the most important rule to remember is that it is not ordinary *correctness* of language that counts, but aesthetic *effectiveness*. In short, whatever works for your story, poem, or play is what you should use. Language is the clay of the art of writing, and it can be molded into some strange and exotic forms. Keep an open mind, but don't forget the basic conventions of your language. Experiment at times, but don't be pointlessly ungrammatical.

1 | Sentence fragments

A sentence needs a subject and a predicate. The sentence has to be about someone or something (the subject), and something has to be said about that subject (the predicate). In general, avoid sentence fragments, unless you have a stylistic reason for using them. They often appear in dialogue, because certain characters talk that way. Some writers consciously use sentence fragments for emphasis. If you do use fragments, you should do so for a reason and not merely by accident.

Examples:

> The best matador in Spain. [fragment]
> Killed by a bull. [fragment]
> The best matador in Spain was killed by a bull.
> [complete]
> Since I was going to England. [fragment]
> Since I was going to England I bought a map.
> [complete]
> Being an only child. [fragment]
> Being an only child is not easy. [complete]

2 | Fused sentences and the comma splice

Don't use a comma when a period is needed. Don't run two sentences together without an appropriate punctuation mark or conjunction. As in the case of the sentence fragment, there are literary exceptions. In a technique called "stream of consciousness," which is used to capture the thoughts of a character, punctuation is often ignored on the assumption that the mind's more primitive mode of expression is not concerned with such details (see Chapter 9).

Examples:

> She decided to go to Chicago, the bus was leaving at eight.
> [comma splice; the comma should be a period]
>
> The train to Paris was fast he would arrive before Maria.
> [fused sentence; it needs a period or a conjunction]
>
> The train to Paris was so fast that he would arrive before Maria. [correct]

3 | Mixed construction

If a sentence begins with one type of construction and ends with a different type, it will contain a *mixed* or *shifted construction*.

Examples:

Because of my lack of ability is why I failed the course. [*correct*: Because of my lack of ability I failed the course; *or*: My lack of ability is why I failed the course.]

Shakespeare is a writer who, although he wanted fame and fortune, he did not sacrifice his art. [*correct*: Shakespeare is a writer who, although he wanted fame and fortune, did not sacrifice his art; *or*: Although Shakespeare wanted fame and fortune, he did not sacrifice his art.]

4 | Coordination

To coordinate two or more words, phrases, or clauses is to place them in a construction that lends equal weight to each element. They can be joined by coordinating conjunctions—*and, but, or, nor, for, so, yet*—as well as correlatives such as *either . . . or*. Coordinate elements are often separated by a comma or semicolon. *And which* and *and who* (*whom*) should not be used to coordinate unless a preceding *which* or *who* has been used. Avoid excessive or illogical coordination.

Examples:

I will go to *France* or *Italy*. [coordinate nouns]
He arrived in America *with high hopes* but *with no money*. [coordinate phrases]

If you have talent, and *if you work hard*, you will succeed. [coordinate clauses]

I gave my last dollar to an old man with a crippled leg, and whom I didn't even know. [*and whom* can be used only after a previous *whom*; *correct*: I gave my last dollar to an old man with a crippled leg, whom I had seen in the village, and whom I didn't even know.]

I went to London, and I went to Paris, and I went to Rome, and I had a very good time. [excessive coordination]

5 | Subordination

When two related ideas of unequal importance appear in a sentence, the relationship between them must be made clear by proper subordination. The *main clause* conveys the basic idea. One or more dependent elements add information. It is necessary to choose the proper subordinating conjunction in order to indicate the exact relationship involved. *Like* is not a subordinating conjunction and should not join two clauses.

Examples:

He returned the money *before anyone realized it was missing*. [The subordinate clause, in italics, indicates *when* the main action takes place.]

If I have enough money, I'll take a trip to London. [The subordinate clause indicates the *condition* under which the main action will take place.]

He climbed to the top of the mountain, *which gave him a good view of the sea*. [The subordinate clause indicates *relation*.]

He looked *like he had seen a ghost*. [incorrect use of *like*, which is not a conjunction; *correct*: He looked *as if he had seen a ghost*.]

6 | Modifiers

Any word, phrase, or clause that describes, limits, qualifies, or defines another element in the sentence is called a *modifier*. Adverbs and adjectives, for instance, are modifiers. One common error is to use an adverb when an adjective should be used, or an adjective when an adverb should be used. Another common error is to leave a modifier dangling, especially a participial phrase. Such phrases function as adjectives and must be clearly linked to a substantive (noun or pronoun). In the following example, the participial phrase should modify the missing subject (*he* or *she*) and not *the sun*. Avoid the habit of starting too many sentences with participial phrases, even if they do not dangle.

Examples:

Coming home late at night, the sun began to rise. [dangling participle; *correct*: Coming home late at night, she saw the sun beginning to rise.]

He ran *swift* and *quiet* through the woods. [should be *swiftly* and *quietly*]

He could not play the violin very *good*. [should be *well*]

The roses smell *sweetly*. [should be *sweet*]

7 | Case

Words can have different forms when they serve different functions in a sentence. *I* as the subject becomes *me* as an object and *my* as a possessive. The objective form is used after a preposition. *Who* is subjective and *whom* is objective. Nouns use an apostrophe in their possessive form. Pronouns do not.

Examples:

> *I* think that *my* novel will make *me* famous. [subjective, possessive, objective]
>
> Between *you* and *me* I think John is a thief. [objective after preposition]
>
> To *whom* did you give the money? *Who* gave you your instructions? [*whom* is an object and *who* is a subject]
>
> It's *John's* first story, but *its* plot is terrific. [correct use of possessive]

8 | Agreement

Agreement between a subject and a verb or between a noun and its pronoun means, in each case, that both items "agree" in (have the same) person and number. A singular subject takes a singular verb, even if a plural noun intervenes between the subject and verb. A plural subject takes a plural verb, even if there is an intervening singular noun between the subject and verb. A pronoun should agree in number and person with its antecedent regardless of what sort of elements are placed between it and its antecedent. If there are two subjects, one of which is plural, the other of which is singular, the verb agrees with the nearer one. Antecedents involving *kind of, sort of, type of* take singular pronouns, but the results are often so awkward that it might be better to avoid the construction. A collective noun can be either singular or plural, depending on the context.

Examples:

> *The bark* of these trees *is* infested with bugs. [The verb *is* agrees with *bark* and not with the intervening plural *trees.*]

Amanda, together with a few others, finished *her* story before the deadline. [*Her* agrees with *Amanda* and not with the intervening plural.]

One or both stories are going to be published in the literary magazine. [When one subject is singular and the other plural, the verb agrees with whichever one is nearer.]

This sort of apples *is* good for applesauce. [correct, but awkward]

The committee is pleased with the decision. [collective noun as singular]

The committee are in serious disagreement. [collective noun as plural]

9 | Tense

Using the wrong tense means choosing a form of the verb that will place the action in the wrong period of time, either in an absolute sense or in relation to what is taking place in the rest of the sentence or paragraph. The six principle tenses are the following: *present* (I see); *past* (I saw); *future* (I shall see); *present perfect* (I have seen); *past perfect* (I had seen); *future perfect* (I shall have seen).

Avoid shifts in tense within a given passage or within the entire narrative. Most stories are told in the past tense, but in certain kinds of stories the present tense can prove effective. In any case, be consistent.

To indicate an action that took place in the past before another action that also took place in the past use the past perfect tense. To indicate an action in the future that will take place before another action in the future use the future perfect tense.

Examples:

> I was visiting Amanda, and we were having a very serious discussion. All of a sudden, in walks Michael and ruins everything. [tense shift]

> By the time he arrived *I had already hidden* the money. [past perfect]

> I shall start writing my book next week, but before then *I shall have finished* all the necessary research. [future perfect]

13B Punctuation

When we speak we naturally break up the flow of language with certain pauses or stops or more subtle indicators in order to make what we are saying as clear as possible. One might call these voice manipulations invisible punctuation marks. We all know what a question sounds like, and we know how to pause parenthetically. Since written language came after spoken language, this invisible punctuation had to be made visible. In English we have developed certain conventions of punctuation.

1 | Period

The period is commonly used to end a declarative sentence or even an imperative sentence. It is also used with some abbreviations, though, over the years, there has been more and more of a tendency to omit periods in abbreviations. For instance, we use *USA* instead of *U.S.A.*, and *NY* instead of *N.Y.* Periods are used with *Mr.* and *Mrs.*, but not with *Ms* and *Miss*. When in doubt consult a good dictionary.

2 | Comma

A comma indicates a slight pause within a sentence and is used in a wide variety of constructions. The following are the most common functions of the comma.

(a) A comma is used before the conjunction that joins two main clauses.

(b) A comma is used after an introductory dependent clause to separate it from the main clause.

(c) Commas are used to separate the parts of a series, unless conjunctions are used instead. They are not used with adjectives that are supplementary.

(d) Nonrestrictive modifiers should be set off by commas. No commas should be used with restrictive modifiers.

(e) Commas should be used with appositives, parenthetical elements, and absolute phrases.

(f) Dates and geographical expressions should contain commas to separate their various parts.

(g) A comma usually precedes a quotation, though there are exceptions (see Chapter 8).

Examples:

You can try to make your living as a writer, or *you can prepare yourself for a more conventional career.* [two main clauses]

If I have enough time this summer, I plan to work on a novel. [introductory dependent clause]

Last week there were demonstrations *in England, in France*, and *in Germany*. [a series of phrases]

I stood under a *big* oak tree with a *little* old lady. [supplementary adjectives]

Angelica, *who has a wonderful sense of humor*, amused us all evening. [nonrestrictive modifier]

The woman who amused us all evening was named Angelica. [restrictive modifier]

He went to Harvard, *one of the best universities in America.* [nonrestrictive appositive]

When Laura was accepted at Harvard, she was, *naturally,* very pleased. [naturally is parenthetical]

She decided, *her novel having failed,* that she would go to graduate school. [absolute phrase]

On *April 2, 1988,* she arrived in *Boston, Massachusetts.* [dates and places]

Spinoza said, "Desire is the very essence of man." [quotation]

3 | Semicolon and colon

A semicolon can often be used instead of a coordinating conjunction between independent clauses. A semicolon can also be used to separate a series of long or complicated elements within a sentence that are themselves subdivided by commas. A colon is usually used to indicate that something will follow.

Examples:

Among Shakespeare's most impressive creations are Hamlet, a confused prince who thinks too much; King Lear, a proud old man who realizes his fault too late; and Lady Macbeth, an ambitious woman who drives her husband to murder. [a series, the parts of which contain commas]

4 | Apostrophe

An apostrophe is a mark used to show the omission of a letter or letters in a word or words forming contractions, or to show possession in nouns and indefinite pronouns. To show joint possession it is only necessary to use the apostrophe with the last owner named (for example, "John and Mary's house"). An apostrophe is not used in personal pronouns. It is used to form plurals of dates, numbers, or words being considered as words. It is used in certain phrases that express time or distance, though they do not really involve possession (for example, "a month's pay").

5 | Quotation marks

Quotation marks are used to enclose all direct quotations except those set apart in different type or distinguished by other mechanical means, such as special spacing. They indicate that the material was written by someone else and is only being reproduced. In fiction they indicate that one of the characters is speaking directly. Quotation marks are also used to enclose titles of shorter works, such as short stories, short plays, poems, paintings, or parts of books. To indicate a quotation within a quotation, use single quotation marks.

6 | Other punctuation marks

(a) The *question mark* is used for direct questions, but not in indirect questions.

(b) An *exclamation point* is used to show some strong emotion or surprise.

(c) A *dash* is used to indicate an interruption in thought. It is very useful in dialogue. Dashes can also be used to set off parenthetical elements.

(d) *Parentheses* and *brackets* are used to set off words, phrases, clauses, or even sentences that are inserted in a sentence by way of comment, explanation, or translation, but which are structurally independent of the sentence. In a parenthetical sentence within another sentence, the normal punctuation falls *outside* of the parentheses. In a separate parenthetical sentence the punctuation falls *inside* the parentheses. Brackets are used for editorial comments and translations. They are also used when a parenthetical remark falls within another parenthetical remark. Example: [Mary (who was Ted's lawyer) disagreed.]

(e) *Ellipses* (. . .) are used to indicate that within a quoted passage certain words have been omitted. If the omission takes place at the end of a sentence, a period is added (. . . .), but under no circumstances should there be more than four dots. In fiction, ellipses are sometimes used in passages of stream of consciousness to indicate a lack of continuity. This device should not be overused.

Examples:

Where did you get that money? [direct question]

He asked him where he got the money. [indirect question]

"Fantastic!" he said when he saw the view. [exclamation point for an emotional expression]

He said, "The murderer is—," but before he could finish he died. [dash indicates interruption]

She bought that house—it is hard to believe—for less than forty thousand dollars. [parenthetical dashes]

Nil desperandum (never despair)! [foreign words in italics, translation in parentheses]

"Nothing appears more surprising . . . than the easiness with which the many are governed by the few." [Ellipses indicate that a phrase has been omitted from this sentence by David Hume.]

13C   Mechanics

1 | Capitals

In prose the first word of every sentence should be capitalized. This is also true of most poetry, but, in addition, the first letter of every line is usually capitalized. There are many exceptions, of course, especially in modern poetry.

Capitals are used in proper names, races, religions, states, cities, streets, societies, historical periods, days of the week, months, the names of courses (History 71), but not for the names of subjects (history). Capitals are used when a title that identifies the position someone holds precedes the name and is thought of as part of the name (for example, President Truman). This is also true of family relationships (Uncle John).

Capitals are used for the major words in all titles. Articles, prepositions, and conjunctions are not capitalized in titles, but the first and last words are always capitalized, no matter what they are. Anyone who has seen the poems of e.e. cummings knows that there are exceptions.

Capitals are used sometimes for emphasis. To attract special attention to a word one might capitalize the first letter or even the entire word. The proper noun *God* (in the Judeo-Christian tradition) and all the pronouns that refer to God are capitalized, but the common noun *god* is not capitalized.

The four directions are not capitalized unless they refer to specific regions of a country (the South, the West, the East, the North).

Examples:

Here's to my comrades, one and all,
Those who will live and those who will fall.
(Anonymous)

[In conventional poetry the first letter of each line is capitalized.]

During the Korean War, President Truman ordered General MacArthur home and relieved him of his command. [Capitalize names of wars and titles that are used as part of a name.]

Columbia University is located in New York City. Sheila took a course there in the Romantic Movement. [Capitalize names of institutions and cities and historical periods.]

Aldous Huxley wrote a novel called *After Many a Summer Dies the Swan*. [Capitalize major words in titles.]

The early Christians believed in God and rejected the pagan gods of other religions. [In the Judeo-Christian tradition *God* is a proper noun, and *gods*, meaning other deities, is a common noun.]

The only god she ever worshiped was Money. [A word can be capitalized at times for special emphasis.]

2 | Abbreviations

In formal writing some abbreviations are acceptable and some are not. Among the acceptable abbreviations are *Mr.*, *Mrs.*, *Dr.*; and A.M., P.M., A.D., and B.C., all of which are usually printed in small capitals; and *Y.M.C.A.* (and certain other organizations). Titles such as *Professor* and *President* should be written out, as should be the names of countries, states, cities, avenues, and streets.

Acronyms are words formed from the first letters of many words or from parts of those words without the benefit of periods. If an acronym is generally recognizable, it is acceptable in formal writing. Otherwise, the entire name of the object or organization should be used. Some of the acronyms that have been in general use for a long time are *NASA*, *NATO*, *SAT*, and *HUD*.

3 | Numbers

Numbers should be written out if it is possible to do so in one or two words. If two words are required, they should be hyphenated. If a number requires more than two words, it should not be written out. Numerals should be used for numbering pages, for numbers in addresses, and for dates.

4 | Italics

Italics can be indicated in unprinted manuscripts by underlining. They are used for titles of publications, for names of ships, and for elements needing emphasis. Italics are also used for used foreign words and expressions.

Examples:

He was reading *Pride and Prejudice* by Jane Austen and enjoying himself immensely on the maiden voyage of the *Titanic* in 1912. [Titles and names of ships are in italics. Dates are in numerals.]

As long as this is *my* house I will do in it what I please. [italics used to emphasize *my*]

It was a case of *de facto* segregation. [Foreign words and expressions are written in italics.]

13D Spelling

Routine spelling questions can usually be handled with the help of a good dictionary and a few basic guidelines.

1 | Compound words

Compound words are made up of two or more words that serve as a single unit or modifier. Some of these are written as one word; some are hyphenated. Consult a good dictionary for specific cases. When they appear before a noun almost any words can be linked by hyphenation to form a single adjective, but the same words are not hyphenated when they appear after the noun.

Examples:

He was a well-known painter. [hyphenated before a noun]

As a painter he was well known. [no hyphenation after a noun]

The Marines established a beachhead with a do-or-die attitude. [hyphenated before a noun]

There were first-rate firemen and fire engines at the scene. [hyphenated before a noun]

2 | Final silent *e*

A final silent *e* is usually dropped when an ending beginning with another vowel is added (*dine, dining*). A final silent *e* is retained in certain words to distinguish them from words that have similar sounds or spellings (*dye, dyeing*). A final silent *e* is usually retained when an ending beginning with a consonant is added (*hate, hateful; shape, shapely*). The final *e* is not dropped in words ending in *ce* and *ge* when an ending beginning in *a* or *o* is added (*change, changeable; notice, noticeable*).

3 | Other spelling rules

(a) A final consonant is doubled when a suffix beginning with a vowel is added if the following conditions are involved: the consonant ends a stressed syllable or a word of one syllable, and the consonant is preceded by a single vowel. The word *begin* meets these conditions. When the suffix *-ing* is added, the consonant *n* is doubled and we get *beginning*. The word *talk* ends in a consonant, but the preceding letter is not a vowel. Therefore, when we add *-ing* we get *talking*.

(b) A final *l* should not be dropped before adding *ly* (*continual, continually*).

(c) Put *i* before *e* except after a *c* that is preceded by a vowel. After an *l*, *i* usually comes first (except *leisure*). After a *c*, *e* usually comes first, except in words ending in *ient* and *iency* (*receive, deceive, relief, science, efficient, proficiency, believe*).

(d) In a word ending in *y* preceded by a consonant, change the *y* to *i* when an ending beginning with anything except *i* is added to it (*lady, ladies*). For words ending in *ie*, drop the *e* and change *i* to *y* before adding *ing* (*tie, tying; lie, lying*).

(e) Only three verbs end in *-ceed* (*exceed, proceed, succeed*). Others that sound similar end in *-cede*, except *supersede*.

13E Diction

One of the most important ingredients in good writing is choosing exactly the right word for every situation. This is especially true for poetry.

1 | Word choice

We all have two kinds of vocabulary. One is *passive* and consists of all the words we can recognize when we read or listen to someone talk. The other is *active* and consists of all the words we are capable of using when we write or speak.

When we write we must depend on the words that we have complete command of in order to guarantee precision and avoid unfortunate connotations. The *denotation* of a word is its literal meaning. Its *connotation* may be more subtle and may include certain feelings, ideas, and value judgments.

Examples:

[Preferred word choice in parentheses]

I want you to vote for Joe Boss, one of the greatest *politicians* (*statesmen*) in America. He has always been *truthful* (*sincere*) and *all tied up in his work* (*devoted to his public duties*).

This little *shack* (*house*) is for sale. It has an *outmoded* (*old-fashioned*) fireplace and *curious* (*quaint*) old windows. It has recently been *scraped and painted* (*redecorated*). It is located on a lovely *plot of earth* (*piece of land*) near an *overgrown* (*wooded*) area.

2 | Triteness (clichés)

The word *trite* comes from the Latin *tritus*, meaning *rubbed* or *worn out*. Trite expressions or clichés are expressions, often similes or metaphors, that have been used so often that they are worn out. They have lost their originality, their color, and their effectiveness. They should be *avoided like the plague* (for example), unless, of course, you are writing dialogue for a boring character who is inclined to use such expressions.

Examples:

Avoid like the plague	Cheap as dirt
Busy as a bee	Clear as a bell
After all is said and done	Dumb as an ox
At one fell swoop	Fat as a pig

Nervous as a cat	Trembling like a leaf
Pretty as a picture	The early bird catches the
Quick as lightning	worm.
Sleep like a log	Something is rotten in
Few and far between	Denmark.
Thin as a rail	In the final analysis
Method in his madness	Last but not least

3 | Jargon

The manner of speaking or writing peculiar to a certain occupation or profession is called *jargon*. The worlds of business, education, medicine, law, sports, and government generate a lot of jargon, a lot of specialized language, some of it evasive and euphemistic, some of it technical. The military long ago turned a *retreat* into a *strategic withdrawal*. Businessmen are fond of making verbs out of nouns such as *priority*, which becomes *prioritize*. In sports, *underdogs* are always out to *upset leading contenders*. Politicians talk about *human rights* and the *democratic process* and often consume a ton of language to tell us that *the future lies ahead*.

If you have characters who talk this way, then write realistic dialogue. Otherwise, try to avoid jargon.

4 | Slang (and other informal language)

The impulse to say things in an informal and colorful way seems to be natural and universal. Every language has its slang, as does every generation. Many of the expressions appear overnight like wild mushrooms, and some of them disappear just as quickly. The word *jazz* has stuck because it describes a kind of music, but expressions such as *jazz up* and *all that jazz* seem to be fading out.

Some slang is created by giving a new meaning to an old word. *Hock*, for instance, is an old word that means "the joint of the hind leg of certain animals." About a hundred years ago it acquired the slang meaning "to pawn" or "to borrow money against some collateral." In more recent decades it came to mean "to shoplift," but that meaning is now disappearing. Other such words include *cool, crazy, grass, acid, swell, haymaker* (a knock-out punch). Some slang requires the combining of words in a new way: *goon* (from *gorilla* and *baboon*), *hangout, hangover, hotshot*. Some slang is sheer invention: *dork, scam, boondoggle*.

Colloquialisms are often informal abbreviations of formal words: *phone, comp, prof, math, auto, psych*. Illiteracies involve errors in grammar or spelling, but are often part of the everyday regional speech: *ain't, hain't, disremember, hisself, theirselfs, heared, sorta, kinda*.

Obviously, you will have to use informal language in dialogue, but keep in mind that such language changes rapidly and can even identify the generation of the speaker. A jazz-age character might say, "We had a swell time at the road-house." A more contemporary character might say, "We partied all night at a club."

How much informal language you use, aside from dialogue, depends on your style. If you are attempting to write formal, classical prose, then you should probably avoid informal expressions or use them with caution.

5 | Accents

Many writers have attempted to capture regional accents in their works. The most famous, perhaps, is Mark Twain. *Huckleberry Finn* is told in the first person by a poorly educated, but very amusing, boy of thirteen. The attempt to put on paper the actual sound of a dialect means abandoning grammar and all the conventions of spelling. It means trying to "sound out" the language. Some readers find this kind of writing hard to read. One way around this difficulty is to suggest the accent in a limited way and to use more normal language otherwise (see Chapter 8).

6 | Glossary (usage)

Listed here are a few samples of the problems in usage that might confront the writer. For more complete coverage see one of the standard reference books on usage, such as H. W. Fowler's *Dictionary of Modern English Usage* or Margaret Nicholson's *Dictionary of American-English Usage*.

accidently An incorrect form of *accidentally*.

advice, advise *Advice* is a noun. *Advise* is a verb.

affect, effect *Affect* is a verb that means "to influence." As a noun *effect* means the "result." As a verb *effect* means "to bring about," as in: *Antibiotics effected a revolution in medicine.*

aggravate Incorrectly used to mean "irritate." It means "to make worse."

allusion, illusion An *allusion* is a reference to something. An *illusion* is a distorted idea of reality.

alot Incorrect spelling of *a lot*.

already, all ready *Already* means "before." *All ready* means "all prepared."

alright Incorrect spelling of *all right*.

altogether, all together *Altogether* means "entirely." *All together* means "all in a group."

among, between *Between* is used with two objects. *Among* is used with three or more.

awhile, a while Awhile is an adverb (*we stayed awhile*). *A while* is used after a preposition (*we stayed for a while*).

being as (that) Incorrect for *because*.

borrow off Incorrect for *borrow from*.

bust Informal for *burst*.

center around Illogical for *center on*.

complement, compliment A *complement* is something that completes. A *compliment* is praise.

consensus of opinion Redundant. Consensus means "majority opinion."

disinterested Means "impartial" not "uninterested."

eminent, imminent *Eminent* means "famous." *Imminent* means "about to happen."

explicit, implicit *Explicit* means "expressed openly." *Implicit* means "implied."

farther, further *Farther* is usually used for distances. *Further* means "additional" in other contexts.

fewer, less *Fewer* is used with things you can count in units. *Less* is used with general quantities (*money, fuel*).

fun Should be used as a noun and not as an adjective.

go, goes Should not be used for *say* (*says*).

hanged *Hanged* means "executed." Otherwise use *hung*.

hanging out Slang when it means "being somewhere without any special purpose."

hopefully Incorrect when used to replace the verb *to hope* (*I hope, he hopes*). Correct when used as an adjective (He looked hopefully toward the sky.)

imply, infer *Imply* means "to suggest." *Infer* means to "conclude."

irregardless Incorrect for *regardless*.

lay Incorrect when used instead of *lie* (I want to lie down).

liable to Informal when used in place of *likely to*.

like Incorrect when used as a conjunction instead of *as* or *as if*.

myself Incorrect when substituted for *I* or *me*.

of Incorrect when used instead of *have* (I could have done it).

okay Informal. Also spelled *O.K.*

principal, principle *Principal* means "main" or "chief." *Principle* is a noun that means "basic truth."

real Informal when used as an adverb instead of *very*.

so Incorrect as a substitute for *very* (She's always so tired).

stationary, stationery *Stationary* means "not moving."
Stationery is paper.

use to Incorrect when used instead of *used to*.

-wise A suffix used in a lot of jargon (*costwise, timewise, comfortwise*). Should be avoided in formal prose.

13F **Good writing is not just a matter of correct grammar and punctuation—it is a matter of effectiveness.**

Here are some other fundamentals to consider.

1 | Logic

Good writing depends in part on precision, and being precise often means being logical. Avoid irrelevancies, hasty general-izations, and contradictions. Use your common sense.

Examples:

[all illogical]

He's probably a war criminal, because everybody in the village hates him and he's an old alcoholic, who reminds me of a horrible sergeant I had when I was in the army.

Although there are portions of the play that are extremely amusing, it is obviously a work of great significance.

I like Hardy's novels because I have always enjoyed reading them.

Television is a menace to society. Look at all the violence it has caused.

2 | Clarity

All writing should be clear, whether it is a description of how to fill out your income tax forms or a novel that looks into the secrets of the human heart. Sometimes it is an overly complex style and a pompous vocabulary that leads to a lack of clarity. Sometimes a statement can be accidentally ambiguous.

Examples:

The cryptical involutions of this megalomaniac drew him into the crepuscular depths.

He met Miranda at the football game, which he thought was terrible.

3 | Emphasis

There are various ways to emphasize those elements in your writing that need special attention. There are simple mechanical devices, such as italics and capitalization. There is the repetition of key words or phrases. Also, there is the rhetorical question and the manipulation of word order. Sometimes, not revealing the full meaning of a sentence until the very end will create suspense. This device is known as a *periodic* sentence. If there is a series in a sentence, it can be arranged so that it builds from the weakest to the strongest element.

Examples:

All you need in life is love. [Periodic sentence. The meaning is not revealed until the final word.]

I believe in *work*, the doctrine of *work*, the religion of *work*. [using italics for emphasis]

Is there anything wrong with materialism? Is there anything wrong with wanting to be comfortable instead of uncomfortable? [rhetorical questions for emphasis]

"Reputation, reputation, reputation! O, I have lost my reputation! I have lost the immortal part of myself, and what remains is bestial. My reputation, Iago, my reputation!" [repetition for emphasis]

—**Shakespeare:** *Othello*

The movie was good; it was brilliant; it was the best movie I had seen all year. [a series that builds from mildest to strongest]

4 | Repetition

Though repetition can be used for emphasis, it can also be misused. The pointless repetition of certain words and phrases can mar your prose, and the excessive repetition of ideas can be boring. Redundancy sometimes means repetition in general, but certain expressions are labeled redundant because a part of them will express the whole meaning, which makes the rest of the expression superfluous. For example, consider "true facts" (what is true is a fact; what is a fact is true).

Examples:

Some writers are better writers than other writers, but sometimes the inferior writers have more commercial success than the superior writers. [excessive repetition]

In the book *Brave New World*, the author, Aldous Huxley, gives us a picture of the future world several hundred years from now. [redundancies: "the book," "the author," and "the future," should be omitted]

5 | Wordiness

Wordiness in prose can be a weakness, but in poetry it can be a disaster. Avoid circumlocutions (roundabout expressions), irrelevancies, and padding.

Examples:

In conclusion, I would like to say that it is, more or less, important, in my opinion, to create characters that are, in a sense, alive and have all the characteristics of living people. [wordy because of pointless qualifying phrases and repetition]

6 | Awkwardness

Awkwardness is something you can detect with your ear. Clumsy writing can be the result of any number of things, such as word choice, word order, sentence length, or a poor combination of sounds. Rhyming may be good for poetry but it is usually damaging to prose.

Examples:

The author, Thomas Hardy, of this story, in my opinion, gives very good details in it. [awkward because of word order]

The object of the game seems to me to be to see who can score the most points. [awkward repetition of sounds]

The slow sloop slid through the soft surf to the glistening shore. [awkward because of excessive alliteration]

7 | Variety

Without some variety in sentence length and pace, your prose can become as monotonous as a metronome.

Examples:

The soldier looked toward the mountain. The mountain looked mysterious. The clouds were very dark. Daylight was fading. The soldier turned back. The path was rough. Soon it was dark. [deadly repetition of the same sentence pattern]

13G   Manuscript form

Over the years, great works of literature have been written in many strange ways, in handwriting difficult to decipher, on scraps of paper of various sizes and color, on scrolls, in folios and notebooks. Before the standardization of spelling, there was a great deal of orthographical inconsistency. Shakespeare sometimes spelled the same word two or three different ways. Even his name comes down to us in a variety of spellings.

Individual eccentricities in the use of language and the preparation of manuscripts will probably always be with us, but certain technological advances have tended to stabilize the language and establish certain manuscript conventions. Movable type, the linotype machine, the typewriter, and the computer have all influenced the way we prepare and present written materials. Modern publishers expect manuscripts to be prepared in a way that is suitable for the publishing process. There are practical considerations, such as sufficient space for editorial and production notations. The exact manuscript form expected depends, to some extent, on the type of material involved. (The form for film and television scripts is taken up in Chapter 12.)

1 | Fiction

If you have ever seen the manuscript of a piece of fiction after it has been through the mill at a publishing house, you will understand the logic of what is considered standard manuscript form. When the author's copy is returned, after the work has been edited, set, and printed, it is full of notations.

There are often several kinds of editing involved in the processing of a manuscript. The *supervising editor* of a project usually edits for content and discusses possible changes with the author. Major changes of this sort take place before the manuscript goes into production. The author makes the negotiated changes and provides the publisher with a clean manuscript. Some authors will allow their editors a free hand in making changes; others will insist on approving all alterations.

Next comes the *copy editor* or *house editor*, who reviews the spelling, punctuation, grammar, and even certain purely factual matters, such as dates or geographical locations. These basic things are called matters of "style" (in a limited sense of the word). Since there is still no universal agreement on all matters of style, every publisher uses some standard style sheet, sometimes one developed in house, such as the *New York Times* style sheet. A widely used reference book is *The Chicago Manual of Style*, now in its sixteenth edition (University of Chicago Press).

The *production editor's* job is to translate design decisions into notations for the printer and typesetter. Typographic instructions are made, involving such things as choices of type, line length, and indentation.

Usually, *proofreading* refers to the reviewing of galleys or a *proof* of the material that has been set in type. Since even the best typesetters make mistakes, both publisher and author review the galleys. Standard proofreaders' marks (see below) are used for making corrections.

The marks of punctuation

⊙ Period

⋀ or ⟋ Comma

=⟋ or ⟍⟋ Hyphen

:⟋ Colon

;⟋ Semicolon

⋁ Apostrophe

⟋ Exclamation mark or
Exclamation point

?⟋ Question mark or
Interrogation point

/en/ or en dash   En dash

/em/ or em   One em dash

/2em/ or 2em   Two em dash

( ) or (⟋) Parentheses

Quotation marks
(double)

Quotation marks
(single)

The marks of typography

⌁ Delete or take out

⌁ Delete and close up

stet Let it stand "as is" or
disregard changes
marked

⋀ Caret. insert

∿ or ⊓ Transpose

⊙ Turn over (letter or cut
upside down)

wf Wrong font

⊗ or ✗ Replace
broken or defective
letter

Insert space

⌒ Close up space

© Cengage Learning

tr	Marginal symbol for transpose	✓	Equalize space
♂	Transfer circled matter to position shown by arrow	⊔	Indent one em or insert one em quad
		caps or <u>Scott</u>	Capital letters
⊟ (2)	Two ems	S.C. or <u>Scott</u>	Small capitals
¶	Paragraph	c+s.c. or <u>Scott</u>	Caps and small caps
No ¶	No paragraph	*rom*	Roman (change from italic to roman)
⊏	Move to left		
⊐	Move to right	*sp*	Spell out
⊐⊏	Center	?	Query to author
⊓	Move up	*out sc*	Out. see copy
⊔	Move down	↪	No paragraph — run in
//	Align	*ld*	Insert 2 point lead
‖	Straighten or justify	↓ or ⊥	Push down space
lc or *l.c.*	Lower case	✱	Asterisk
ital or <u>Scott</u>	Italic	⌄3	Superior figure or letter
bf or <u>Scott</u>	Boldface	⌃3	Inferior figure or letter

© Cengage Learning

The main points to keep in mind about standard manuscript form for fiction are the following:

(A) Paper

Use standard 8½" by 11" white typing paper of a reasonable weight, usually a number 1 grade of 20-pound bond.

(B) Margins

Leave 1½" at the top and left-hand side; 1" at the bottom and right-hand side.

(C) Page numbers

Page numbers should be in Arabic numerals in the upper right-hand corner, about ½" in and ½" down from the corner.

(D) Indentation

Standard indentation is five spaces. Indent all paragraphs. Some designers prefer that first paragraphs and paragraphs following major headings (if any) be set flush left.

(E) Titles

Titles of short stories or chapters of longer works should be placed three inches below the top of the page and should be typed in upper-case letters (capitals).

(F) Spacing

Use a double-space between all lines. Between major parts of stories or chapters use four spaces.

A diagram of standard manuscript form for fiction follows.

2 | Poetry

Since poetry has a typographical dimension, it is difficult to define a standard presentation. Poems depend heavily on line length and spacing. These are determined by the author, not by editors or printers. Freely structured poetry should be typed on 8½" by 11" white paper, and it should include the title of the poem and the author's name, either in the upper left-hand corner or at the end of the poem.

If the style of the poem permits, it is single-spaced, centered on the page, and usually uses a capital letter at the beginning of each line.

Untitled poems are usually referred to by their first line in brackets: [I Wake and Feel the Fell of Dark, not Day].

Author's name   Page number here 2
                                        can be omitted on title page

Top margin 1 1/2"

STANDARD INDENTATION FIVE SPACES

Title 3" from top   TITLE IN UPPER CASE
of page

Left-hand margin 1 1/2"

Right-hand margin 1"

Double double space after title. Begin first
paragraph with or without indentation.
Subsequent paragraphs indented five spaces.

Double space the entire manuscript. Use
double double spacing to indicate breaks,
parts, or subdivisions. Pica type is preferred to
elite. Avoid fancy typefaces such as italic. Use a
good grade of twenty-pound bond. Do not use
erasable bond.
Use mechanical correction, if possible.
Avoid handwritten corrections or insertions.
Save the text in your computer or make a
carbon as insurance against losing the
manuscript.

Bottom margin 1"

© Cengage Learning

Standard Form for Fiction

EXERCISES

The fundamentals of writing can be improved in the following passages. Rewrite these passages, eliminating the weaknesses in grammar, punctuation, mechanics, spelling, diction, and effectiveness:

1. She was a child of the streets. Abandoned by her parents at the age of 10. She lived in the ruined rubble of collapsing buildings in the south bronx. There were other wild orphans in those ruins without parents. They herded together for survival and prayed on unsuspecting victims, and whom even pitied them thus being lured into a trap. Her name was Jennifer she could have been a star an actress or something on account of her beautiful looks, but no her life was wasted. They found her dead when she was only 12.

2. He thought of education like he thought of being fed by his mother when he was a small little child. She was always forcing food into his mouth, parting his teeth with the hard spoon, hurting him. Growing up his mother's voice haunted him, because she was always scolding him for this and that. So he could not open his mind to education and he rejected education and remained uneducated for a long time. One day when he was laying on his bed and starring out the window he saw a white seagull. Gliding on the wind, the freedom it epitomized stirred his heart and soul. He suddenly knew what he had to do and everything was different from that point in time onward.

Writing as a Career

There have been drastic changes in the world of books in the past decade. Those cozy old bookstores in which we may have browsed for hours are now mostly gone. Even the large chains of bookstores are in financial jeopardy. For instance, Border's has gone into bankruptcy, and other large outlets are on the brink, wondering what they can do to survive.

One of the most important factors is the e-book, a book that is not a book as we know it. It is not bound paper. It is electronic. To see and read it you need a gadget with a screen, a small, lightweight gadget within which there can be hundreds or thousands of titles. What the impact of the *Kindles* and *Nooks* will be in the long run we don't know. There are many predictions.

Another thing in the world of writers that is changing drastically is research. Through information sources such as *Google* and *Wikipedia* a reader can gather information about almost anything in the world. For instance, in early editions of this *Handbook* there were many lists. Lists of publishers, magazines, newspapers, agents, bookstores, reviewers, creative writing programs, contests and grants. Now, all of this information can be had in a flash on a computer.

In spite of this *Brave New World* atmosphere, there are still plenty of writers around. Some of them even earn money. Most of them are sensible enough to have backup jobs. Many of them teach English in high school or college. Some of the more adventurous writers like to emulate the writers of the early twentieth century, like Hemingway and Fitzgerald. The successful ones celebrated in Paris. Those who did not earn enough money took "mindless" jobs that only require putting in time and do not interfere with what is going on in their head. Alan Dugan, for instance, a Pulitzer Prize–winning poet, once worked in a factory that made plastic anatomical parts for medical students. It used to be traditional for young writers (and actors) to support themselves by holding jobs in restaurants or resorts.

There are some things that all writers should keep in mind, things that are part of the trade or craft. All that you must know can be found in LMP (*Literary Market Place*) which you can find in your local library or on your computer.

After you have created a wonderful story or book, you will be confronted by the difficult job of finding a publisher. You can find lists of agents and publishers on your computer. You will also find warnings about agents that might ask for money from you before they can place your book with a publisher. Stay away from these people. A good agent can be very helpful, but they will usually ask for 15% of everything you earn. In most cases it's worth it.

Sending out your manuscript directly to an editor is liable to be futile. Chances are the editor will never see it. A letter of inquiry might be better in most cases. But even then you can expect a form letter of rejection.

If your work is accepted, you can celebrate any which way you please, but don't forget to get some help with the contract that is offered to you. You may have a lawyer for such things, or an agent. In fact, it might be fairly easy at this point to get an agent interested. Consult lists from the information on your computer, or look up a reliable organization for writers, an organization such as the Authors Guild. They can answer all your questions. You would do well to join such a group.

If you plan to do the transaction yourself with a publisher, you might consult a book called *Negotiating a Book Contract* by Mark L. Levine.

If you are lucky enough to earn royalties or fees for your work, you must remember to include this income in your tax form. Consult your accountant for details, or study a tax book. There are many on the internet.

As examples for this chapter you will find two articles to give you a sample of how writers think.

EXAMPLE 14A

WHY WE WRITE
by Laura Maylene Walter

My writing career, as it appeared from my perspective as a twenty-two-year-old college graduate, looked pretty darn promising. By the time I won Washington College's Sophie Kerr Prize, which came with a check for the obscene amount of $61,000, for my first (and still unpublished) novel, I had already won six National Scholastic Writing awards, attended the Pennsylvania Governor's School for the Arts fiction program, published a few pieces of short fiction, and been featured in a local newspaper that proclaimed I was "The County's Best Writer." The day after I won the Sophie Kerr Prize, my picture appeared on the front page of the *Baltimore Sun* and of the *Washington Post* Metro section.

I entered my postgraduate life with instant (if fleeting) fame and fortune—in short, a totally unrealistic windfall for a literary fiction writer.

I wasted no time putting pressure on myself. I wanted to prove that I deserved to win that prize. I wanted to break the so-called curse that apparently has prevented any winner of the Sophie Kerr Prize, given annually since 1968, from going on to an illustrious literary career. Back then, I thought the answer lay in the novel that won me the prize in the first place.

I submitted "Developing Olivia" to more than sixty agents. I received requests for the manuscript, then personal letters, and even a few phone calls. One agent gave me a twenty-minute critique over the phone, ending with, "It's rare for me to make these calls. You definitely have what it takes to have your first novel published by a major house." She did not take my novel on, however, and when I later sent her a second manuscript—more flawed than the first, it turns out—she sent me a form rejection. I can't blame her.

Once I'd admitted that the second novel was a flop, I took a hard look at my writing. What I found was not encouraging. My short story attempts were forgettable, even embarrassing. I tried to start another novel but couldn't get it off the ground. Finally, I saw that I couldn't get by on promise. I was going to have to work.

Over the next few years, I joined writing groups and churned out story after story. After a few mostly unsuccessful attempts at placing my work in select literary magazines, I gave up the idea of publishing my stories at all. I simply wrote, and revised, and then wrote and revised some more.

As time passed and my stories grew stronger, I knew I had to write another novel. But I was still afraid. Trying to find an agent had been heartbreaking, and my second novel was such a failure that I refuse even today to pull out the manuscript and look at it. How could I put myself through that again? It was starting to seem hopeless. I began to face the possibility that despite all my hopes and expectations I might not make it after all. Maybe I wasn't meant to be a writer. Maybe I wasn't talented enough or hardworking enough to achieve what I once felt capable of. I could quit, and that would be that. I'd be just another failed writer giving up on her dreams.

After confiding in my friends about my fears (and, I admit, shedding a few tears), I thought about why I had started writing in the first place. All my young life I had been told I was talented. That I had promise. That I was one of the best. If I quit, all of that would disappear. But so what? So what if I never published another word, or won another prize, or was mentioned in another newspaper article? When I first began writing I didn't do it for the praise and attention. I wrote for the writing itself—for the times it was just me, at a desk, putting one word down after another.

And so I wrote. I wrote for practice. I wrote for fun. I wrote to discover, to explore, to play. I wrote because I was never more content than when I was sitting quietly at my writing desk, churning out pages. I put the pressure of publication, of the Sophie Kerr Prize, behind me. I'd already faced my fears of never living up to that hype, and so I wrote as if I had lost everything. I just wrote.

Time passed. Eventually I finished book-length collection of short stories and developed an idea for that elusive third novel. Over the next few years that idea evolved into a manuscript. I believe in more than my first two novels put together. I also started submitting stories to literary magazine again—and of course I've racked up scores of rejections. While the rejections certainly outnumber everything else, the news hasn't all been bad. I've received several acceptances, I was named a finalist in two short fiction competitions, and my new novel became a semifinalist for a fellowship. These are small steps, and certainly nothing accompanied by a paycheck or a profile in the *Baltimore Sun*, but it is a start. I finally feel as if I'm on the right track. I've learned to write without the glow of praise and awards. I've learned how to write around a full time job and other real life obligations. I'm just learning to write.

I will always be grateful for the Sophie Kerr Prize. It was a lovely gift. But from my perspective now, those years of disappointment, rejection and struggle mean more than the day my name was called at commencement and I walked onstage to receive a check. Because by pushing through the self-doubt and working without recognition, I discovered that my love of writing is not motivated by praise of awards. And in the process, I learned something else: I believe in myself again.

Editor's Postscript: Several weeks after she submitted this essay for publication, Laura Maylene Walter informed us that her story collection, *Living Arrangements*, won the G. S. Sharat Chandra Prize for Short Fiction and will be published by BkMk Press next year.

Source: From Poets & Writers, Nov-Dec. 2010. Reprinted with permission.

EXAMPLE 14B

THE MAKING OF A WRITER
by Joyce Carol Oates

Telling stories, I discovered at the age of three or four, is a way of being told stories. One picture yields another; one set of words, another set of words. Like our dreams, the stories we tell are also the stories we are told. If I say that I write with the enormous hope of altering the world—and why write without that hope?—I should first say that I write to discover what it is *I will have written*. A love of reading stimulates the wish to write—so that one can read, as a reader, the words one has written. Storytellers may be finite in number but stories appear to be inexhaustible.

For many days—in fact for weeks—I have been tormented by the proposition that if I could set down, in reasonably lucid prose, the story of "the making of the writer Joyce Carol Oates," I might in some rudimentary way be defined, at least to myself. Stretched upon a grammatical framework, who among us does not appear to make sense? But the story will not cohere. The necessary words will not arrange themselves. Of the forty-odd pages I have written (each, I should confess, with the rapt, naïve certainty, *At last I have it*) very little strikes me as useful. The miniature stories I have told myself, by way of analyzing "myself," are not precisely lies; but, since each contains so small a fraction of the truth, it is untrue. Each angle of vision, each voice, yields (by way of that process of fictional abiogenesis[1] all storytellers know) a separate writer-self, an alternative Joyce Carol Oates. Each miniature story exerts so powerful an appeal (to the author, that is) that it could, in time, evolve

---

[1] **abiogenesis** Creation of life from lifeless material.

into a novel—for me the divine form, the ultimate artwork, toward which all the arts aspire. Consequently this "story" you are reading is an admission of failure, or, at the very most, a record of failed attempts. If knowing oneself is an alphabet, I seem to be stuck at *A*, and take solace from the elderly Yeats's remark in a letter: "Man can embody truth but he cannot know it."

One of the stories I tell myself has to do with the dream of a "sacred text."

Perhaps it is a dream, an actual dream: to set down words with such talismanic precision, such painstaking love, that they cannot be altered—that they constitute a reality of their own, and are not merely referential. It is one of the enigmas of our craft (so my writer friends agree) that, with the passage of time, *how* becomes an obsession, rather than *what*: it becomes increasingly more difficult to say the simplest things. Content yields to form, theme to "voice." But we don't know what voice is.

The story of the elusive sacred text has something to do with a childlike notion of omnipotent thoughts, a wish for immortality through language, a command that time stand still. What is curious is that writing, the act of writing, often satisfies these demands. We throw ourselves into it with such absorption, writing eight or ten hours at a time, writing in our daydreams, composing in our sleep; we enter that fictional world so deeply that time seems to warp or to fold back in upon itself. Where do you find the time, people ask, to write so much? But the time I inhabit is protracted; my interior clock moves with frustrating slowness.

The melancholy secret at the heart of all creative activity (we are not talking here of quality, that ambiguous term) has something to do with our desire to complete a work and to perfect it—this very desire bringing with it our exclusion from that phase of our lives. Though a novel must be begun, often with extraordinary effort, it eventually acquires its own rhythm, its own voice, and begins to write itself; and when it is completed, the writer is expelled—the door closes slowly upon him or her, but it does close. A work of prose may be many things to many people, but to the author it is a monument to a certain chunk of time: so many pulse-beats, so much effort. [1982]

Glossary of Literary Terms

abstract General and theoretical, without reference to specifics. Often applied to word choice. *Beauty* and *truth* are abstract.

absurd Illogical or senseless. In literary works certain artistic effects can be achieved by using absurd elements.

accent 1. The stress placed on a syllable in poetry. 2. A way of pronouncing a word that reveals a regional or foreign background.

act A major subdivision of a play or opera.

action The events that occur in any literary work. Action is presented through narration in fiction and poetry and through visual devices in drama and film. Dialogue and thoughts can also be considered part of the action. Compare *plot*, which requires action with form and significance.

adventure Usually applied to works that concentrate on suspenseful happenings rather than subtleties of theme or depth of character.

alexandrine A line of iambic hexameter (from French romances about Alexander the Great): "Beware the man who has no faith, no hope, no love."

allegory A kind of literary work in which the characters stand for certain ideas. Bunyan's *The Pilgrim's Progress* is often cited as an example.

alliteration The repetition of the initial sounds of certain words within a single line of poetry. "When I do count the clock that tells the time ..." (Shakespeare).

allusion A reference to a specific person, place, or thing, usually in a figure of speech: "Like Sisyphus he could have worked at his job forever without getting anywhere."

ambiguity Having more than one meaning. When it is accidental, ambiguity can be a flaw; when it is purposeful, it can add richness to a passage.

anachronism The placing of material in the wrong time period. Shakespeare, for instance, refers to a clock in

Julius Caesar, though clocks were not yet invented in Caesar's time.

anagram A rearrangement of the letters of one word to form another, as in *god-dog*.

analogy A comparison, as in a simile or metaphor, in which one thing is like another thing. "Achieving success is like climbing a ladder. It requires a series of steps."

anapest A metrical foot in poetry consisting of two unstressed syllables followed by a stressed syllable.

androgynous Having both male and female characteristics. Sometimes applied to literary works.

anecdote A brief narrative, usually designed to make a point.

angst *Anxiety* in German. A term associated with existentialism.

antagonist The opponent of the protagonist, who is usually the hero.

anticlimax Any action that takes place after the climax or resolution of a literary work. It is either a dramatic letdown or totally unnecessary.

antihero A modern type of hero, who does not have the stature and qualities of the classical hero, and is often an ordinary person.

aphorism A concise statement of some belief or truth. "Men are but children of a larger growth" (Dryden).

archetype An idea, character, or plot that is fundamental to the human imagination and recurs frequently in literature.

assonance The recurrence of vowel sounds, often used in poetry. "The squat pen rests; snug as a gun" (Heaney).

atmosphere The dominant mood in a literary work.

avant-garde A nontraditional work that is innovative or experimental.

ballad A narrative poem or song, sometimes anonymous and belonging to folk art. In poetry the standard ballad stanza has four lines that rhyme *abcb*. There are four stresses in the first and third lines and three stresses in the second and fourth lines.

beat A notation in scriptwriting meaning a pause in dialogue.

bildungsroman A novel that deals with the growth and development of a young person and his or her emergence into maturity.

biographical fallacy An error that assumes that a literary work can be interpreted entirely in terms of the author's biography.

black humor Humor that stems from a morbid and negative view of life.

blank verse Passages of iambic pentameter without end-rhyme.

burlesque Humor that ridicules ideas, characters, and events through the use of exaggeration and other distortions.

cadence The beat or rhythm of prose or free verse that is not conventionally structured or metrical.

caesura A pause in a line of poetry because of meaning or syntax. "Beauty is truth, truth beauty" (Keats).

canto A subdivision of a long poem, as in Dante's *The Divine Comedy*.

caricature The humorous distortion of the physical characteristics of recognizable personalities, as in political cartoons.

character 1. The traits or nature of a particular person. 2. A person, usually fictitious, who participates in the action of some work of literature.

characterization The process of presenting and developing literary characters through various devices.

chronology An order of events as they occur in time, from earliest to latest.

classic A literary work that has endured for a long time because of its impressive qualities and universal appeal.

classicism In all the arts, including literature, an approach that involves formalism, discipline, restraint, and strong conventions, as opposed to romanticism, which is more subjective, unrestrained, and emotional.

cliché A word or phrase that is worn out from overuse and loses much of its impact. "The ship of state."

cliff-hanger An adventure full of suspense that leaves its hero or heroine in danger at the end of each chapter or episode, used frequently in film or magazine serials, and especially popular several decades ago.

climax The moment of peak drama in a literary work. It often includes some sort of resolution of the conflict that has caused the drama.

closure The literary resolution of a text.

coherence Holding together. A coherent literary work is one in which all the parts are clearly put together.

colloquialism A word or phrase more appropriate to informal conversation than to formal writing. Realistic dialogue cannot avoid colloquialisms.

comedy A general event that is amusing, or, specifically, a play designed to amuse, as opposed to tragedy. Comedy can result from many sources, and can be farcical, satirical, slapstick, witty, situational, or even tragicomic.

comic relief An amusing episode in an otherwise serious or tragic work, designed to alleviate the tension momentarily.

conflict In literature, characters or forces in opposition. There are social and psychological and political conflicts, as well as individual conflicts, internal and external. From conflict grows drama and suspense.

connotation Extended meanings of words beyond their strict definition. Compare *politician* and *statesman*.

consonance The similarity of consonant sounds, used especially in poetry.

continuity A connected series of events that builds a plot. A technical term in scriptwriting that refers to the notations in a shooting script.

convention An established practice in any area. There are many literary conventions, such as capitalizing each new line of a poem. In popular adventures, the triumph of good over evil might be considered a convention.

cosmic irony Situational irony, in which the individual is seen as insignificant in the context of an immense and indifferent universe.

counterpoint A musical term sometimes applied to literature to describe the simultaneous development of two or more sets of circumstances that have parallel elements.

couplet A pair of lines of poetry, often rhyming and metrically similar.

crisis A period of severe conflict during which significant changes take place, often the high point of a literary work.

criticism In literature, the evaluation or analysis of a work. Sometimes the word is misunderstood as purely negative commentary.

cut In scriptwriting, a notation at the end of a scene. In editing, the shortening of a passage by omitting certain things.

dactyl In poetry, a metrical unit made up of one stressed syllable followed by two unstressed syllables.

deconstruction A critical movement associated with the French theorist Jacques Derrida, who holds that there is no stability between words and meaning and that the textual analysis of a work can generate innumerable and often contradictory meanings.

denotation The literal meaning of a word, without additional connotations.

denouement The final outcome or solution of a drama or narrative, in which all is explained.

description That aspect of narration that tells you what things are like, usually as perceived by the five senses.

dialect The particular way that a language is used by people of different regions or classes.

dialogue The words spoken to each other by characters in any form of literature.

diction The words chosen by an author. Diction is a major factor in tone and style.

didactic A term applied to literary works that are primarily designed to teach or preach.

dimeter A line of poetry with only two metrical feet. "Roses are red."

dirge A poem or song that mourns the dead.

discourse The language context in which certain subjects are discussed, a context that has its own terminology and agreed upon meanings and values (i.e. feminine discourse, Christian discourse).

dissonance An unappealing combination of sounds; sometimes, however, used consciously and effectively.

documentary A film of actual events, using a variety of sources. It can explore a subject in any field or dramatize episodes in history.

double entendre From the French, meaning "double meaning." A conscious device often found in satire and comedy, but also in more serious works. For instance, Hamlet asks Ophelia, "Are you fair?" Naturally, she is puzzled by the double entendre. It is a reference to both honesty and beauty.

double rhyme Words of two syllables that rhyme: *reaching, teaching.*

downstage That part of the stage closest to the audience. Used in stage directions.

drama Human events portrayed by actors on a stage with an audience in attendance.

dramatis personae Characters in the play.

elegy A poem for a funeral; a lamentation for the dead.

empathy A sharing of other people's feelings. In literature a reader or member of the audience often feels what the characters in a book or on stage feel.

end rhyme The similar sounds at the ends of two or more lines of poetry.

end-stopped line A line of poetry in which a pause comes at the end because of meaning or grammar.

English sonnet Also known as the *Shakespearean sonnet.* Fourteen lines of iambic pentameter, rhyming *abab, cdcd, efef, gg.*

enjambment A line of poetry that runs on in meaning to the next line: "My spirit is too weak—mortality Weighs heavily on me like unwilling sleep" (Keats)

epic A long poem with larger-than-life characters and universal themes often drawn from legends—Homer's *Iliad* and *Odyssey,* for example.

epigram A brief, witty saying expressed usually in one sentence. "Two's company; three's a crowd."

epigraph A quotation at the beginning of a literary work.

epilogue A brief statement added to a literary work after it has been essentially concluded.

epiphany A revelation or sudden insight.

episode A brief event in a longer narrative.

epistle A formal and literary letter.

epistolary An adjective used to describe novels made up exclusively of letters.

epitaph A poem or inscription suitable for a tombstone, but not always put to that use.

epithet A descriptive word added to a person's name: "Eric the Red."

essay A short discussion of some theme or topic in prose. The word was first used by Montaigne to describe his personal thoughts and comments (1580).

eulogy Formal praise, written or spoken, for someone who has died.

euphemism A mild expression used in place of one that might be offensive: *passed away* instead of *died*.

euphony A pleasing combination of sounds.

exposition Any definition or explanation of something, either written or spoken.

expressionism The use of distortions, symbols, and subjectivity in any of the arts.

fable A simple story that makes a moral point and often uses animals as characters.

fairy tale A story involving imaginary and magical creatures such as fairies, elves, and spirits.

fantasy A story involving purely imaginary creatures in imaginary places.

farce An obvious and exaggerated comedy that draws on loud and silly devices for its humor.

feminine rhyme The rhyming of words with two or more syllables: *meeting-greeting*.

feminist criticism An approach to criticism that assumes that female readers have a unique way of reacting to literature, since they bring to the experience special attitudes, values, and concerns.

fiction Any literary work that involves invented elements. More specifically, fiction refers to novels and short stories.

figure of speech An expression that cannot be taken literally, often a simile, metaphor, or allusion. Nonliteral comparisons: "How sharper than a serpent's tooth it is / To have a thankless child!" (Shakespeare).

first person The point of view (*I, we*) from which much fiction and poetry is written.

flashback Going back to an earlier time period than the period established for a literary work in order to insert a scene, often a memory or reverie.

flat character A character without depth, sometimes a mere stereotype.

foil Usually a lesser character who provides a contrast to the main character (i.e. Watson and Sherlock Holmes).

folklore A body of traditions and legends expressed orally or in various kinds of literary works, usually anonymous, from proverbs and work songs to myths and ballads.

foot A metrical unit consisting of two or more syllables, one of which is stressed.

foreshadowing A clue or hint of things to come in a literary work with some kind of plot.

form A clearly defined arrangement of the parts of a work. Some forms have become traditional, such as the sonnet or ballad; others are highly individual.

format The physical (visual) presentation of a literary work.

formula A very conventional way of developing stories and plays, usually of a commercial nature and without much literary depth or originality. There are formulas for detective stories, westerns, situation comedies, romances, and other popular genres.

free verse Verse without a fixed pattern of rhythm and rhyme, but with a pleasing cadence of some sort.

genre A broad subdivision of literature, such as fiction, poetry, and drama, but also further divisions into more specific categories, such as lyric, romance, and docudrama.

gothic A term that describes literary works that contain mysterious, supernatural, and other strange ingredients, including settings such as dungeons, castles, and graveyards.

hackneyed Words and phrases that have become colorless from overuse are described as hackneyed or trite.

haiku A Japanese verse form that usually uses three lines and a total of seventeen syllables and makes some kind of comment or comparison. There is some question about whether or not the form can be carried over into English.

heptameter A line of poetry consisting of seven feet.

hero 1. A hero or heroine, in general, is a person of courage and other admirable qualities. 2. In literature, the central character is often called the hero or heroine, no matter what qualities he or she possesses.

heroic couplet In poetry, two lines of iambic pentameter that rhyme.

heroic stanza A quatrain in iambic pentameter.

hexameter A line of poetry consisting of six feet, or metrical units.

historical criticism An approach to criticism that holds that a literary work can be understood mainly in terms of the author's life and the historical period in which it was written.

historical novel A novel that uses real characters and events in history, but with varying degrees of accuracy. Some are quite scholarly; others are almost pure fiction.

hubris From the Greek, meaning arrogance or excessive pride, a serious tragic flaw.

humor The comic appreciation of human foibles, absurdities, and amusing situations.

hyperbole Obvious but literary exaggeration. Othello says to Desdemona that if he cannot love her, "Chaos is come again."

iamb A metric foot of two syllables, the first of which is unstressed, and the second of which is stressed. The adjectival form is *iambic*.

idyll A piece of poetry or prose in which the pastoral life and innocence are idealized.

image A picture conjured up by a literary device such as a metaphor or simile or symbol. Images appeal to the senses and are essential to all imaginative literature.

impressionism An approach to the arts, including literature, that stresses the subjective, the feelings of the author or of the characters.

incantation The use of words to invoke supernatural powers, usually in the form of a chant.

intentional fallacy A modern approach to criticism that claims that it is an error to accept the author's stated intention as the true meaning of the work.

interior monologue The interior thoughts of a character, recorded in literature in a variety of styles from formal soliloquies to the poetic passages in Virginia Woolf and the cruder levels of thought in James Joyce.

internal rhyme Similar sounds of two or more words within a single line of poetry.

invocation An appeal to a supernatural being for help or guidance.

irony Saying one thing but meaning something quite opposite. An ironic ending is one in which one thing is intended, but the opposite occurs, as in *Hamlet* when a poisoned drink intended for him is drunk instead by his mother.

Italian sonnet Also known as the *Petrarchan sonnet*, it consists of fourteen lines, an octave and a sestet, rhyming *abbaabba* and *cdecde*.

jargon The terminology of a particular activity, trade, or profession, such as sports, education, or law. When it is introduced pointlessly into standard English, it can weaken one's prose.

lament Any literary expression of grief, such as an elegy.

lampoon A criticism of characters, groups, or ideas through ridicule.

legend A story of unknown origin handed down from generation to generation, and often about a colorful, heroic, or saintly figure.

limerick A humorous and sometimes naughty form of verse, made up of five lines that rhyme *aabba*. The first, second, and fifth lines contain three stresses; the third and fourth lines contain two stresses.

lyric A short poem that is subjective, musical, and full of feeling.

madrigal A short, musical love poem that can easily be set to music, and often was in Italy, France, and England as early as the sixteenth century.

malapropism The ridiculous misuse of words. A device often used in comedy. "I can't visit the country because I have an allegory to wild flowers."

melodrama A play with implausibly exaggerated actions and emotions and not much depth or literary value.

metafiction A literary work that is about fiction itself and the way it achieves meaning.

metaphor A nonliteral comparison, a figure of speech: "His friend's betrayal was a dagger in his heart."

meter Poetic measure, using units called *feet*, which are made up of combinations of stressed and unstressed syllables. Some poems are made of measured lines; others are free of meter but rely on cadence.

mixed metaphor The illogical mixture of two or more metaphors within the same passage: "The rose of love is the altar at which he worshiped."

monologue Something spoken by one person: a speech, a soliloquy, a narrative, a comic routine. An internal monologue tries to capture the thoughts of one person in some literary form.

motivation The desires or other psychological conditions that cause the actions of characters. Motivations must be plausible if characters are to be believable.

myth A traditional story of unknown origin that often contains a nonscientific explanation of some aspect of nature or the human condition. Myths of creation, for instance.

narration An account of a series of events either in prose or poetry.

narrator The one who tells the story, sometimes the author, sometimes one of the characters, sometimes an omniscient, anonymous speaker. See also *persona*.

naturalism The approach to literature and other arts that tries to present human experience and the world as it actually is, without idealism or sentimentality.

new criticism A modern approach to criticism that focuses on the work itself without reference to the author's life, the author's intention, or the historical or cultural context in which the work was created. It depends on a close verbal analysis of the text.

novel A coherent piece of fiction of a certain length, sometimes fixed at a minimum of about 50,000 words. Works shorter than that but longer than short stories are often called *novellas*.

ode A formal, lyrical poem on a serious theme. See "Ode on a Grecian Urn," by John Keats.

octave In poetry, a stanza of eight lines.

octameter A line of poetry consisting of eight feet.

off-rhyme A rhyme that involves sounds that are close but not precisely the same: *kiss-chess*.

omniscient All-knowing. A frequently used point of view in literature.

onomatopoeia The use of words that sound like what they mean: *crash, bang*.

ottava rima A stanza of eight lines of iambic pentameter with a rhyme pattern of *abababcc*.

parable A story designed to illustrate a moral principle or universal truth.

paradox An apparent contradiction that proves to be true in another sense.

parody A humorous imitation of a person, events, society, or ideas, intended to be satirical or critical.

pastoral A literary work dealing with the simple rural life, especially its charm and innocence.

pathos That which evokes pity, sorrow, or compassion.

pentameter A line of poetry that consists of five feet.

persona A narrator created to tell the reader what happens, not necessarily the author, even in works written in the first or third person. Even in the most personal works, a distinction must be made between the author's real voice and his or her literary voice.

personification A literary device in which inanimate objects, animals, and abstractions are endowed with human qualities.

Petrarchan sonnet See *Italian sonnet*.

picaresque A type of fiction made up loosely of the adventurous episodes in the life of a rascal or rogue.

plot A carefully arranged series of events in a narrative work. The sequence is designed to lead to a certain effect, a revelation or emotional impact.

poetic justice The obsolete concept, once very influential in literature, that good is rewarded and evil is punished.

poetic license The occasional violation of the conventional uses of language in order to achieve a special artistic effect. Gerard Manley Hopkins, for instance, sometimes uses archaic diction.

point of view The position of the narrator, who can be a participant or a nonparticipant in the action. If the narrator is a participant, the story is usually told in the first person (I). If the narrator is not a participant, the story can be told in the second person, but that is rare and not advisable. The narrator will probably use the third person. In that case, there are two major options: to see the action from the point of view of one of the characters, or to use an omniscient (all-knowing) point of view. In a long work, such as a novel, several different points of view might be involved.

polemic A term used to describe literary works in which the author's main purpose is to present his or her views on a subject that is often controversial.

postmodern A term used to describe innovative works of the past thirty years or so that break with tradition, even with the ideas and techniques of earlier so-called "modern" writers.

prose All forms of written expression except poetry, which has special requirements. Works of nonfiction as well as fiction are prose compositions.

prosody The principles of poetic structure, including meter, rhyme, rhythm, and stanza forms.

protagonist The main character in a literary work, no matter what his or her qualities are.

pun An amusing play on words, such as this description of a poker game: "Chips that pass in the night."

quatrain A stanza of four lines, or a complete poem if it consists of only one such stanza.

quintet A stanza consisting of five lines.

realism An approach to literature in which ordinary life is depicted with objective and photographic accuracy. Because this approach has so often focused on the harsh and sordid aspects of ordinary life, the word realism has taken on an additional connotation.

refrain A portion of a poem that is repeated at certain intervals, often at the end of each stanza.

resolution That portion of the final part of a literary work that ends the dramatic tension with some kind of solution of the problem or resolution of the conflict.

rhyme Identical sounds in poetry, whether they occur within a line (internal rhyme) or at the end of certain lines (end rhyme).

rhyme royal A rhyme scheme of *ababbcc* in a seven-line stanza of iambic pentameter.

rhythm A pattern of beats or accents either in conventional or unconventional forms. There is rhythm in prose as well as in poetry, though it may be impossible to scan.

romance Once a term used to describe literary works with heroic characters and fanciful events; now used almost exclusively to describe a love story, sometimes of a superficial and commercial nature.

romanticism An approach to literature marked by a freedom from classical rules and the expression of strong emotions, often subjectively.

round character A fully developed, three-dimensional character that is utterly plausible, as opposed to flat characters that tend to be superficial and not altogether convincing.

saga A long narrative about the adventures and achievements of an extraordinary or legendary character.

sarcasm The use of harsh and wounding remarks with a touch of irony.

satire A literary technique that uses ridicule, humor, and irony to point out the faults of an individual or a society or all of mankind.

scansion The analysis of the meter and rhyme of a poem, using certain standard marks for stressed syllables, unstressed syllables, pauses, and rhyme patterns.

scenario The sequence of events, including dialogue and characters, described in a script intended for film or television. A scenario can also be a hypothetical sequence of events, whether written down or not.

scene A subdivision of an act in a play, a clearly defined unit of action in a longer work.

science fiction A narrative that makes plausible use of scientific materials but remains within the realm of fiction. Often distinguished from fantasy, which includes fanciful and supernatural ingredients.

second person In literature, an occasionally used point of view (*you*).

semiotics The study of any method of signifying meaning: words, sounds, gestures, body language, and so on.

sentimentality A preoccupation with exaggerated emotions that can weaken the quality of a literary work.

septet A stanza of seven lines.

sestet A stanza of six lines.

setting The place where the action occurs in any literary work. The setting is formally named at the beginning of a play and any of its subdivisions (acts and scenes).

Shakespearean sonnet See *English sonnet*.

short story A short narrative, usually under 10,000 words, that deals with a single dramatic event or central conflict that is developed and then resolved.

simile A figurative comparison that states that one thing is *like* (*as*) another, but not in a literal sense. "He was like a bull in a china shop."

slant rhyme See *off rhyme*.

slice of life A literary work that allows one to have a look at a segment of "real life" without much concern for plot. However, there is significance in the segment, often a commentary on a particular character or way of life.

soliloquy A speech spoken aloud but intended as a representation of the character's thoughts.

sonnet A poem consisting of fourteen lines of iambic pentameter and a rhyme scheme in which there might be slight variations. See also *English sonnet*.

Spenserian stanza Eight lines of iambic pentameter followed by a line of iambic hexameter, rhyming *ababbcbcc*. The basic stanza of *The Faerie Queene* by Edmund Spenser.

spondee In poetry, a metric unit consisting of two stressed syllables.

stanza A subdivision of a poem with some kind of structure: couplet, quatrain, Spenserian stanza, and so on. A poem can consist of just one stanza.

stereotype A simplistic and traditional view of things, a stock character, usually two-dimensional.

stock character A figure with traditional characteristics but not much depth or individuality, such as the butler, the workaholic businessperson, the wide-eyed innocent.

stream of consciousness A technique used in literature to capture human thoughts as they actually occur, however distorted and ungrammatical.

stress Accent, emphasis. In poetry, the accent on a syllable.

structure A logical pattern or plan in a literary work, such as the sequence of events in a story, the acts in a play, the rhyme and rhythm pattern of a poem.

style The individual and characteristic manner of writing, influenced by the personality of the author and reflecting the author's attitudes.

subjectivity The tendency to see the outside world from inside the characters. A preoccupation with the thoughts and feelings of the characters.

suspense Uncertainty and anxiety about the outcome of a series of events.

suspension of disbelief The willingness of the reader or audience to accept, for the moment, that fiction is fact, in order to experience literary works as though they were true.

symbol Something specific that stands for something more abstract and complex. Moby Dick is a whale, but he stands for certain mysterious forces in the universe.

synopsis A short summary of a longer work. A synopsis sometimes appears at the beginning of a novel when it is sent to an editor, and even more frequently at the beginning of a screenplay.

tags In dialogue, the labels that indicate who is speaking: *he said, she said.*

tercet A three-line stanza.

terza rima A form of verse made up of tercets and a rhyme scheme in which the middle line of the tercet rhymes with the first and third lines of the following tercet: *aba, bcb, cdc.* The lines are iambic and eleven syllables long.

tetrameter A poetic line of four feet.

theme The central idea or impact of a literary work.

theoretical criticism A field of study that focuses on the fundamental principles of artistic expression, as opposed to the individual work of art, which is the realm of *practical criticism.*

third person The most common point of view used in fiction (*he, she, they*).

tone The quality of a literary work that reveals the author's attitude: for example, satirical, sardonic, gloomy.

tragedy Any literary drama about the downfall of a sympathetic hero or heroine, who often dies at the end. Classically, a tragic flaw is involved, but in modern times blame is sometimes shifted to society or circumstances.

flaw A defect in the character of an otherwise good or noble person. The defect leads to tragedy, as in the case of Macbeth and his "vaulting ambition."

tragic hero Classically, a person of good qualities who makes an error in judgment because of a tragic flaw (such as pride or ambition). In Greek tragedy the hero was a person in a high position, often a king. The same is true, slightly modified, in Shakespeare (Hamlet, Lear, Macbeth). In modern times, a tragic hero is often a more ordinary person.

trimeter A poetic line of three feet.

triplet A three-line stanza.

triteness Writing marked by worn-out phrases or ideas.

trochee A metric unit in poetry (a *foot*) with a stressed syllable followed by an unstressed syllable.

unity A quality that occurs in literature when all the parts are related by some central theme or artistic concept.

upstage The back of the stage.

verse Sometimes a single line of poetry, but more often merely a synonym for poetry in general.

villanelle A poem consisting of five tercets and a quatrain with a rhyme scheme that uses only two rhymes: *aba, aba, aba, aba, aba, abaa*. The lines tend to have five stresses and to be iambic.

whodunit An informal expression for a story or drama about crime. The suspense stems from the reader's curiosity about who committed the crime.

wit A form of humor that depends largely on language and ideas rather than actions and situations.